# ICHIROH! 2

MIKAGE

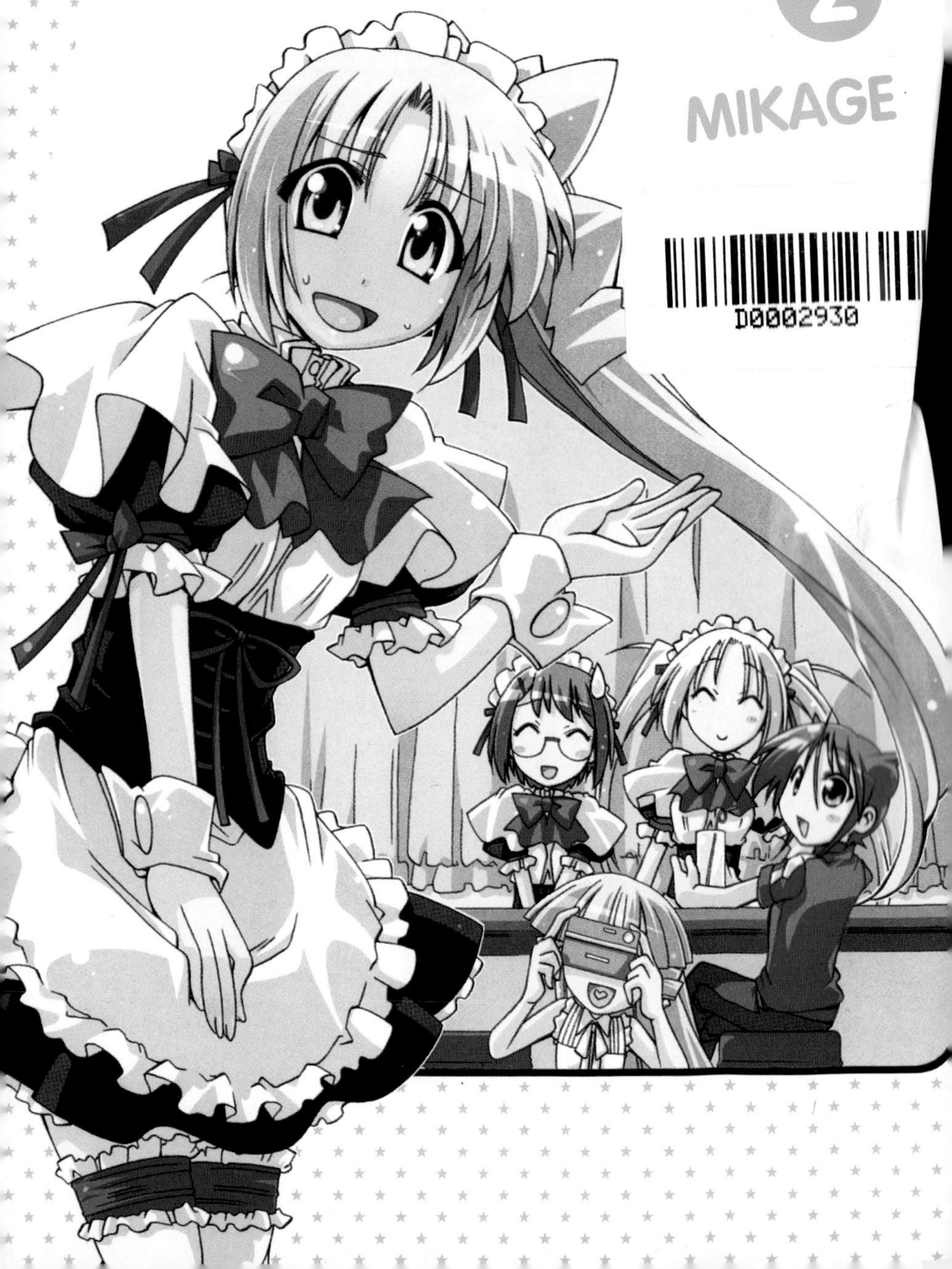

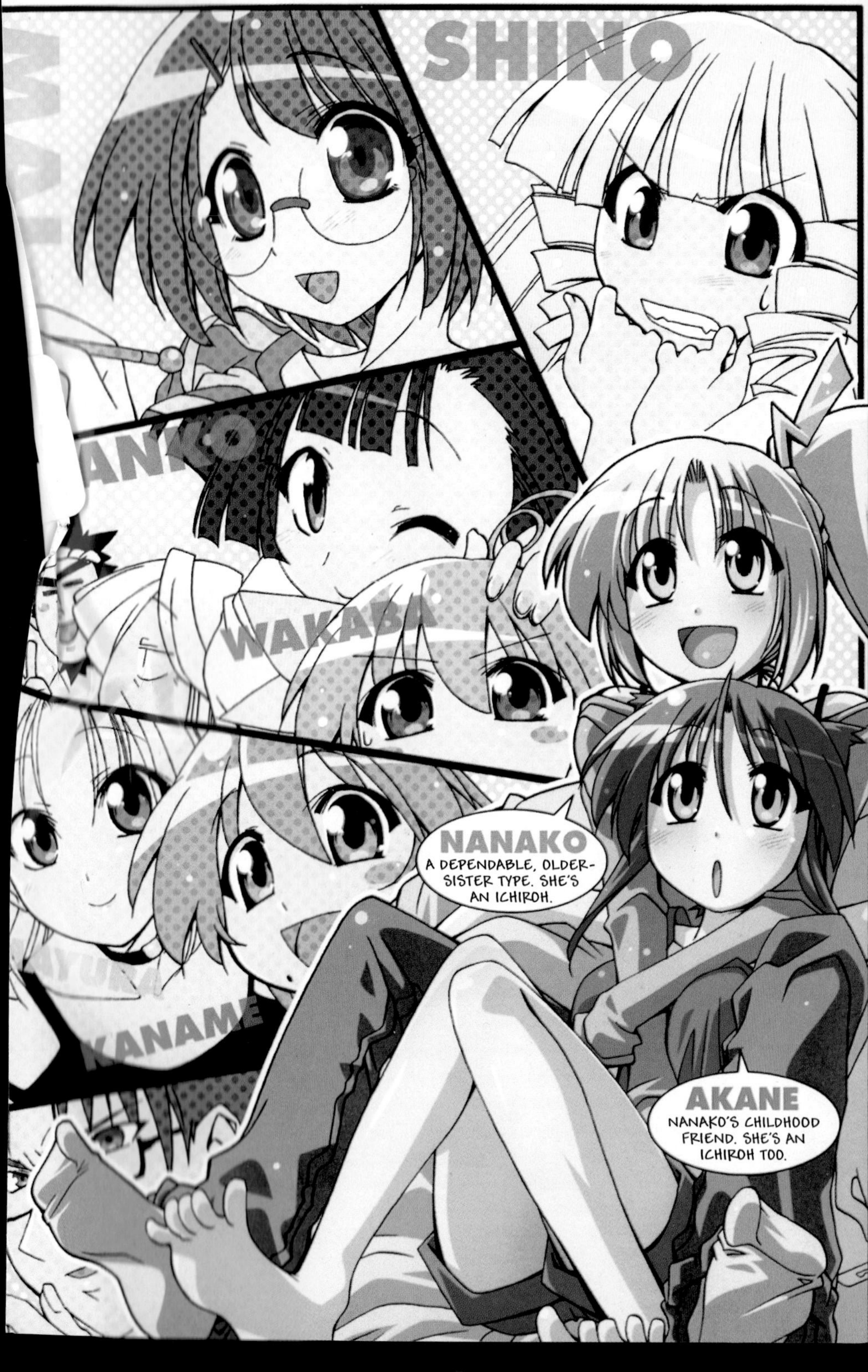
SHINO
MAYU
NANAKO
A DEPENDABLE, OLDER-SISTER TYPE. SHE'S AN ICHIROH.
WAKABA
AKANE
NANAKO'S CHILDHOOD FRIEND. SHE'S AN ICHIROH TOO.
MAYURA
KANAME

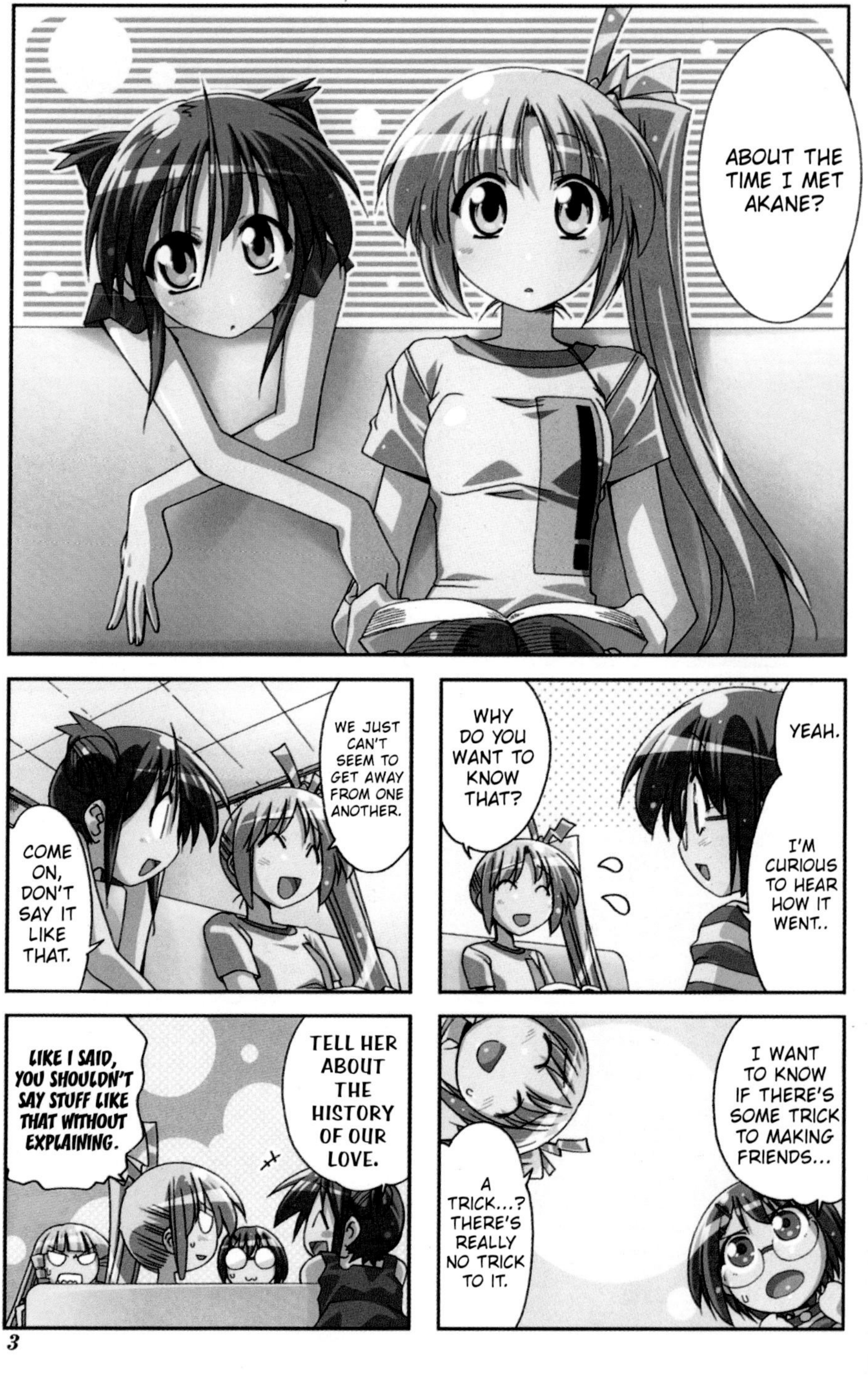
ABOUT THE TIME I MET AKANE?
YEAH.
I'M CURIOUS TO HEAR HOW IT WENT..
WHY DO YOU WANT TO KNOW THAT?
WE JUST CAN'T SEEM TO GET AWAY FROM ONE ANOTHER.
COME ON, DON'T SAY IT LIKE THAT.
I WANT TO KNOW IF THERE'S SOME TRICK TO MAKING FRIENDS...
A TRICK...? THERE'S REALLY NO TRICK TO IT.
TELL HER ABOUT THE HISTORY OF OUR LOVE.
LIKE I SAID, YOU SHOULDN'T SAY STUFF LIKE THAT WITHOUT EXPLAINING.

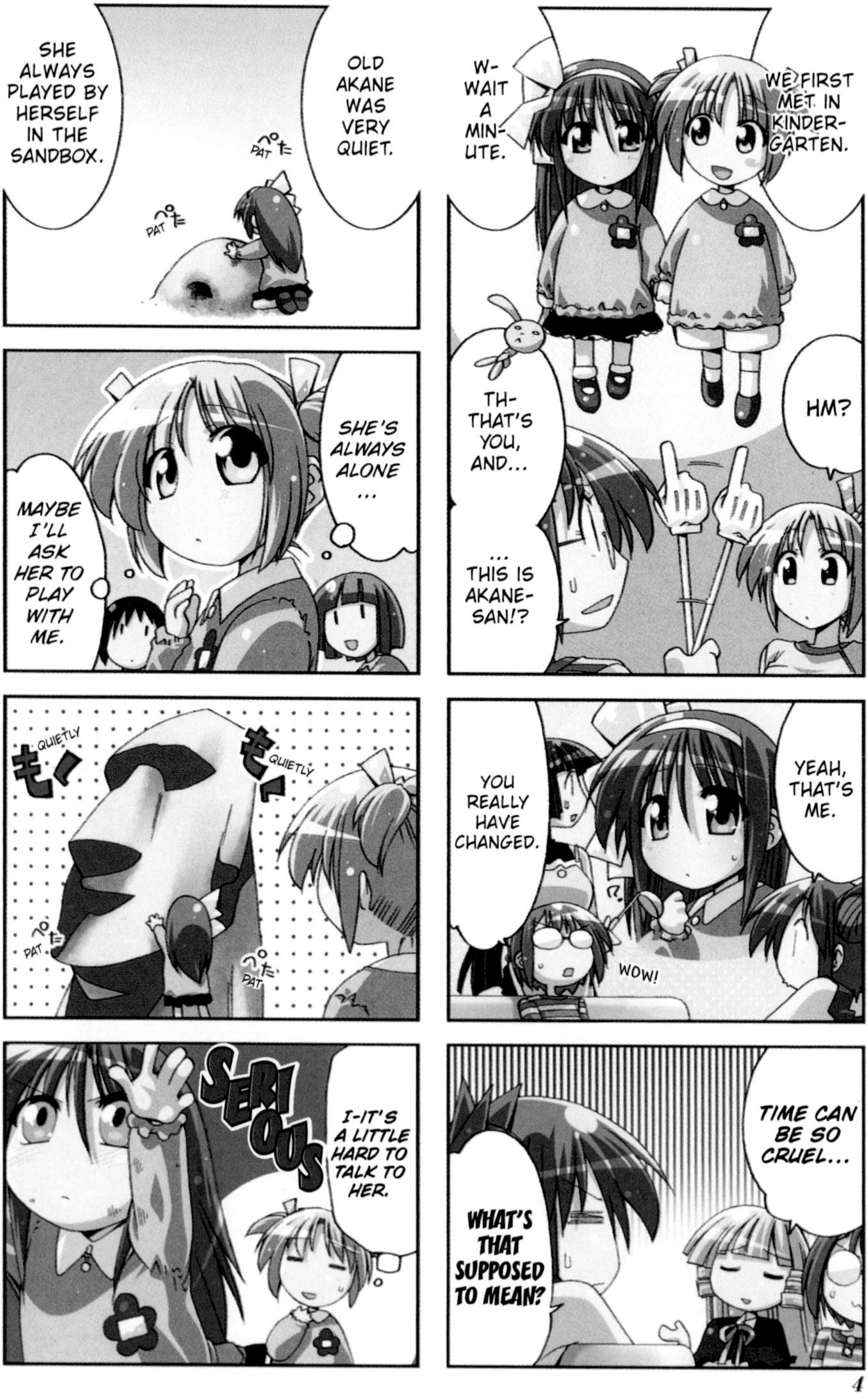
WE FIRST MET IN KINDER-GARTEN.
W-WAIT A MIN-UTE.
HM?
TH-THAT'S YOU, AND...
...THIS IS AKANE-SAN!?
YEAH, THAT'S ME.
YOU REALLY HAVE CHANGED.
WOW!
TIME CAN BE SO CRUEL...
WHAT'S THAT SUPPOSED TO MEAN?
OLD AKANE WAS VERY QUIET.
SHE ALWAYS PLAYED BY HERSELF IN THE SANDBOX.
ぺた PAT
ぺた PAT
SHE'S ALWAYS ALONE...
MAYBE I'LL ASK HER TO PLAY WITH ME.
もく QUIETLY
もく QUIETLY
ぺた PAT
ぺた PAT
SERIOUS
I-IT'S A LITTLE HARD TO TALK TO HER.

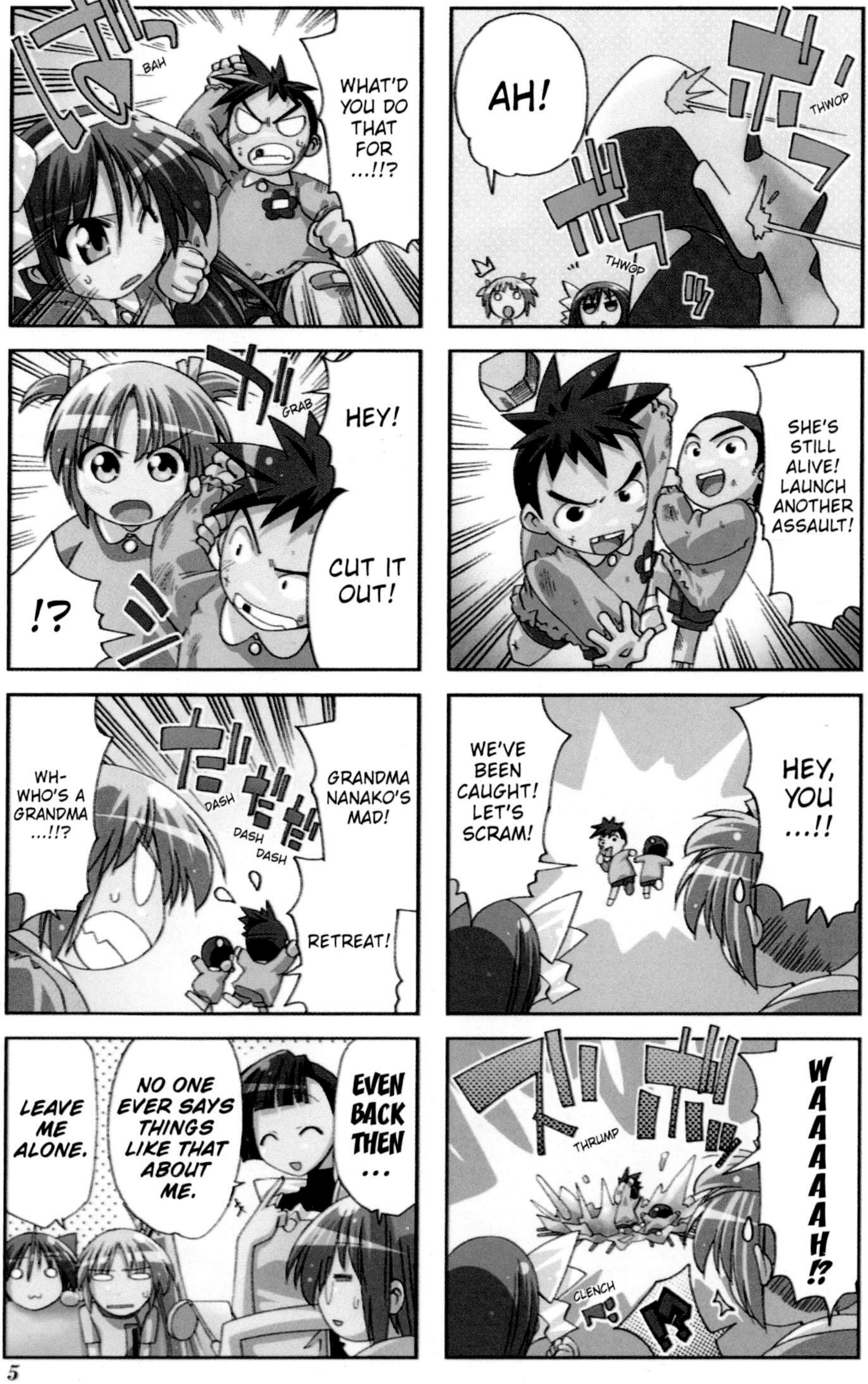
THWOP
AH!
THWOP
WHAT'D YOU DO THAT FOR ...!!?
BAH
SHE'S STILL ALIVE! LAUNCH ANOTHER ASSAULT!
HEY!
GRAB
CUT IT OUT!
!?
HEY, YOU ...!!
WE'VE BEEN CAUGHT! LET'S SCRAM!
GRANDMA NANAKO'S MAD!
RETREAT!
DASH
DASH
DASH
WH-WHO'S A GRANDMA ...!!?
WAAAAAAAH!!?
THRUMP
CLENCH
EVEN BACK THEN ...
NO ONE EVER SAYS THINGS LIKE THAT ABOUT ME.
LEAVE ME ALONE.

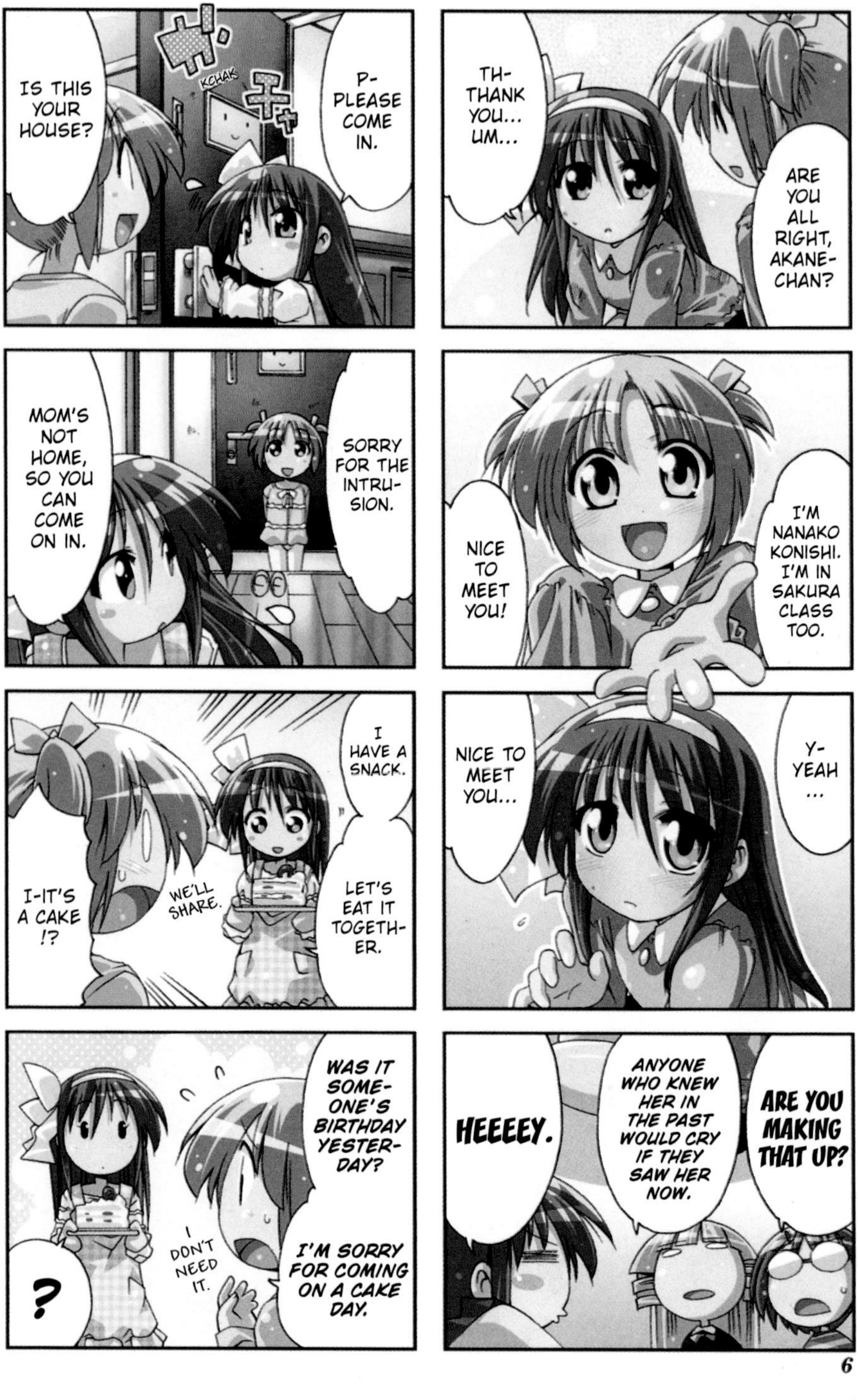
ARE YOU ALL RIGHT, AKANE-CHAN?
TH-THANK YOU... UM...
I'M NANAKO KONISHI. I'M IN SAKURA CLASS TOO.
NICE TO MEET YOU!
Y-YEAH ...
NICE TO MEET YOU...
ARE YOU MAKING THAT UP?
ANYONE WHO KNEW HER IN THE PAST WOULD CRY IF THEY SAW HER NOW.
HEEEEY.
P-PLEASE COME IN.
KCHAK
IS THIS YOUR HOUSE?
SORRY FOR THE INTRU-SION.
MOM'S NOT HOME, SO YOU CAN COME ON IN.
I HAVE A SNACK.
LET'S EAT IT TOGETH-ER.
WE'LL SHARE.
I-IT'S A CAKE !?
WAS IT SOME-ONE'S BIRTHDAY YESTER-DAY?
I'M SORRY FOR COMING ON A CAKE DAY.
I DON'T NEED IT.
?

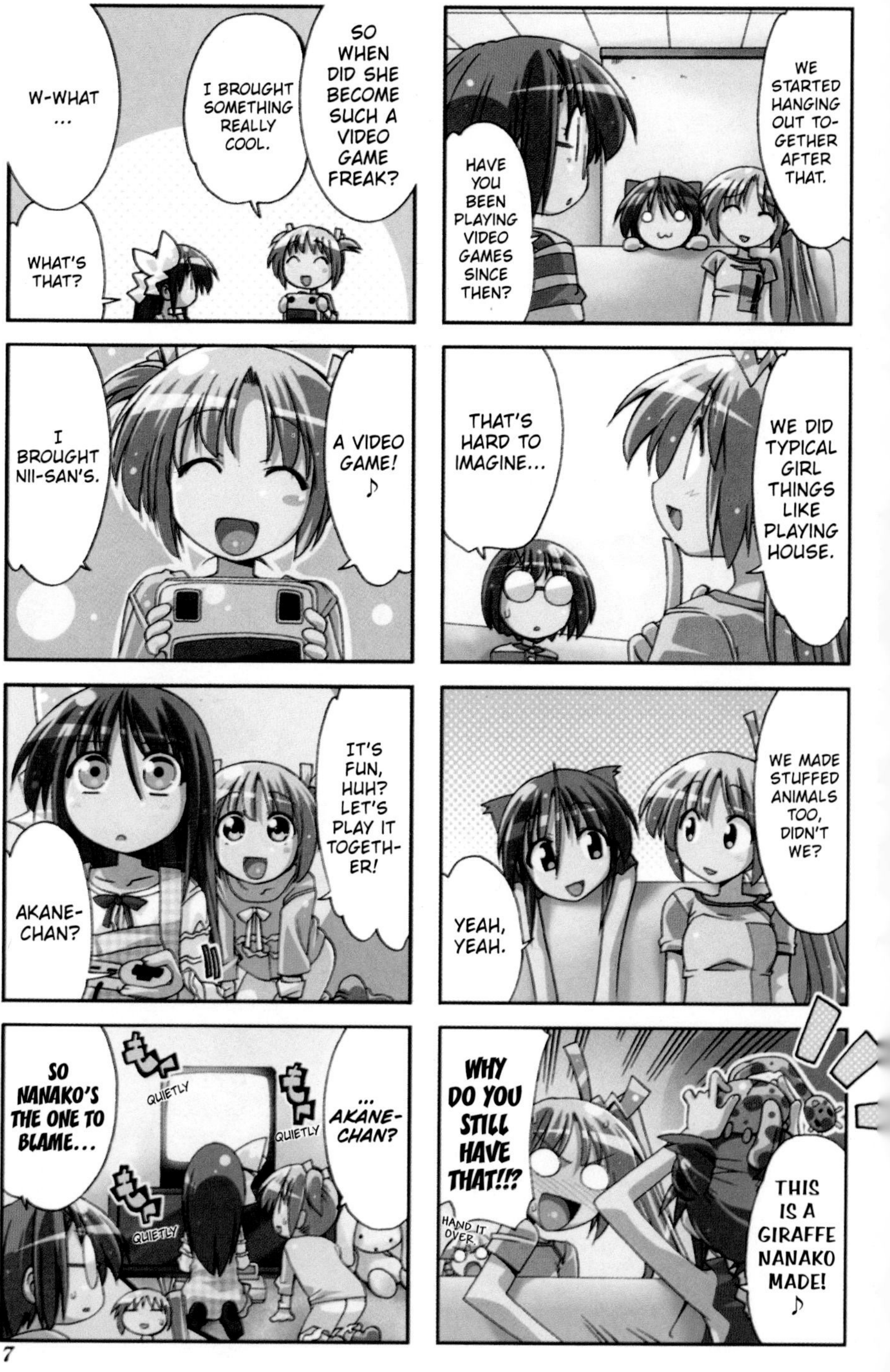
WE STARTED HANGING OUT TOGETHER AFTER THAT.
HAVE YOU BEEN PLAYING VIDEO GAMES SINCE THEN?
WE DID TYPICAL GIRL THINGS LIKE PLAYING HOUSE.
THAT'S HARD TO IMAGINE...
WE MADE STUFFED ANIMALS TOO, DIDN'T WE?
YEAH, YEAH.
THIS IS A GIRAFFE NANAKO MADE! ♪
WHY DO YOU STILL HAVE THAT!!?
HAND IT OVER.
SO WHEN DID SHE BECOME SUCH A VIDEO GAME FREAK?
I BROUGHT SOMETHING REALLY COOL.
W-WHAT...
WHAT'S THAT?
A VIDEO GAME! ♪
I BROUGHT NII-SAN'S.
IT'S FUN, HUH? LET'S PLAY IT TOGETHER!
AKANE-CHAN?
...AKANE-CHAN?
QUIETLY
QUIETLY
QUIETLY
SO NANAKO'S THE ONE TO BLAME...

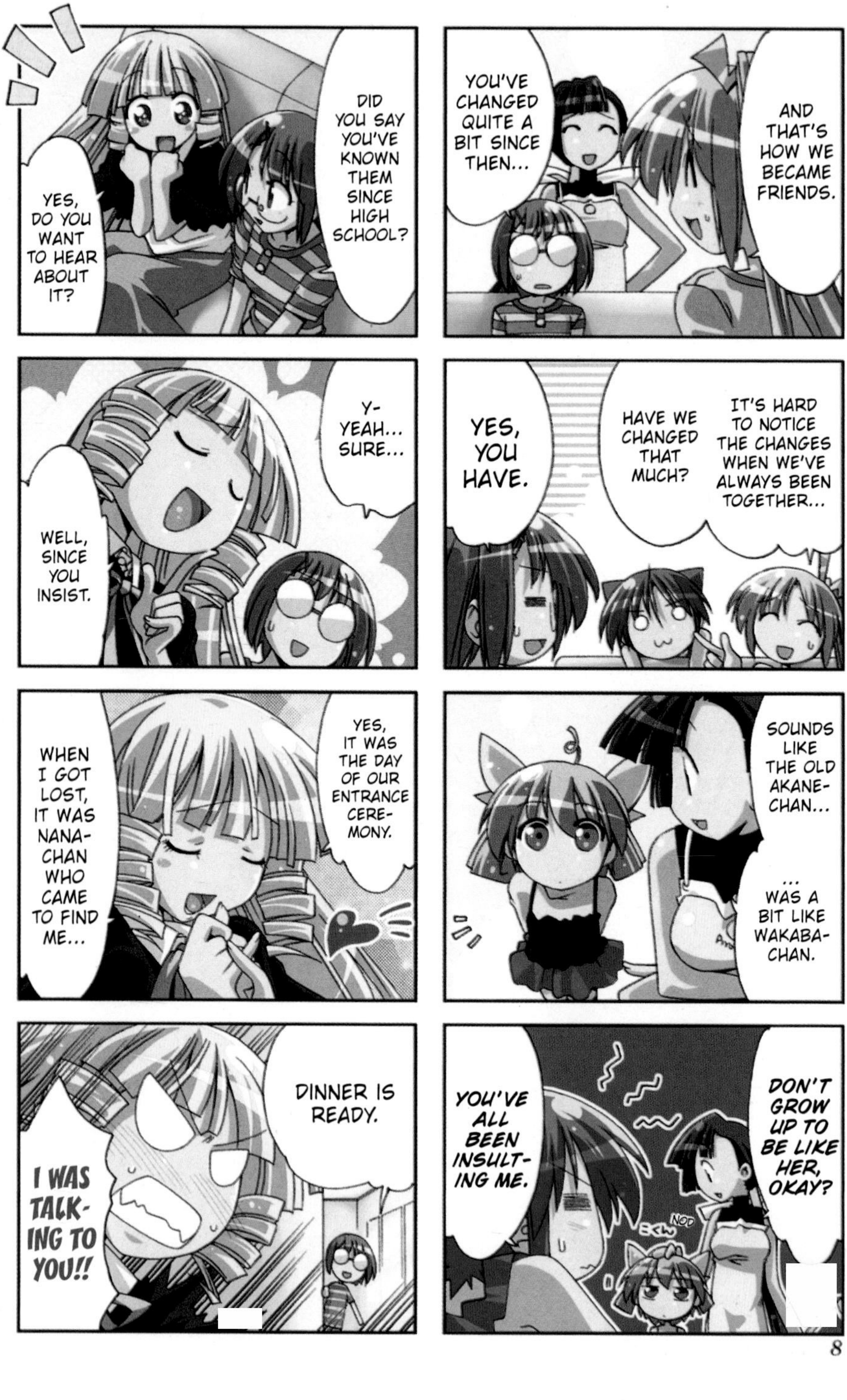
AND THAT'S HOW WE BECAME FRIENDS.
YOU'VE CHANGED QUITE A BIT SINCE THEN...
IT'S HARD TO NOTICE THE CHANGES WHEN WE'VE ALWAYS BEEN TOGETHER...
HAVE WE CHANGED THAT MUCH?
YES, YOU HAVE.
SOUNDS LIKE THE OLD AKANE-CHAN...
...WAS A BIT LIKE WAKABA-CHAN.
DON'T GROW UP TO BE LIKE HER, OKAY?
NOD
YOU'VE ALL BEEN INSULTING ME.
DID YOU SAY YOU'VE KNOWN THEM SINCE HIGH SCHOOL?
YES, DO YOU WANT TO HEAR ABOUT IT?
Y-YEAH... SURE...
WELL, SINCE YOU INSIST.
YES, IT WAS THE DAY OF OUR ENTRANCE CERE-MONY.
WHEN I GOT LOST, IT WAS NANA-CHAN WHO CAME TO FIND ME...
DINNER IS READY.
I WAS TALK-ING TO YOU!!

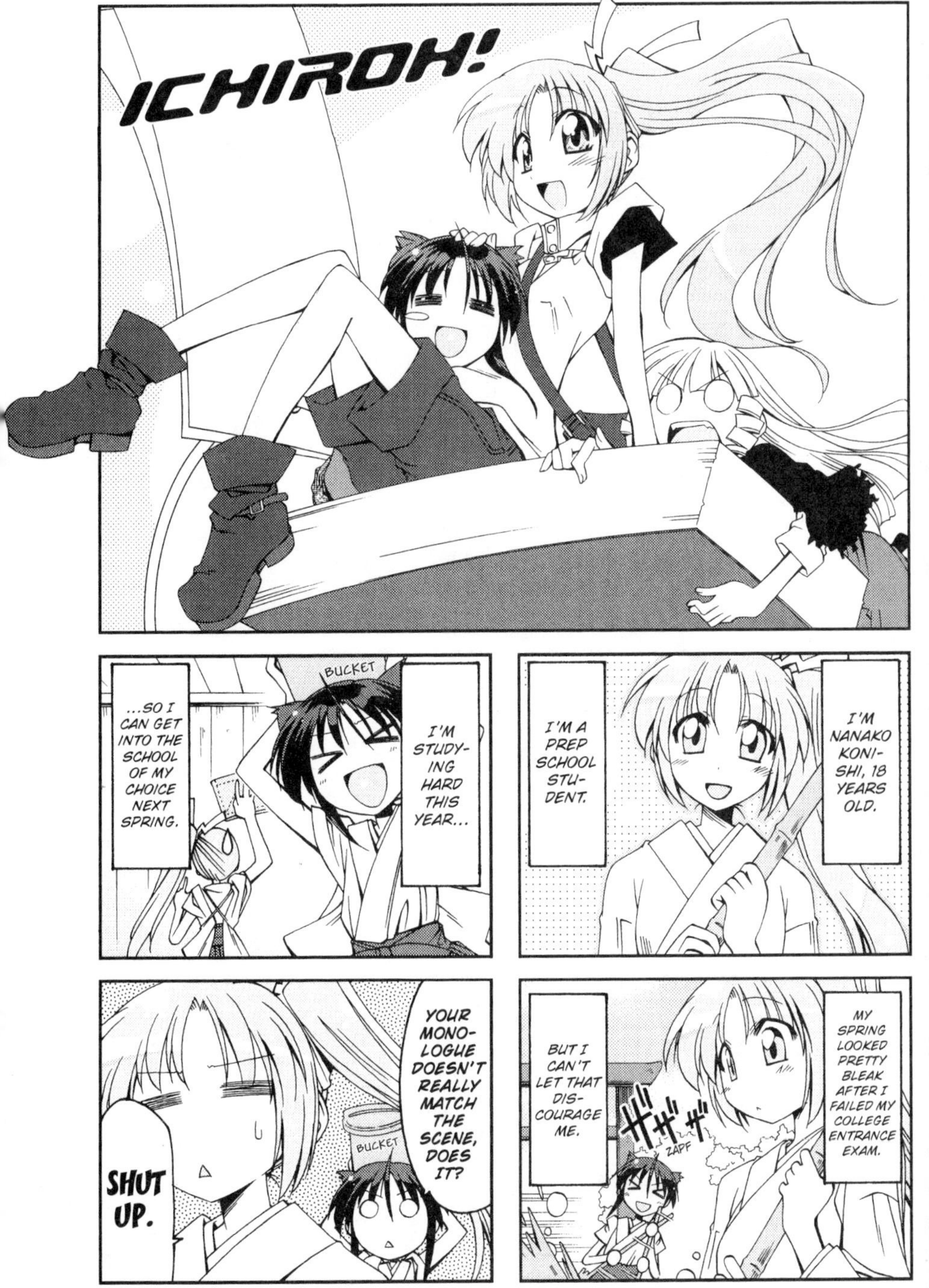
ICHIROH!
I'M NANAKO KONISHI, 18 YEARS OLD.
I'M A PREP SCHOOL STUDENT.
BUCKET
I'M STUDYING HARD THIS YEAR...
...SO I CAN GET INTO THE SCHOOL OF MY CHOICE NEXT SPRING.
MY SPRING LOOKED PRETTY BLEAK AFTER I FAILED MY COLLEGE ENTRANCE EXAM.
BUT I CAN'T LET THAT DISCOURAGE ME.
ZAPF
YOUR MONOLOGUE DOESN'T REALLY MATCH THE SCENE, DOES IT?
BUCKET
SHUT UP.

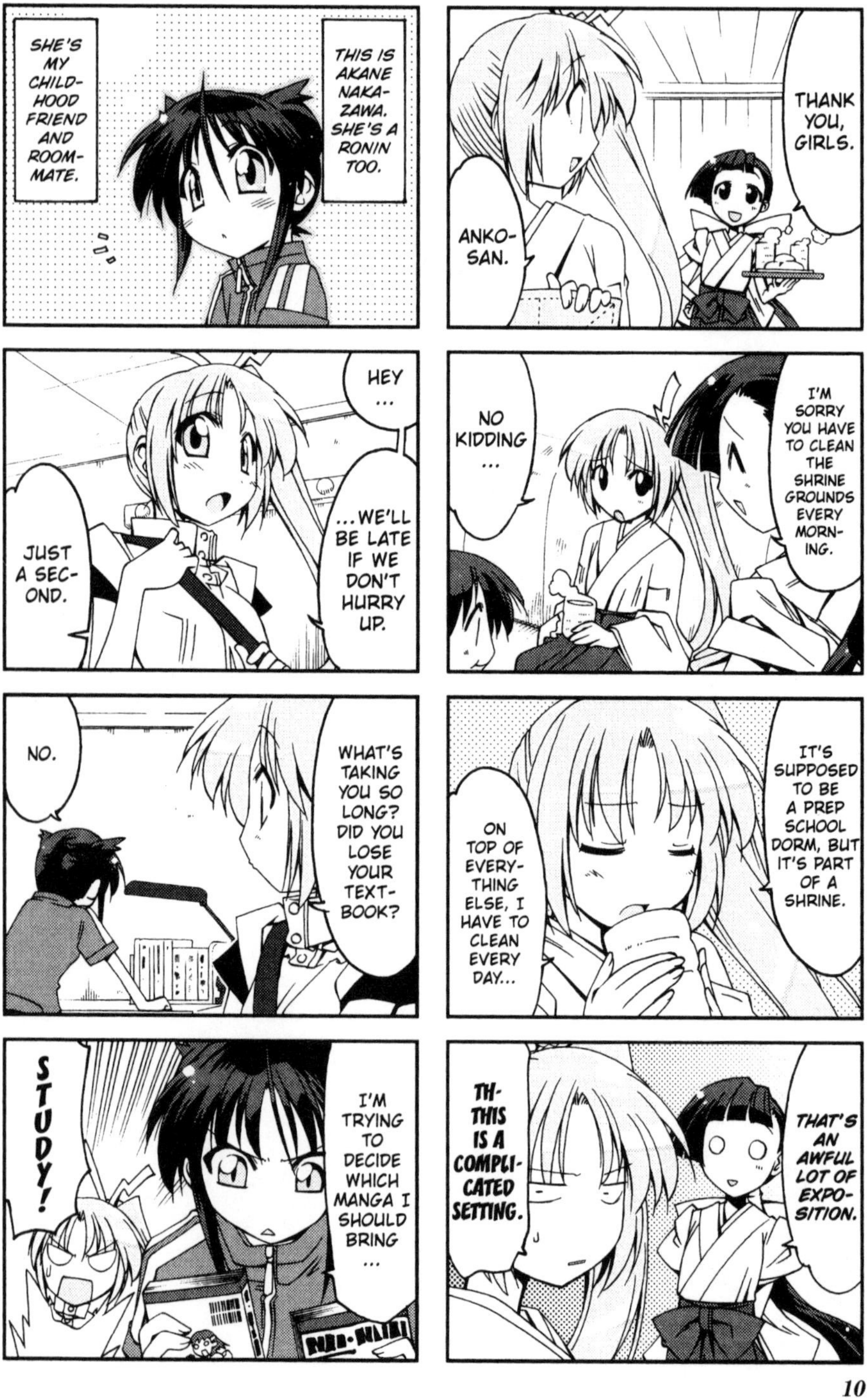
THANK YOU, GIRLS.
ANKO-SAN.
I'M SORRY YOU HAVE TO CLEAN THE SHRINE GROUNDS EVERY MORNING.
NO KIDDING ...
IT'S SUPPOSED TO BE A PREP SCHOOL DORM, BUT IT'S PART OF A SHRINE.
ON TOP OF EVERYTHING ELSE, I HAVE TO CLEAN EVERY DAY...
THAT'S AN AWFUL LOT OF EXPOSITION.
TH-THIS IS A COMPLICATED SETTING.
THIS IS AKANE NAKAZAWA. SHE'S A RONIN TOO.
SHE'S MY CHILDHOOD FRIEND AND ROOMMATE.
HEY ...
...WE'LL BE LATE IF WE DON'T HURRY UP.
JUST A SECOND.
WHAT'S TAKING YOU SO LONG? DID YOU LOSE YOUR TEXTBOOK?
NO.
I'M TRYING TO DECIDE WHICH MANGA I SHOULD BRING ...
STUDY!

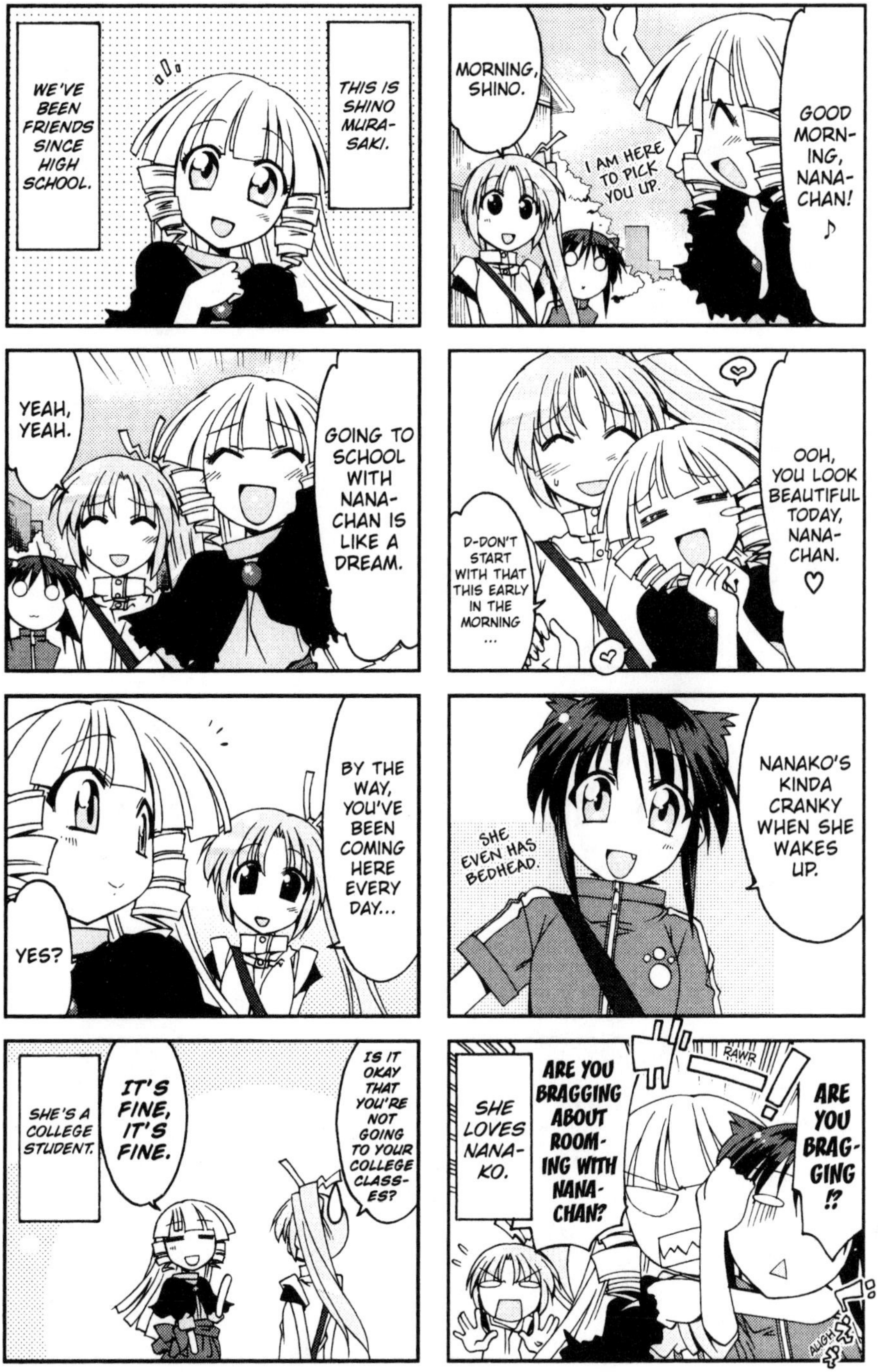
GOOD MORNING, NANA-CHAN! ♪
MORNING, SHINO.
I AM HERE TO PICK YOU UP.
OOH, YOU LOOK BEAUTIFUL TODAY, NANA-CHAN. ♡
D-DON'T START WITH THAT THIS EARLY IN THE MORNING...
NANAKO'S KINDA CRANKY WHEN SHE WAKES UP.
SHE EVEN HAS BEDHEAD.
ARE YOU BRAGGING!?
RAWR
ARE YOU BRAGGING ABOUT ROOMING WITH NANA-CHAN?
SHE LOVES NANAKO.
AUGH
THIS IS SHINO MURASAKI.
WE'VE BEEN FRIENDS SINCE HIGH SCHOOL.
GOING TO SCHOOL WITH NANA-CHAN IS LIKE A DREAM.
YEAH, YEAH.
BY THE WAY, YOU'VE BEEN COMING HERE EVERY DAY...
YES?
IS IT OKAY THAT YOU'RE NOT GOING TO YOUR COLLEGE CLASSES?
IT'S FINE, IT'S FINE.
SHE'S A COLLEGE STUDENT.

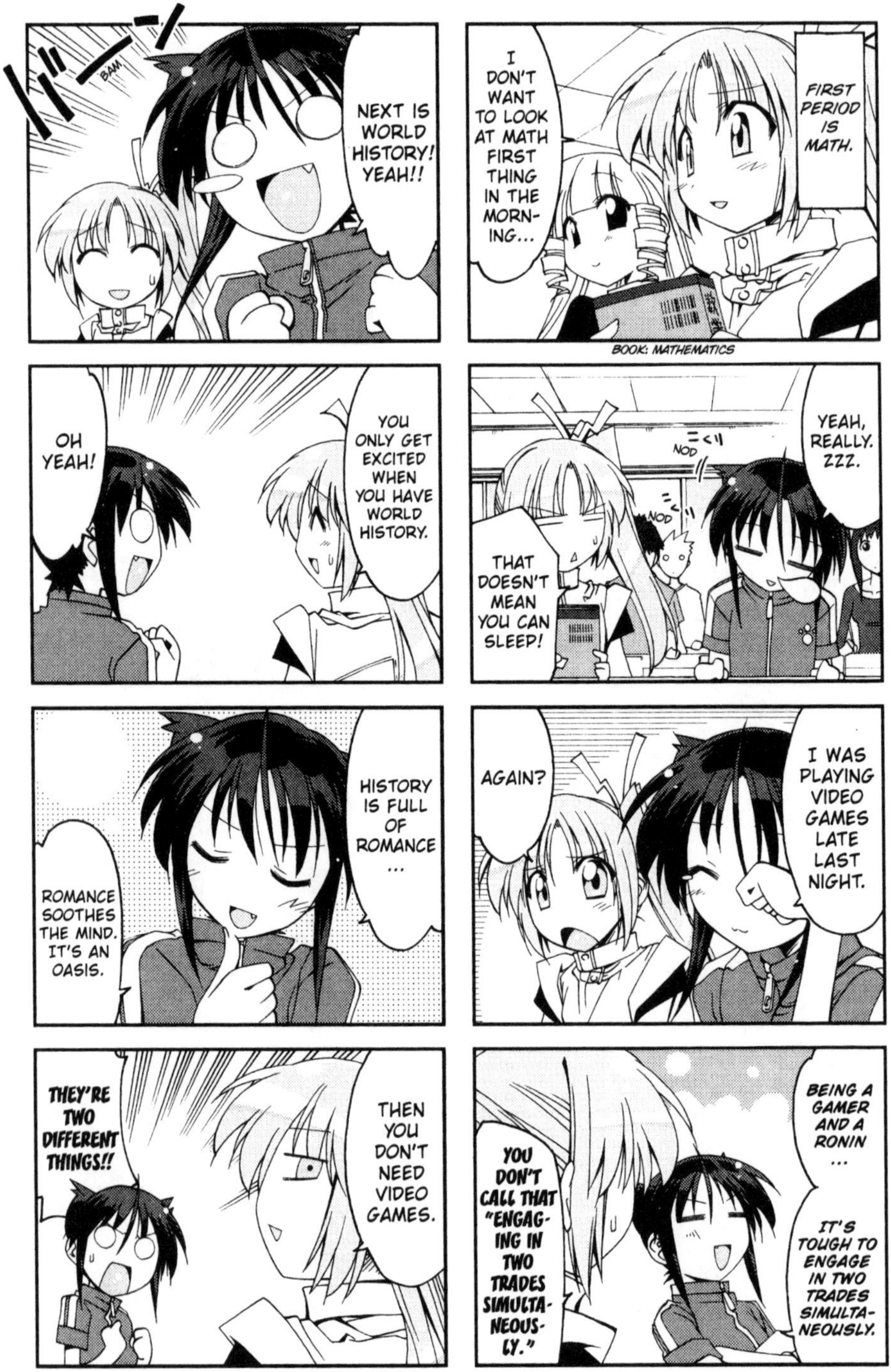
FIRST PERIOD IS MATH.
I DON'T WANT TO LOOK AT MATH FIRST THING IN THE MORNING...
BOOK: MATHEMATICS
BAM
NEXT IS WORLD HISTORY! YEAH!!
YEAH, REALLY. ZZZ.
NOD
NOD
THAT DOESN'T MEAN YOU CAN SLEEP!
YOU ONLY GET EXCITED WHEN YOU HAVE WORLD HISTORY.
OH YEAH!
I WAS PLAYING VIDEO GAMES LATE LAST NIGHT.
AGAIN?
HISTORY IS FULL OF ROMANCE...
ROMANCE SOOTHES THE MIND. IT'S AN OASIS.
BEING A GAMER AND A RONIN...
IT'S TOUGH TO ENGAGE IN TWO TRADES SIMULTANEOUSLY.
YOU DON'T CALL THAT "ENGAGING IN TWO TRADES SIMULTANEOUSLY."
THEN YOU DON'T NEED VIDEO GAMES.
THEY'RE TWO DIFFERENT THINGS!!

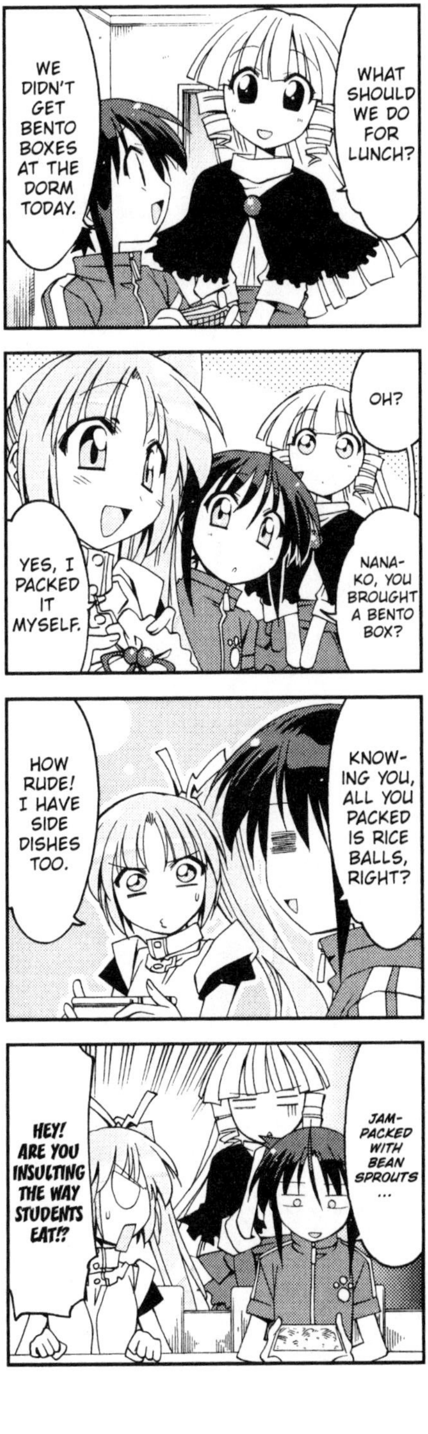
WHAT SHOULD WE DO FOR LUNCH?
WE DIDN'T GET BENTO BOXES AT THE DORM TODAY.
OH?
NANAKO, YOU BROUGHT A BENTO BOX?
YES, I PACKED IT MYSELF.
KNOWING YOU, ALL YOU PACKED IS RICE BALLS, RIGHT?
HOW RUDE! I HAVE SIDE DISHES TOO.
JAM-PACKED WITH BEAN SPROUTS ...
HEY! ARE YOU INSULTING THE WAY STUDENTS EAT!?
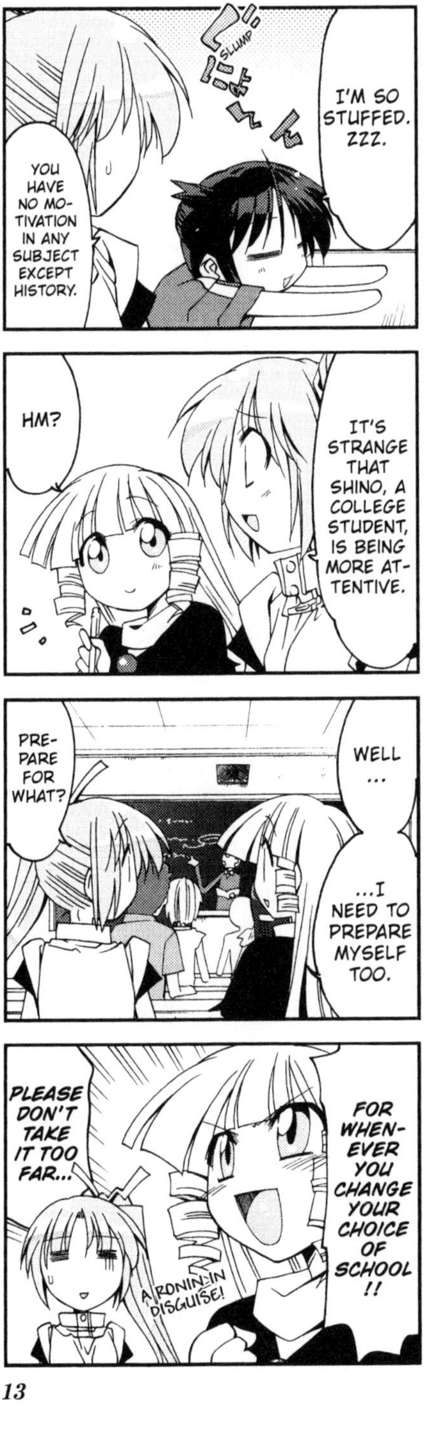
I'M SO STUFFED. ZZZ.
SLUMP
YOU HAVE NO MOTIVATION IN ANY SUBJECT EXCEPT HISTORY.
IT'S STRANGE THAT SHINO, A COLLEGE STUDENT, IS BEING MORE ATTENTIVE.
HM?
WELL ...
...I NEED TO PREPARE MYSELF TOO.
PREPARE FOR WHAT?
FOR WHENEVER YOU CHANGE YOUR CHOICE OF SCHOOL !!
A RONIN IN DISGUISE!
PLEASE DON'T TAKE IT TOO FAR...

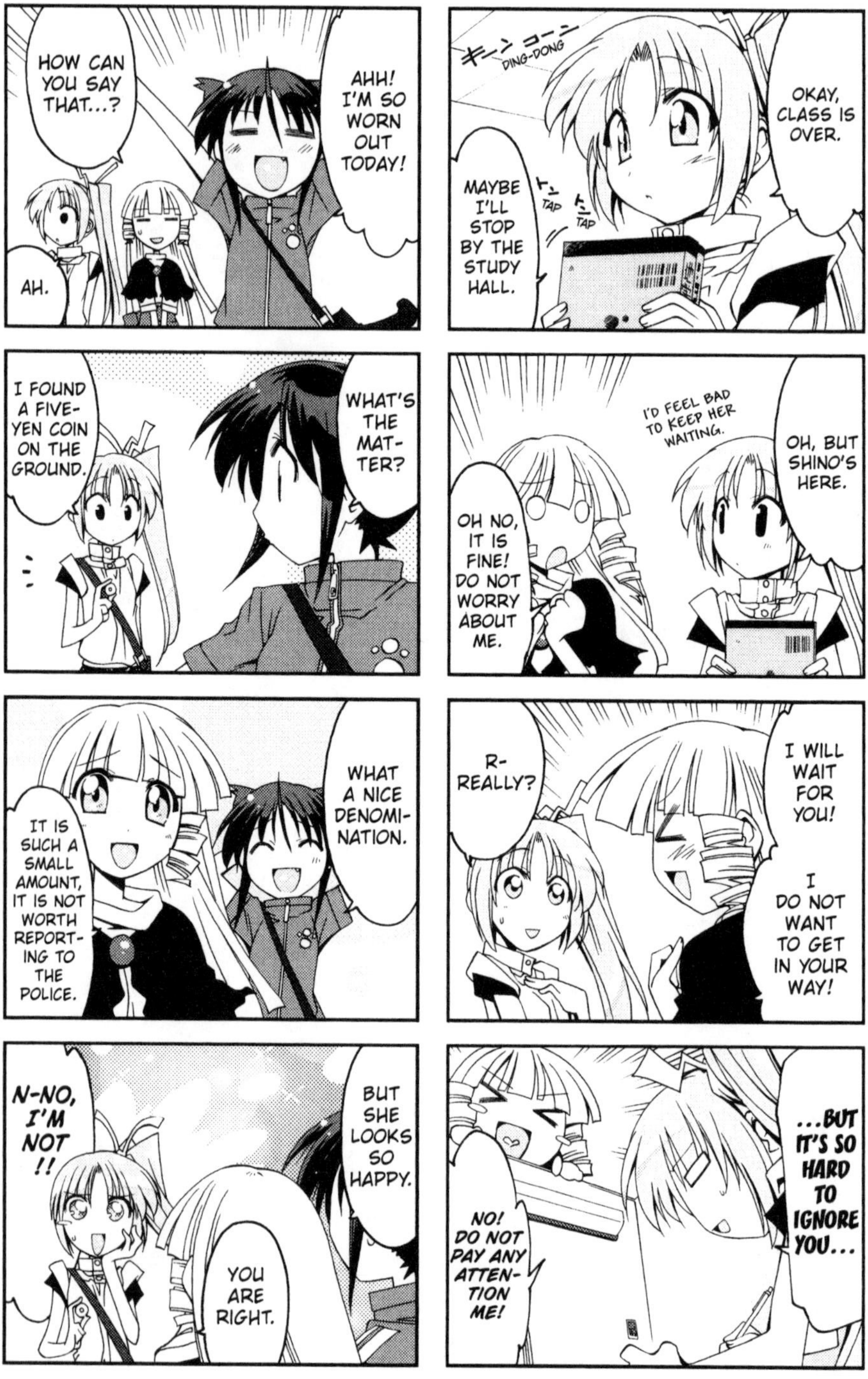
キーン コーン
DING-DONG
OKAY, CLASS IS OVER.
MAYBE I'LL STOP BY THE STUDY HALL.
トン
TAP
トン
TAP
OH, BUT SHINO'S HERE.
I'D FEEL BAD TO KEEP HER WAITING.
OH NO, IT IS FINE! DO NOT WORRY ABOUT ME.
I WILL WAIT FOR YOU!
I DO NOT WANT TO GET IN YOUR WAY!
R-REALLY?
...BUT IT'S SO HARD TO IGNORE YOU...
NO! DO NOT PAY ANY ATTENTION ME!
AHH! I'M SO WORN OUT TODAY!
HOW CAN YOU SAY THAT...?
AH.
WHAT'S THE MATTER?
I FOUND A FIVE-YEN COIN ON THE GROUND.
WHAT A NICE DENOMINATION.
IT IS SUCH A SMALL AMOUNT, IT IS NOT WORTH REPORTING TO THE POLICE.
BUT SHE LOOKS SO HAPPY.
N-NO, I'M NOT !!
YOU ARE RIGHT.

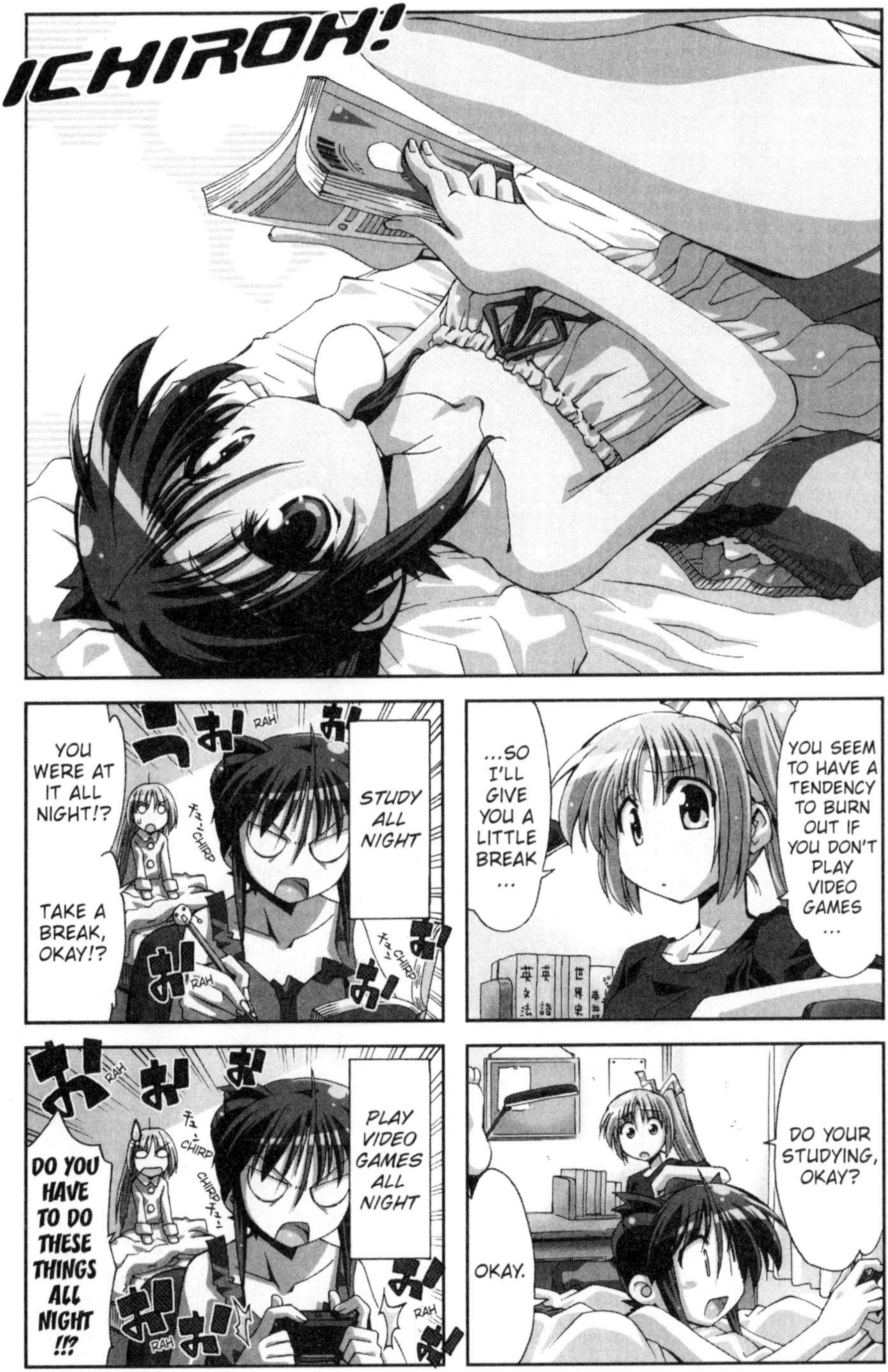
ICHIROH!
YOU SEEM TO HAVE A TENDENCY TO BURN OUT IF YOU DON'T PLAY VIDEO GAMES ...
...SO I'LL GIVE YOU A LITTLE BREAK ...
STUDY ALL NIGHT
RAH
YOU WERE AT IT ALL NIGHT!?
CHIRP
TAKE A BREAK, OKAY!?
CHIRP
RAH
DO YOUR STUDYING, OKAY?
OKAY.
PLAY VIDEO GAMES ALL NIGHT
RAH
CHIRP
CHIRP
DO YOU HAVE TO DO THESE THINGS ALL NIGHT!!?
RAH
RAH

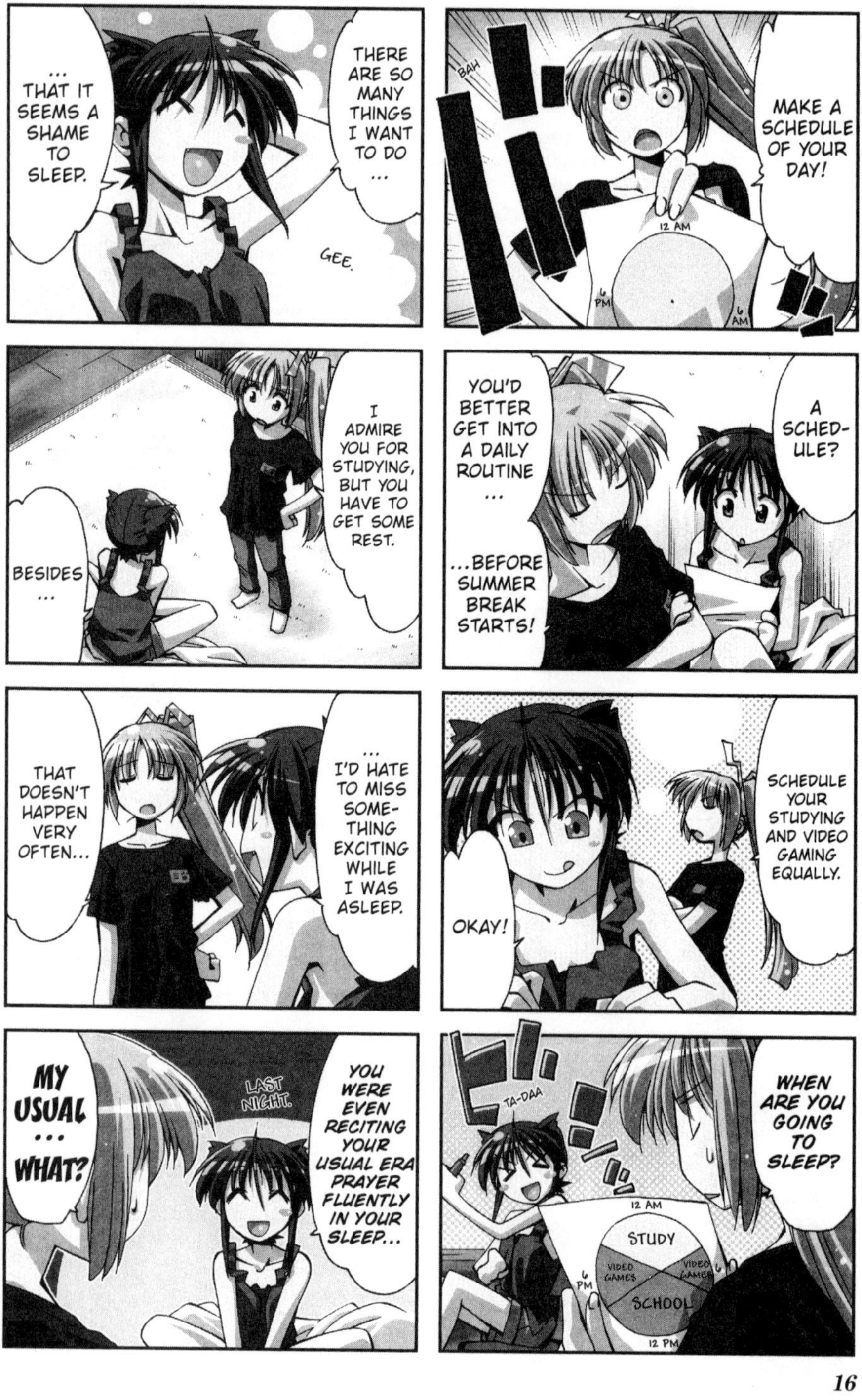
BAH
MAKE A SCHEDULE OF YOUR DAY!
12 AM
6 PM
6 AM
A SCHED-ULE?
YOU'D BETTER GET INTO A DAILY ROUTINE ...
...BEFORE SUMMER BREAK STARTS!
SCHEDULE YOUR STUDYING AND VIDEO GAMING EQUALLY.
OKAY!
TA-DAA
WHEN ARE YOU GOING TO SLEEP?
12 AM
STUDY
VIDEO GAMES
VIDEO GAMES
6 PM
6
SCHOOL
12 PM
THERE ARE SO MANY THINGS I WANT TO DO ...
... THAT IT SEEMS A SHAME TO SLEEP.
GEE.
I ADMIRE YOU FOR STUDYING, BUT YOU HAVE TO GET SOME REST.
BESIDES ...
... I'D HATE TO MISS SOME-THING EXCITING WHILE I WAS ASLEEP.
THAT DOESN'T HAPPEN VERY OFTEN...
LAST NIGHT.
YOU WERE EVEN RECITING YOUR USUAL ERA PRAYER FLUENTLY IN YOUR SLEEP...
MY USUAL ... WHAT?

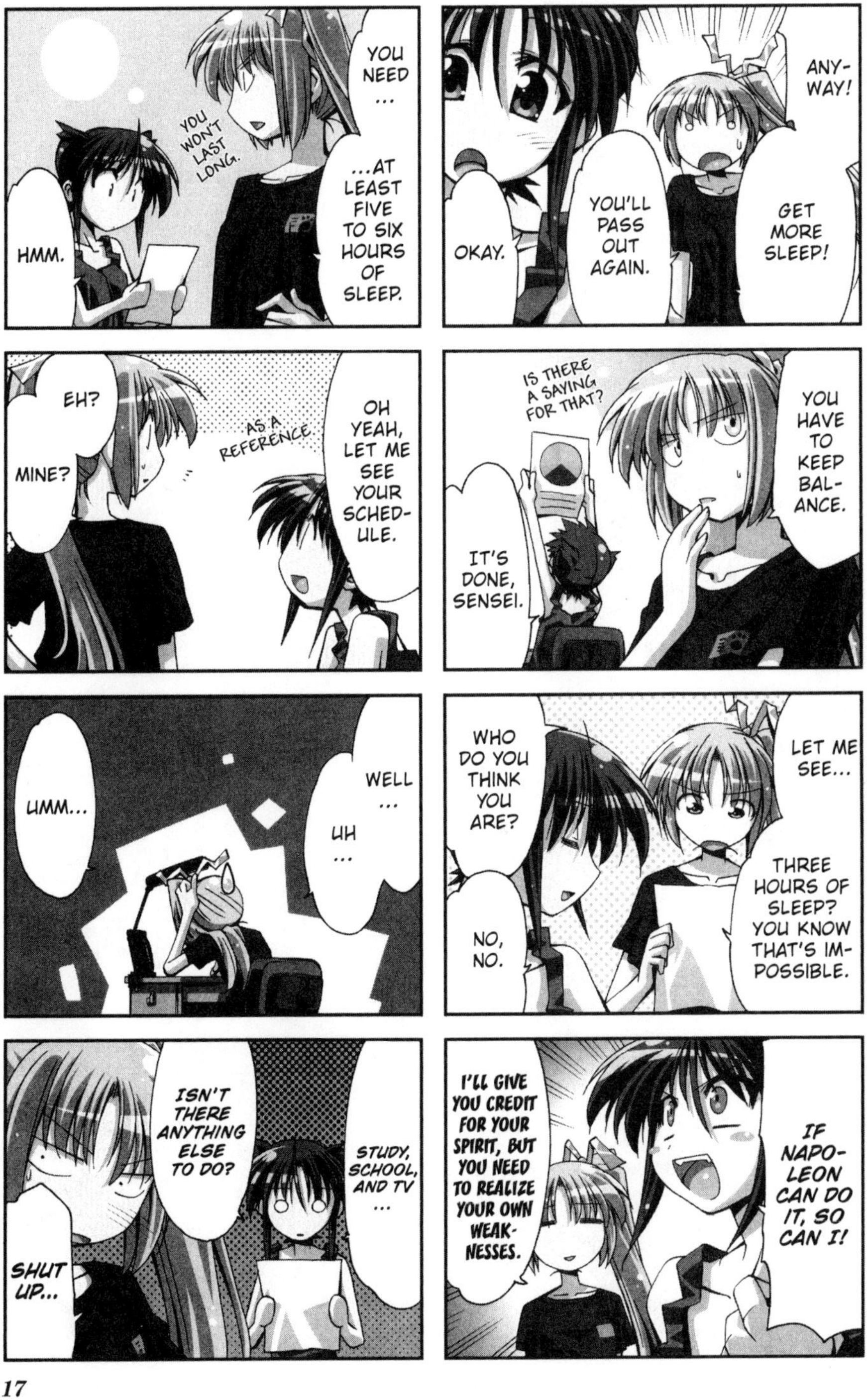
ANY-WAY!
GET MORE SLEEP!
YOU'LL PASS OUT AGAIN.
OKAY.
YOU HAVE TO KEEP BAL-ANCE.
IS THERE A SAYING FOR THAT?
IT'S DONE, SENSEI.
LET ME SEE...
THREE HOURS OF SLEEP? YOU KNOW THAT'S IM-POSSIBLE.
WHO DO YOU THINK YOU ARE?
NO, NO.
IF NAPO-LEON CAN DO IT, SO CAN I!
I'LL GIVE YOU CREDIT FOR YOUR SPIRIT, BUT YOU NEED TO REALIZE YOUR OWN WEAK-NESSES.
YOU NEED ...
...AT LEAST FIVE TO SIX HOURS OF SLEEP.
YOU WON'T LAST LONG.
HMM.
OH YEAH, LET ME SEE YOUR SCHED-ULE.
AS A REFERENCE.
EH?
MINE?
WELL ...
UH ...
UMM...
ISN'T THERE ANYTHING ELSE TO DO?
STUDY, SCHOOL, AND TV ...
SHUT UP...

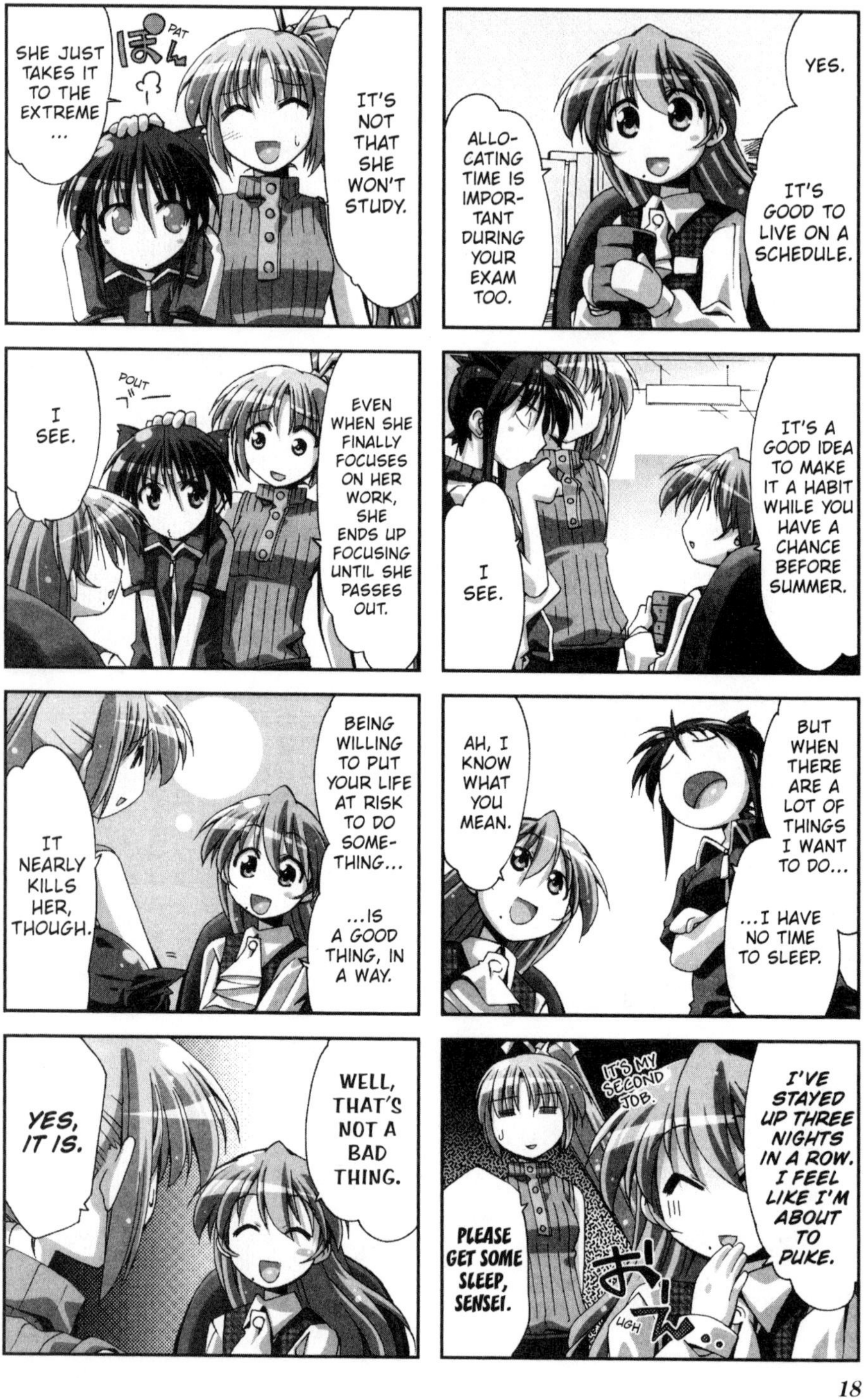
YES.
IT'S GOOD TO LIVE ON A SCHEDULE.
ALLOCATING TIME IS IMPORTANT DURING YOUR EXAM TOO.
IT'S NOT THAT SHE WON'T STUDY.
PAT
SHE JUST TAKES IT TO THE EXTREME...
IT'S A GOOD IDEA TO MAKE IT A HABIT WHILE YOU HAVE A CHANCE BEFORE SUMMER.
I SEE.
EVEN WHEN SHE FINALLY FOCUSES ON HER WORK, SHE ENDS UP FOCUSING UNTIL SHE PASSES OUT.
POUT
I SEE.
BUT WHEN THERE ARE A LOT OF THINGS I WANT TO DO...
...I HAVE NO TIME TO SLEEP.
AH, I KNOW WHAT YOU MEAN.
BEING WILLING TO PUT YOUR LIFE AT RISK TO DO SOMETHING...
...IS A GOOD THING, IN A WAY.
IT NEARLY KILLS HER, THOUGH.
I'VE STAYED UP THREE NIGHTS IN A ROW. I FEEL LIKE I'M ABOUT TO PUKE.
IT'S MY SECOND JOB.
PLEASE GET SOME SLEEP, SENSEI.
UGH
WELL, THAT'S NOT A BAD THING.
YES, IT IS.

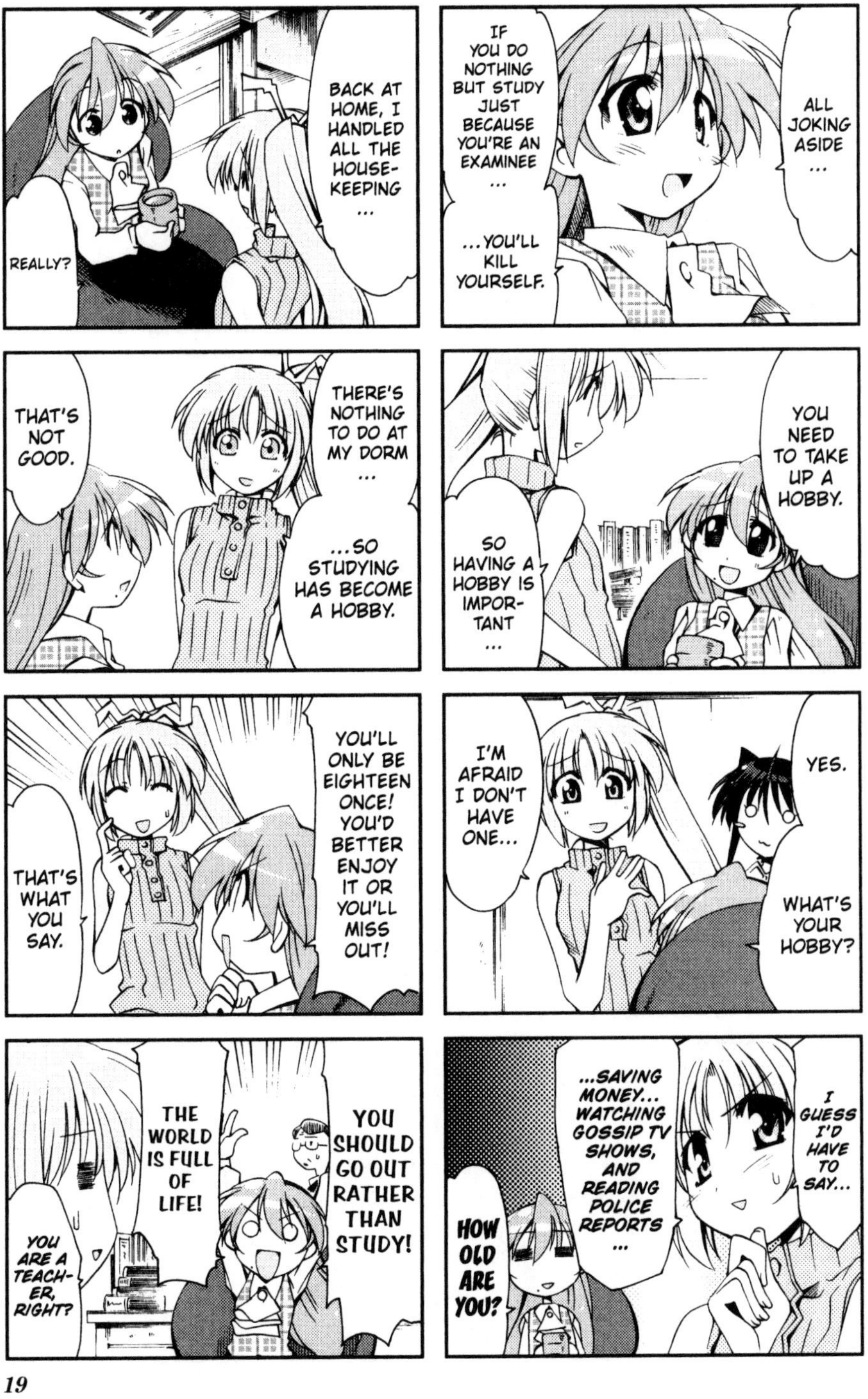
ALL JOKING ASIDE ...
IF YOU DO NOTHING BUT STUDY JUST BECAUSE YOU'RE AN EXAMINEE ...
...YOU'LL KILL YOURSELF.
YOU NEED TO TAKE UP A HOBBY.
SO HAVING A HOBBY IS IMPORTANT ...
YES.
WHAT'S YOUR HOBBY?
I'M AFRAID I DON'T HAVE ONE...
I GUESS I'D HAVE TO SAY...
...SAVING MONEY... WATCHING GOSSIP TV SHOWS, AND READING POLICE REPORTS ...
HOW OLD ARE YOU?
BACK AT HOME, I HANDLED ALL THE HOUSE-KEEPING ...
REALLY?
THERE'S NOTHING TO DO AT MY DORM ...
...SO STUDYING HAS BECOME A HOBBY.
THAT'S NOT GOOD.
YOU'LL ONLY BE EIGHTEEN ONCE! YOU'D BETTER ENJOY IT OR YOU'LL MISS OUT!
THAT'S WHAT YOU SAY.
YOU SHOULD GO OUT RATHER THAN STUDY!
THE WORLD IS FULL OF LIFE!
YOU ARE A TEACHER, RIGHT?

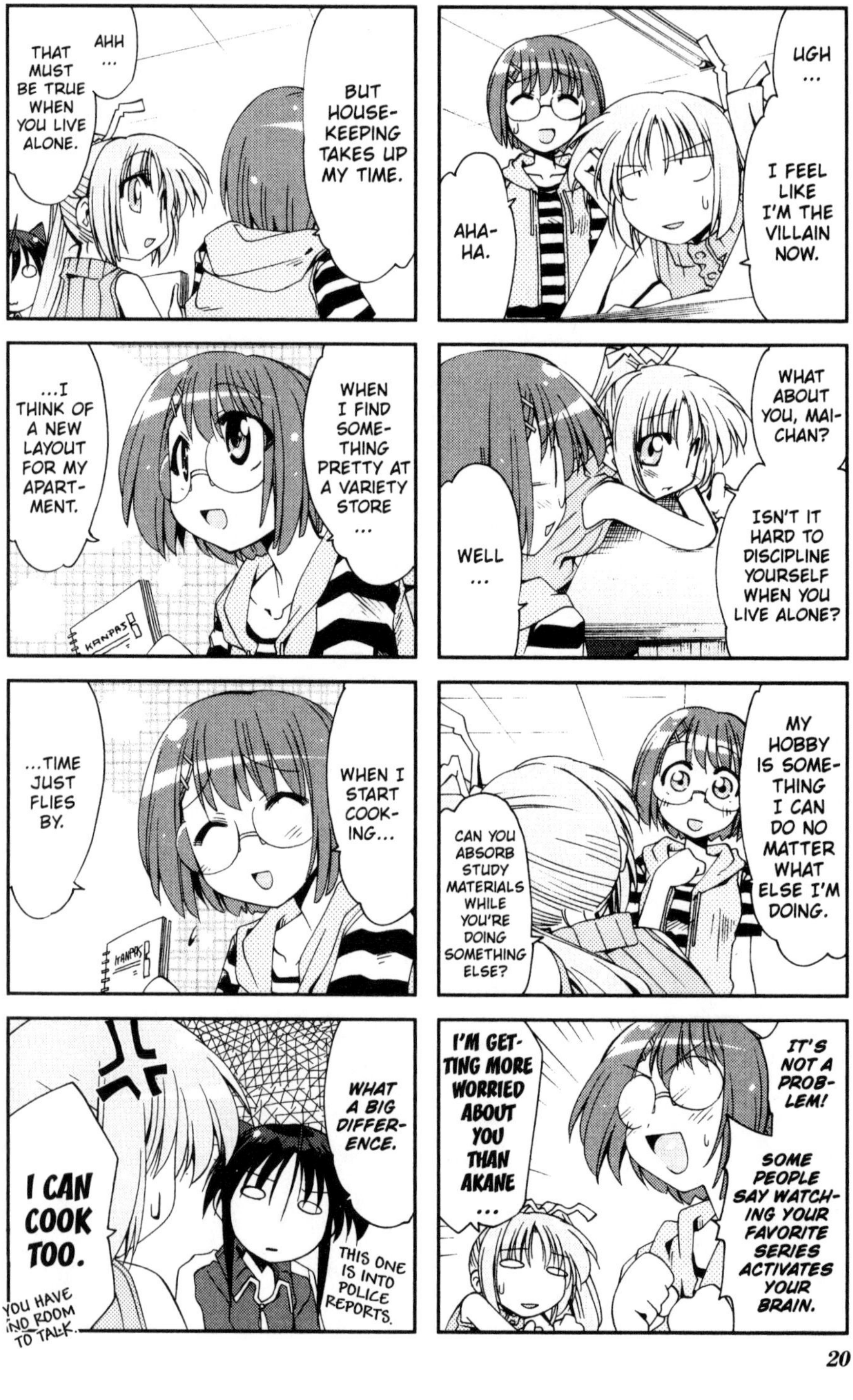
UGH ...
I FEEL LIKE I'M THE VILLAIN NOW.
AHA-HA.
BUT HOUSE-KEEPING TAKES UP MY TIME.
AHH ...
THAT MUST BE TRUE WHEN YOU LIVE ALONE.
WHAT ABOUT YOU, MAI-CHAN?
ISN'T IT HARD TO DISCIPLINE YOURSELF WHEN YOU LIVE ALONE?
WELL ...
WHEN I FIND SOME-THING PRETTY AT A VARIETY STORE ...
...I THINK OF A NEW LAYOUT FOR MY APART-MENT.
KANPAS
MY HOBBY IS SOME-THING I CAN DO NO MATTER WHAT ELSE I'M DOING.
CAN YOU ABSORB STUDY MATERIALS WHILE YOU'RE DOING SOMETHING ELSE?
WHEN I START COOK-ING...
...TIME JUST FLIES BY.
KANPAS
IT'S NOT A PROB-LEM!
SOME PEOPLE SAY WATCH-ING YOUR FAVORITE SERIES ACTIVATES YOUR BRAIN.
I'M GET-TING MORE WORRIED ABOUT YOU THAN AKANE ...
WHAT A BIG DIFFER-ENCE.
I CAN COOK TOO.
THIS ONE IS INTO POLICE REPORTS.
YOU HAVE NO ROOM TO TALK.

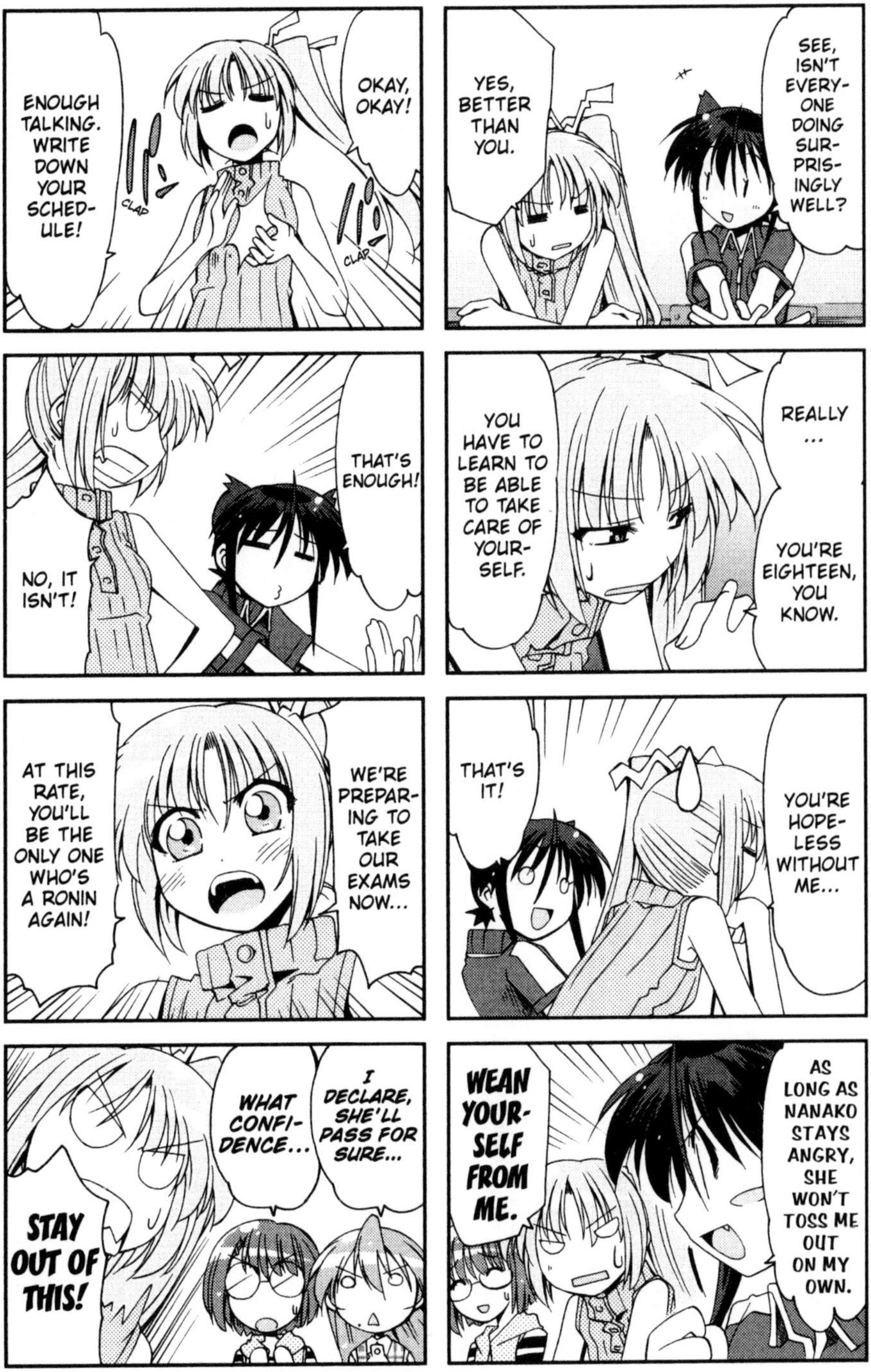
SEE, ISN'T EVERYONE DOING SURPRISINGLY WELL?
YES, BETTER THAN YOU.
OKAY, OKAY!
CLAP
CLAP
ENOUGH TALKING. WRITE DOWN YOUR SCHEDULE!
REALLY...
YOU'RE EIGHTEEN, YOU KNOW.
YOU HAVE TO LEARN TO BE ABLE TO TAKE CARE OF YOURSELF.
THAT'S ENOUGH!
NO, IT ISN'T!
YOU'RE HOPELESS WITHOUT ME...
THAT'S IT!
WE'RE PREPARING TO TAKE OUR EXAMS NOW...
AT THIS RATE, YOU'LL BE THE ONLY ONE WHO'S A RONIN AGAIN!
AS LONG AS NANAKO STAYS ANGRY, SHE WON'T TOSS ME OUT ON MY OWN.
WEAN YOURSELF FROM ME.
I DECLARE, SHE'LL PASS FOR SURE...
WHAT CONFIDENCE...
STAY OUT OF THIS!

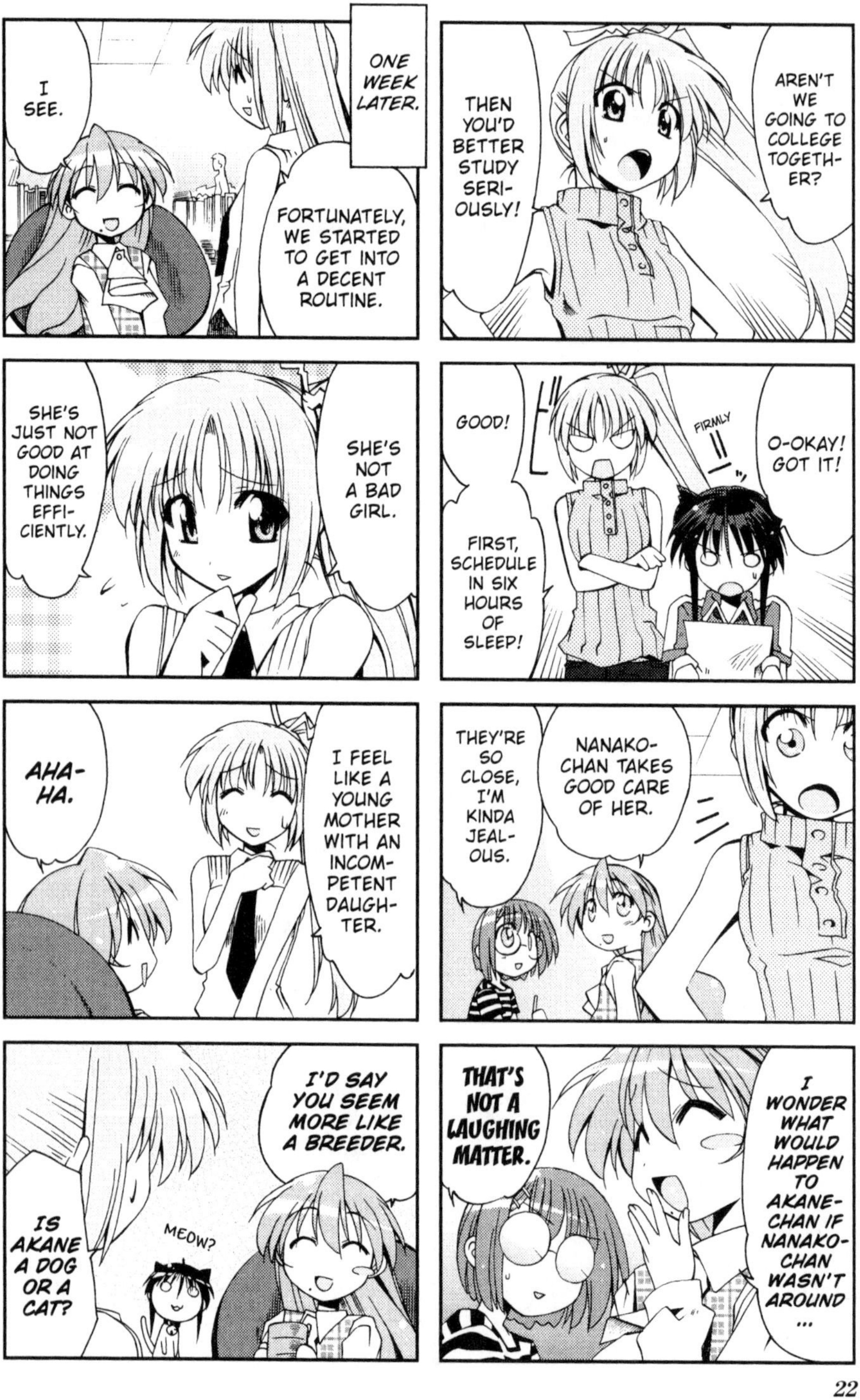
AREN'T WE GOING TO COLLEGE TOGETHER?
THEN YOU'D BETTER STUDY SERIOUSLY!
ONE WEEK LATER.
FORTUNATELY, WE STARTED TO GET INTO A DECENT ROUTINE.
I SEE.
O-OKAY! GOT IT!
FIRMLY
GOOD!
FIRST, SCHEDULE IN SIX HOURS OF SLEEP!
SHE'S NOT A BAD GIRL.
SHE'S JUST NOT GOOD AT DOING THINGS EFFICIENTLY.
NANAKO-CHAN TAKES GOOD CARE OF HER.
THEY'RE SO CLOSE, I'M KINDA JEALOUS.
I FEEL LIKE A YOUNG MOTHER WITH AN INCOMPETENT DAUGHTER.
AHAHA.
I WONDER WHAT WOULD HAPPEN TO AKANE-CHAN IF NANAKO-CHAN WASN'T AROUND...
THAT'S NOT A LAUGHING MATTER.
I'D SAY YOU SEEM MORE LIKE A BREEDER.
MEOW?
IS AKANE A DOG OR A CAT?

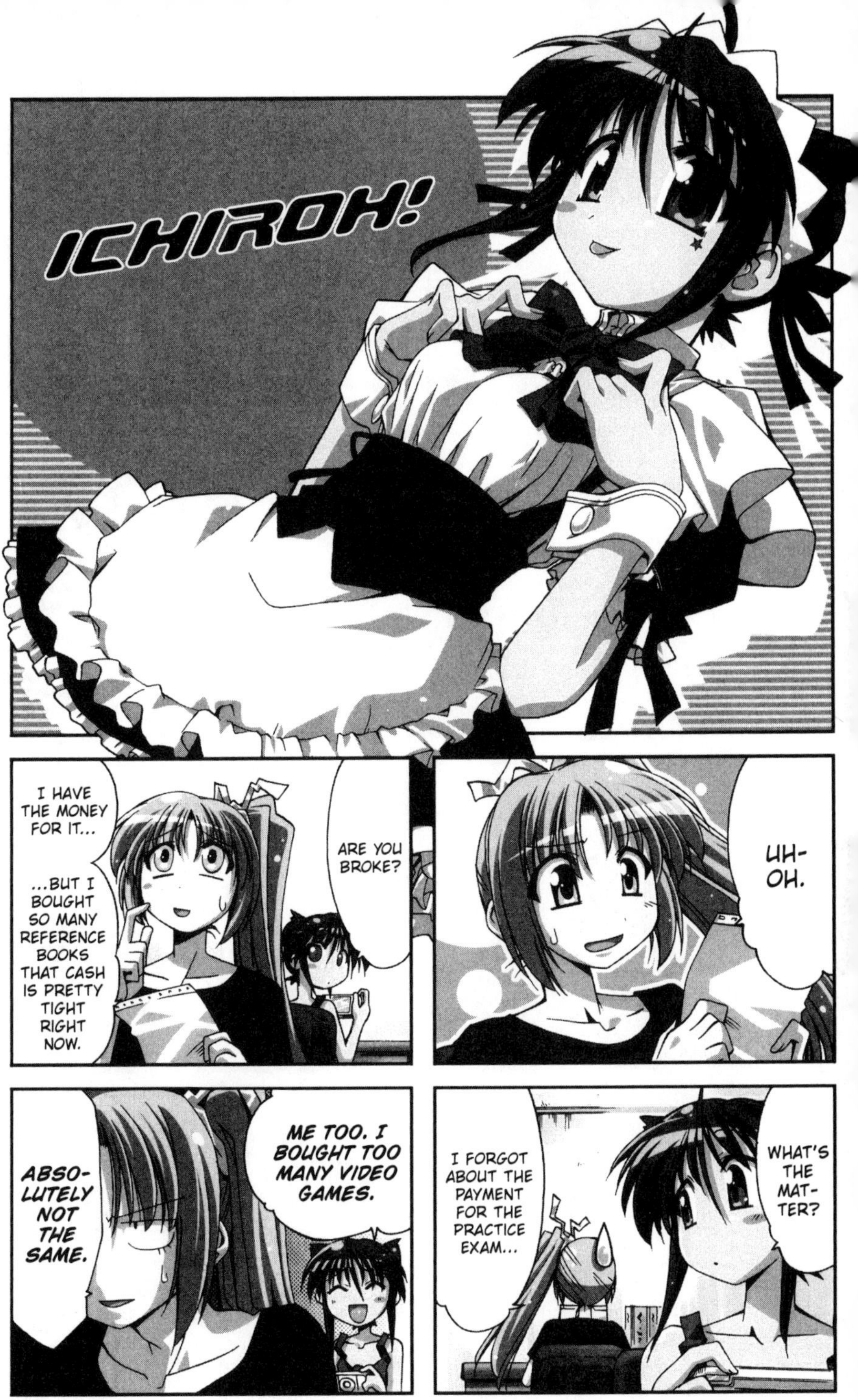
ICHIROH!
UH-OH.
ARE YOU BROKE?
I HAVE THE MONEY FOR IT...
...BUT I BOUGHT SO MANY REFERENCE BOOKS THAT CASH IS PRETTY TIGHT RIGHT NOW.
WHAT'S THE MAT-TER?
I FORGOT ABOUT THE PAYMENT FOR THE PRACTICE EXAM...
ME TOO. I BOUGHT TOO MANY VIDEO GAMES.
ABSO-LUTELY NOT THE SAME.

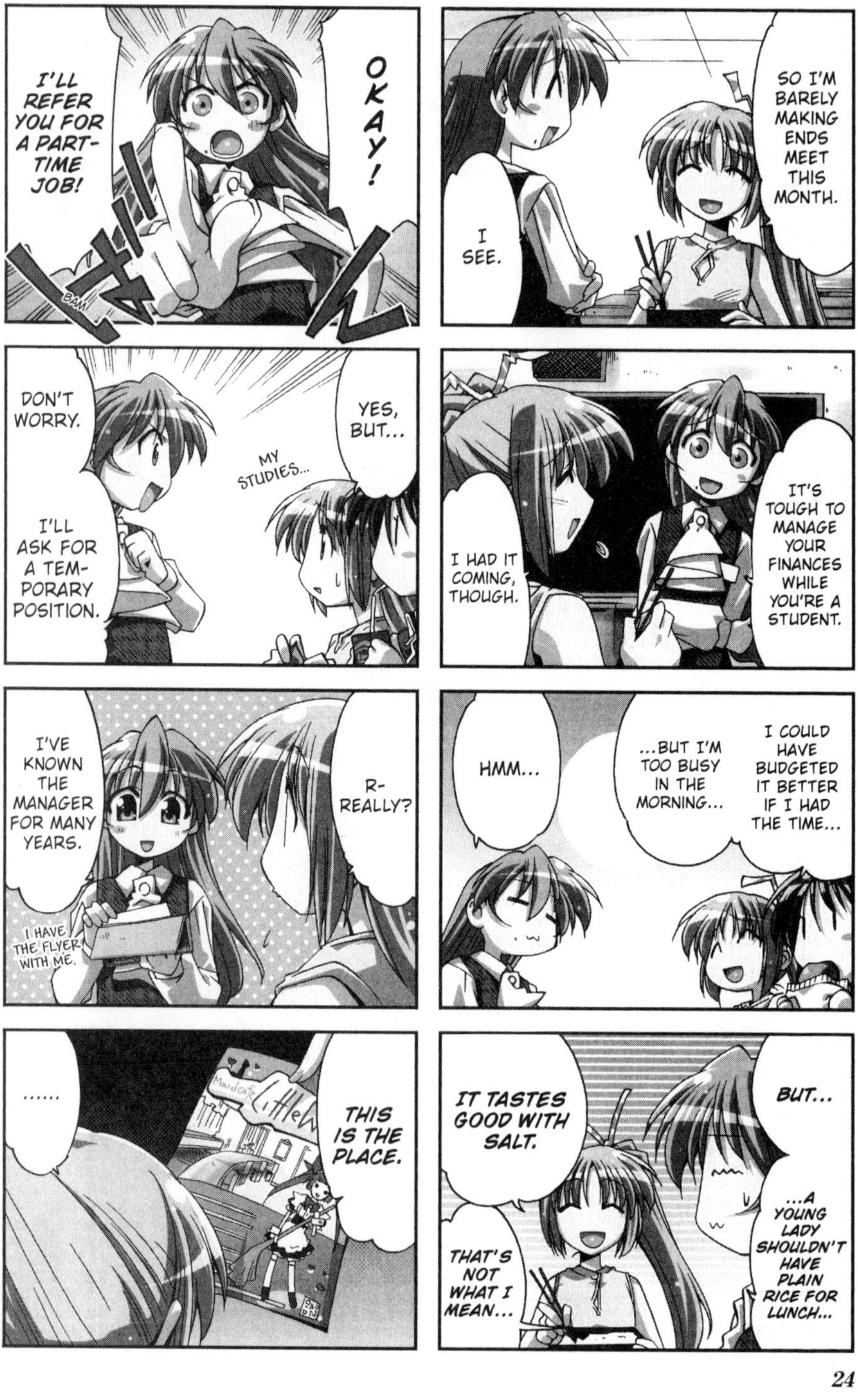
SO I'M BARELY MAKING ENDS MEET THIS MONTH.
I SEE.
IT'S TOUGH TO MANAGE YOUR FINANCES WHILE YOU'RE A STUDENT.
I HAD IT COMING, THOUGH.
I COULD HAVE BUDGETED IT BETTER IF I HAD THE TIME...
...BUT I'M TOO BUSY IN THE MORNING...
HMM...
BUT...
...A YOUNG LADY SHOULDN'T HAVE PLAIN RICE FOR LUNCH...
IT TASTES GOOD WITH SALT.
THAT'S NOT WHAT I MEAN...
OKAY!
I'LL REFER YOU FOR A PART-TIME JOB!
BAM
YES, BUT...
MY STUDIES...
DON'T WORRY.
I'LL ASK FOR A TEMPORARY POSITION.
R-REALLY?
I'VE KNOWN THE MANAGER FOR MANY YEARS.
I HAVE THE FLYER WITH ME.
THIS IS THE PLACE.
......

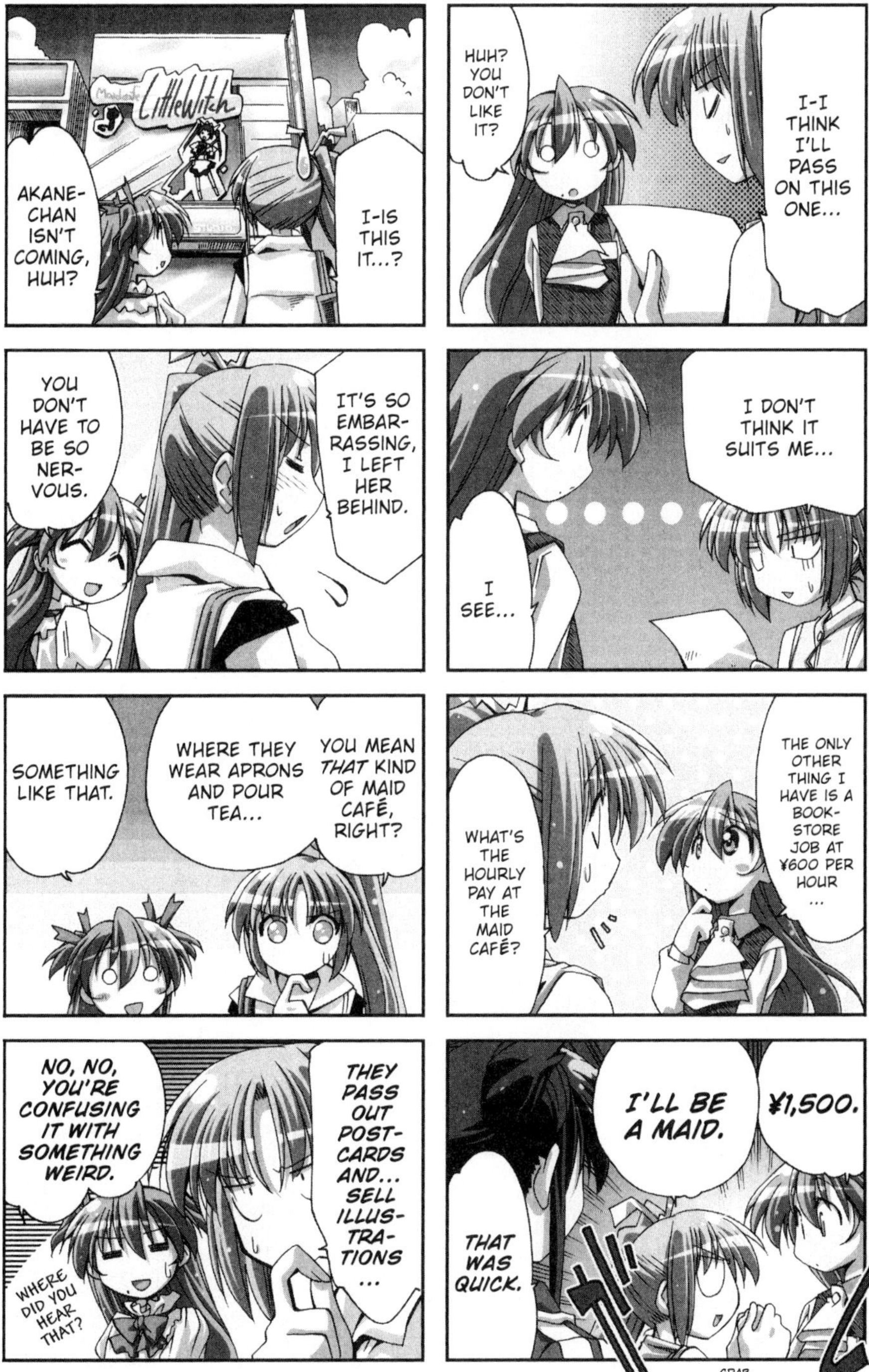
I-I THINK I'LL PASS ON THIS ONE...
HUH? YOU DON'T LIKE IT?
LittleWitch
I-IS THIS IT...?
AKANE-CHAN ISN'T COMING, HUH?
I DON'T THINK IT SUITS ME...
I SEE...
IT'S SO EMBARRASSING, I LEFT HER BEHIND.
YOU DON'T HAVE TO BE SO NERVOUS.
THE ONLY OTHER THING I HAVE IS A BOOKSTORE JOB AT ¥600 PER HOUR...
WHAT'S THE HOURLY PAY AT THE MAID CAFÉ?
YOU MEAN *THAT* KIND OF MAID CAFÉ, RIGHT?
WHERE THEY WEAR APRONS AND POUR TEA...
SOMETHING LIKE THAT.
¥1,500.
I'LL BE A MAID.
THAT WAS QUICK.
GRAB
THEY PASS OUT POSTCARDS AND... SELL ILLUSTRATIONS...
NO, NO, YOU'RE CONFUSING IT WITH SOMETHING WEIRD.
WHERE DID YOU HEAR THAT?

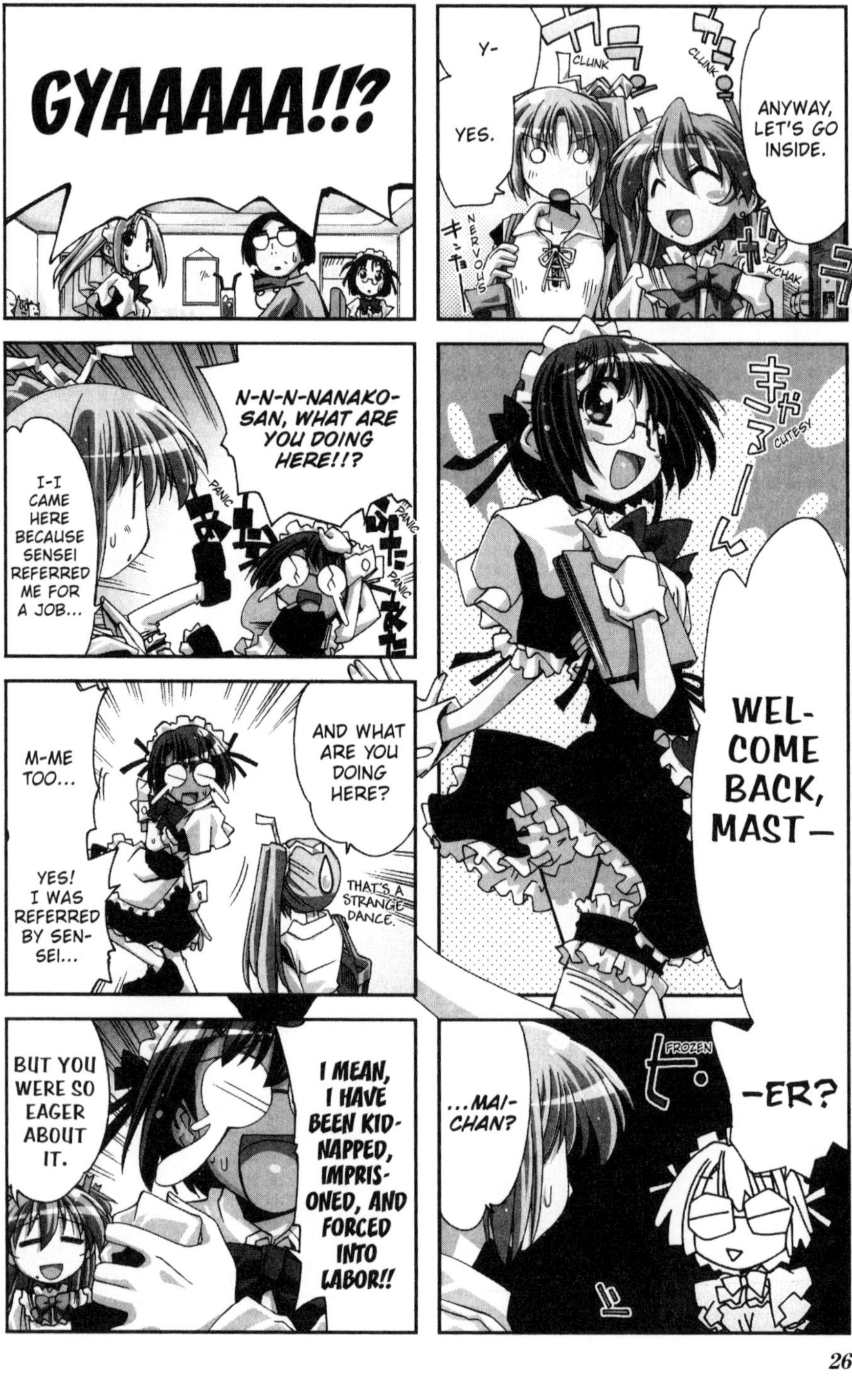
CLUNK
CLUNK
ANYWAY, LET'S GO INSIDE.
Y-
YES.
NERVOUS
KCHAK
GYAAAAA!!?
CUTESY
WELCOME BACK, MAST—
N-N-N-NANAKO-SAN, WHAT ARE YOU DOING HERE!!?
PANIC
PANIC
PANIC
I-I CAME HERE BECAUSE SENSEI REFERRED ME FOR A JOB...
AND WHAT ARE YOU DOING HERE?
M-ME TOO...
THAT'S A STRANGE DANCE.
YES! I WAS REFERRED BY SENSEI...
FROZEN
-ER?
...MAI-CHAN?
I MEAN, I HAVE BEEN KIDNAPPED, IMPRISONED, AND FORCED INTO LABOR!!
BUT YOU WERE SO EAGER ABOUT IT.

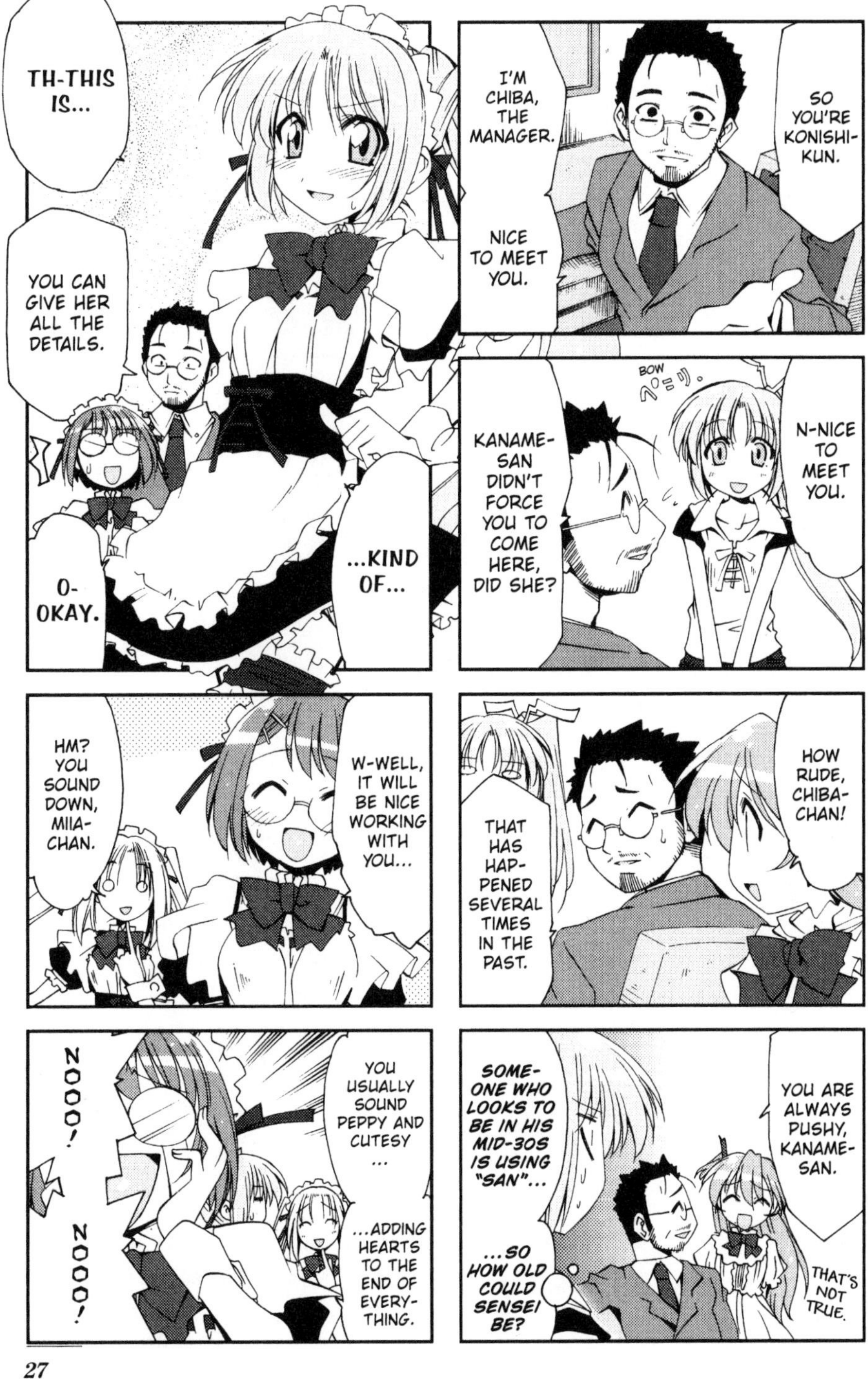
SO YOU'RE KONISHI-KUN.
I'M CHIBA, THE MANAGER.
NICE TO MEET YOU.
BOW
N-NICE TO MEET YOU.
KANAME-SAN DIDN'T FORCE YOU TO COME HERE, DID SHE?
TH-THIS IS...
YOU CAN GIVE HER ALL THE DETAILS.
...KIND OF...
O-OKAY.
HOW RUDE, CHIBA-CHAN!
THAT HAS HAPPENED SEVERAL TIMES IN THE PAST.
W-WELL, IT WILL BE NICE WORKING WITH YOU...
HM? YOU SOUND DOWN, MIIA-CHAN.
YOU ARE ALWAYS PUSHY, KANAME-SAN.
THAT'S NOT TRUE.
SOMEONE WHO LOOKS TO BE IN HIS MID-30S IS USING "SAN"...
...SO HOW OLD COULD SENSEI BE?
YOU USUALLY SOUND PEPPY AND CUTESY ...
...ADDING HEARTS TO THE END OF EVERYTHING.
NOOO!
NOOO!

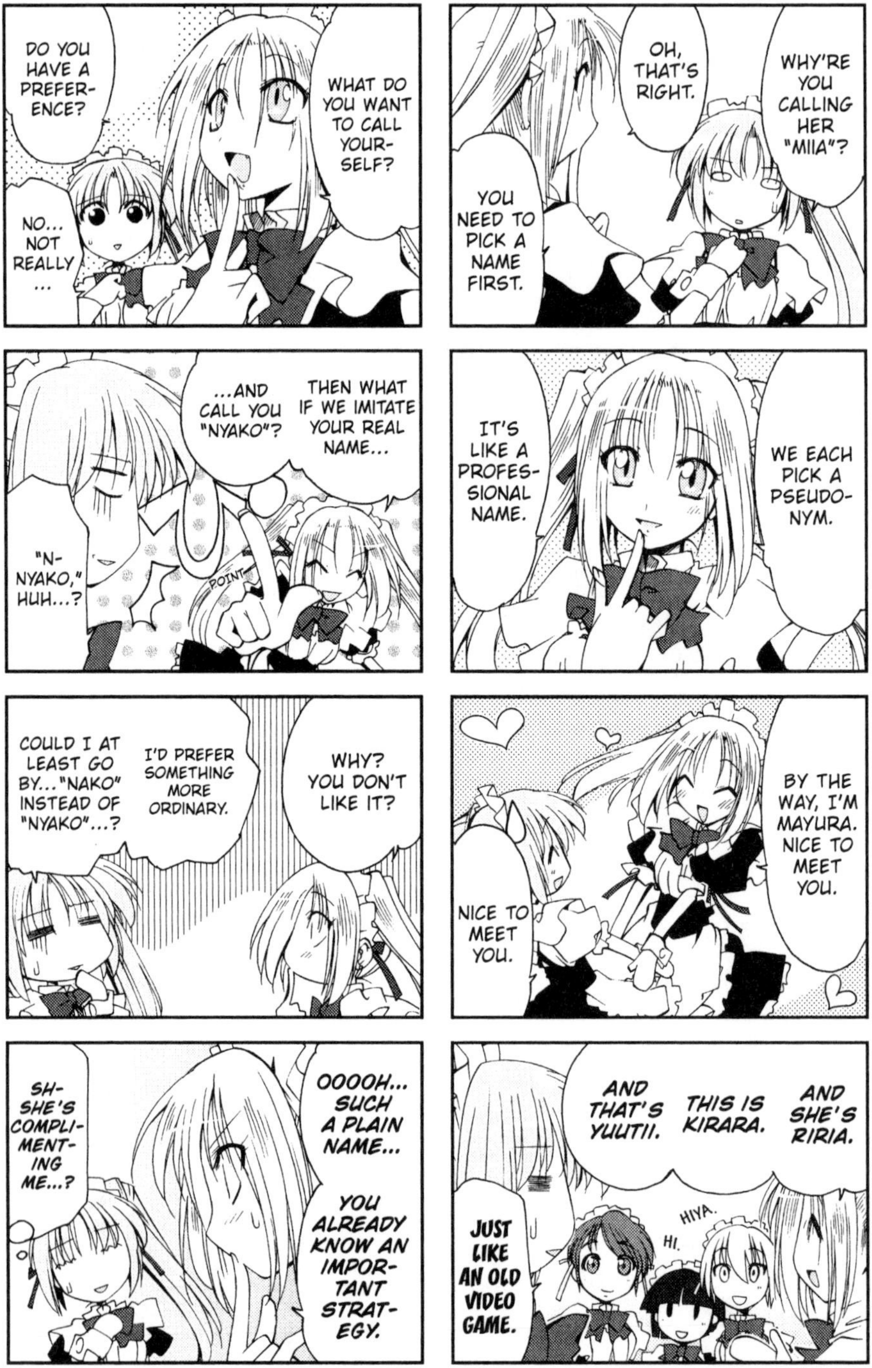
WHY'RE YOU CALLING HER "MIIA"?
OH, THAT'S RIGHT.
YOU NEED TO PICK A NAME FIRST.
WE EACH PICK A PSEUDONYM.
IT'S LIKE A PROFESSIONAL NAME.
BY THE WAY, I'M MAYURA. NICE TO MEET YOU.
NICE TO MEET YOU.
AND SHE'S RIRIA.
THIS IS KIRARA.
AND THAT'S YUUTII.
HIYA.
HI.
JUST LIKE AN OLD VIDEO GAME.
WHAT DO YOU WANT TO CALL YOURSELF?
DO YOU HAVE A PREFERENCE?
NO... NOT REALLY...
THEN WHAT IF WE IMITATE YOUR REAL NAME...
...AND CALL YOU "NYAKO"?
POINT
"N-NYAKO," HUH...?
WHY? YOU DON'T LIKE IT?
I'D PREFER SOMETHING MORE ORDINARY.
COULD I AT LEAST GO BY..."NAKO" INSTEAD OF "NYAKO"...?
OOOOH... SUCH A PLAIN NAME...
YOU ALREADY KNOW AN IMPORTANT STRATEGY.
SH-SHE'S COMPLIMENTING ME...?

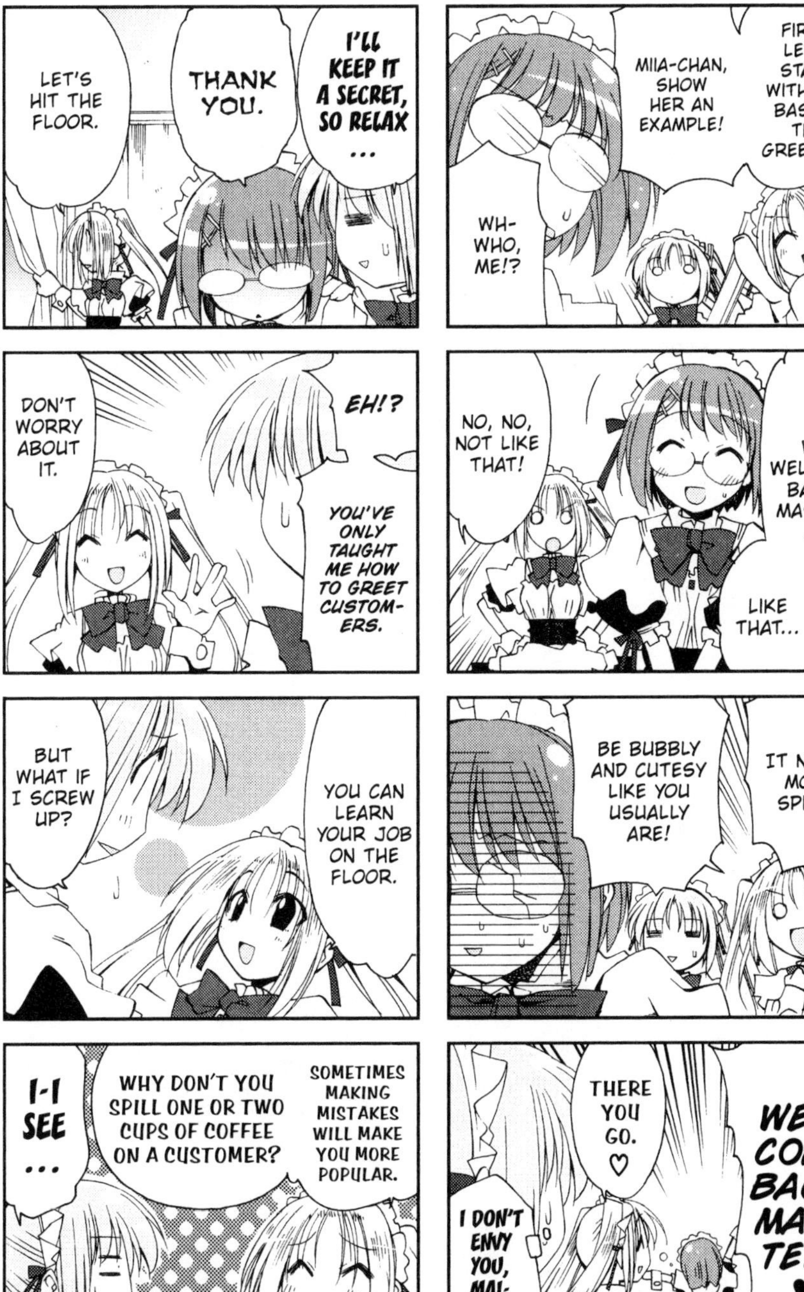

FIRST, LET'S START WITH THE BASICS: THE GREETING.
MIIA-CHAN, SHOW HER AN EXAMPLE!
WH-WHO, ME!?
W-WELCOME BACK, MASTER ...
LIKE THAT...
NO, NO, NOT LIKE THAT!
IT NEEDS MORE SPIRIT!
BE BUBBLY AND CUTESY LIKE YOU USUALLY ARE!
WEL-COME BACK, MAS-TER! ♥
THERE YOU GO. ♡
I DON'T ENVY YOU, MAI-CHAN ...
I'LL KEEP IT A SECRET, SO RELAX ...
THANK YOU.
LET'S HIT THE FLOOR.
EH!?
YOU'VE ONLY TAUGHT ME HOW TO GREET CUSTOM-ERS.
DON'T WORRY ABOUT IT.
YOU CAN LEARN YOUR JOB ON THE FLOOR.
BUT WHAT IF I SCREW UP?
SOMETIMES MAKING MISTAKES WILL MAKE YOU MORE POPULAR.
WHY DON'T YOU SPILL ONE OR TWO CUPS OF COFFEE ON A CUSTOMER?
I-I SEE ...

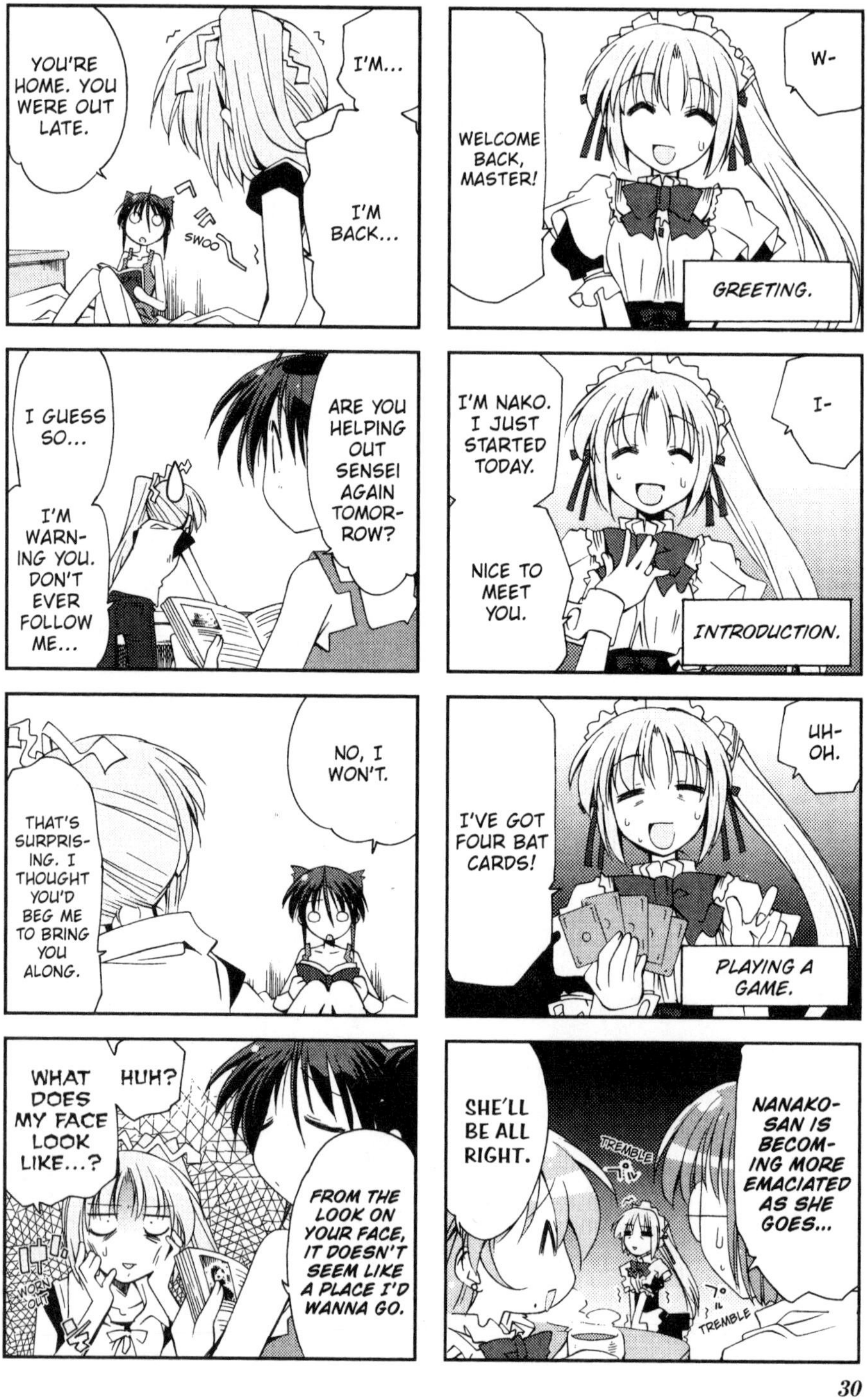
W-
WELCOME BACK, MASTER!
GREETING.
I-
I'M NAKO. I JUST STARTED TODAY.
NICE TO MEET YOU.
INTRODUCTION.
UH-OH.
I'VE GOT FOUR BAT CARDS!
PLAYING A GAME.
NANAKO-SAN IS BECOMING MORE EMACIATED AS SHE GOES...
TREMBLE
SHE'LL BE ALL RIGHT.
TREMBLE
I'M...
I'M BACK...
SWOO
YOU'RE HOME. YOU WERE OUT LATE.
ARE YOU HELPING OUT SENSEI AGAIN TOMORROW?
I GUESS SO...
I'M WARNING YOU. DON'T EVER FOLLOW ME...
NO, I WON'T.
THAT'S SURPRISING. I THOUGHT YOU'D BEG ME TO BRING YOU ALONG.
HUH?
WHAT DOES MY FACE LOOK LIKE...?
FROM THE LOOK ON YOUR FACE, IT DOESN'T SEEM LIKE A PLACE I'D WANNA GO.
WORN OUT

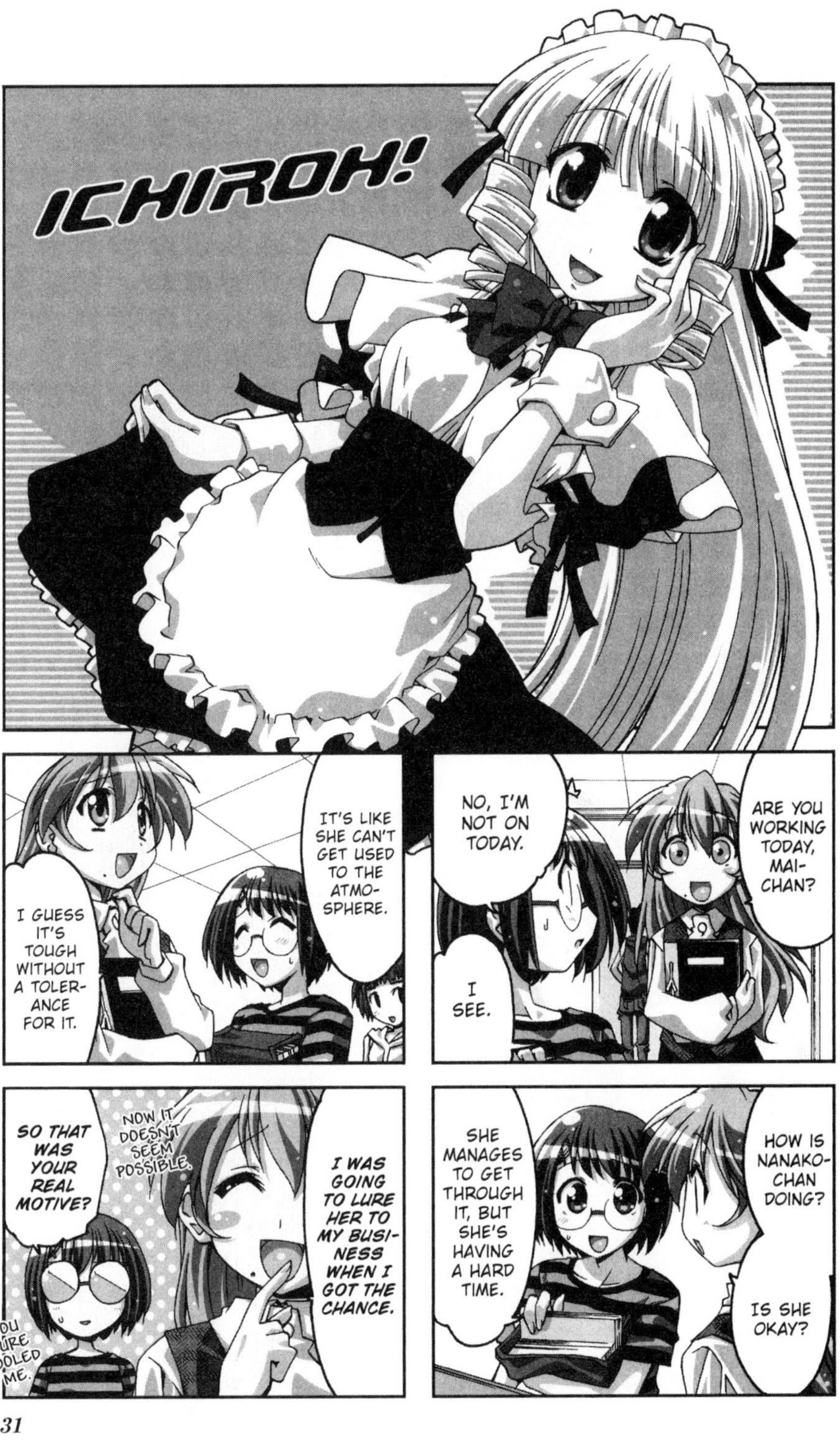
ICHIROH!
ARE YOU WORKING TODAY, MAI-CHAN?
NO, I'M NOT ON TODAY.
I SEE.
IT'S LIKE SHE CAN'T GET USED TO THE ATMOSPHERE.
I GUESS IT'S TOUGH WITHOUT A TOLERANCE FOR IT.
HOW IS NANAKO-CHAN DOING?
SHE MANAGES TO GET THROUGH IT, BUT SHE'S HAVING A HARD TIME.
IS SHE OKAY?
I WAS GOING TO LURE HER TO MY BUSINESS WHEN I GOT THE CHANCE.
NOW IT DOESN'T SEEM POSSIBLE.
SO THAT WAS YOUR REAL MOTIVE?
YOU SURE FOOLED ME.

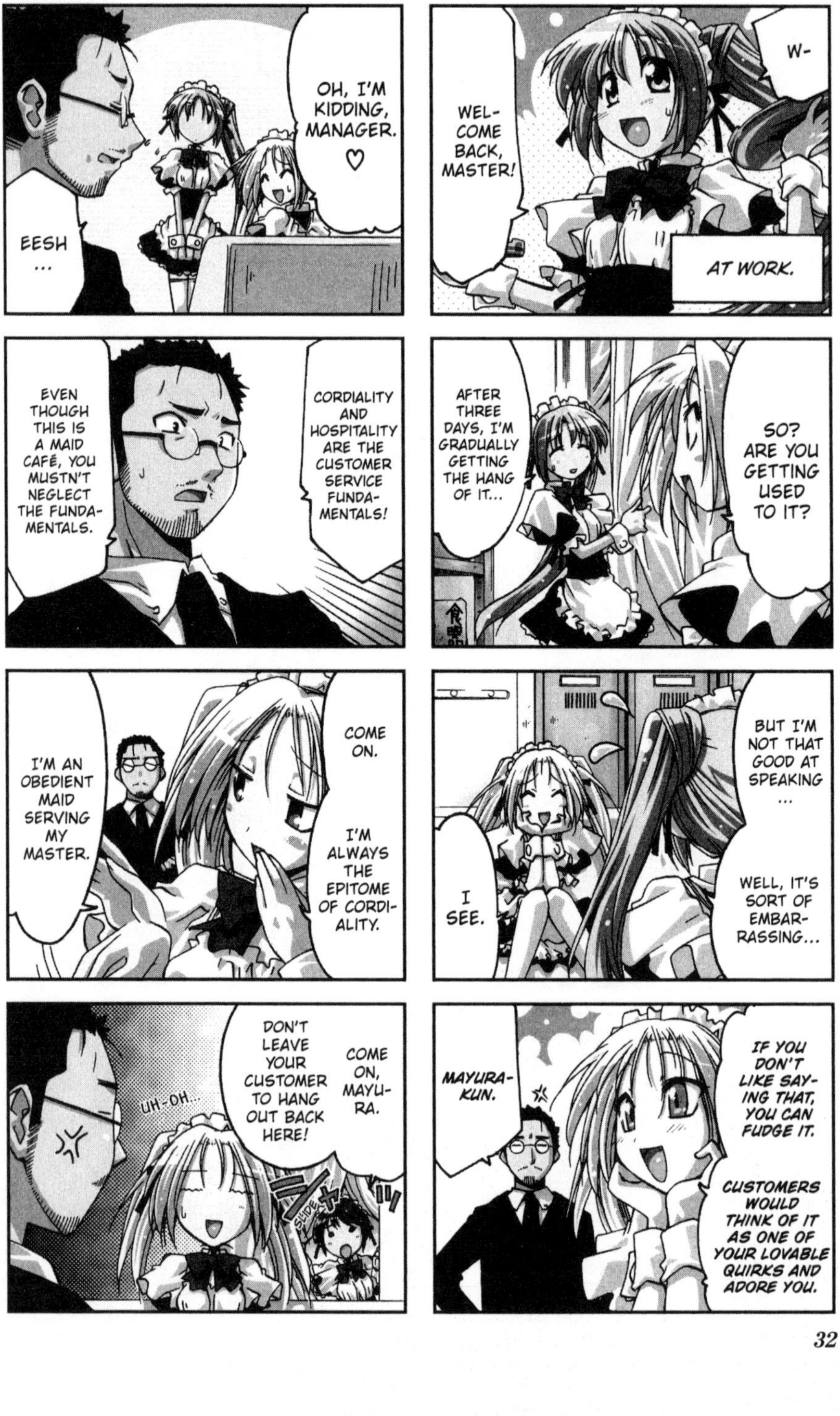
W-
WEL-COME BACK, MASTER!
AT WORK.
OH, I'M KIDDING, MANAGER. ♡
EESH...
SO? ARE YOU GETTING USED TO IT?
AFTER THREE DAYS, I'M GRADUALLY GETTING THE HANG OF IT...
CORDIALITY AND HOSPITALITY ARE THE CUSTOMER SERVICE FUNDA-MENTALS!
EVEN THOUGH THIS IS A MAID CAFÉ, YOU MUSTN'T NEGLECT THE FUNDA-MENTALS.
BUT I'M NOT THAT GOOD AT SPEAKING...
WELL, IT'S SORT OF EMBAR-RASSING...
I SEE.
COME ON.
I'M ALWAYS THE EPITOME OF CORDI-ALITY.
I'M AN OBEDIENT MAID SERVING MY MASTER.
IF YOU DON'T LIKE SAY-ING THAT, YOU CAN FUDGE IT.
CUSTOMERS WOULD THINK OF IT AS ONE OF YOUR LOVABLE QUIRKS AND ADORE YOU.
MAYURA-KUN.
COME ON, MAYU-RA.
DON'T LEAVE YOUR CUSTOMER TO HANG OUT BACK HERE!
UH-OH...
SLIDE

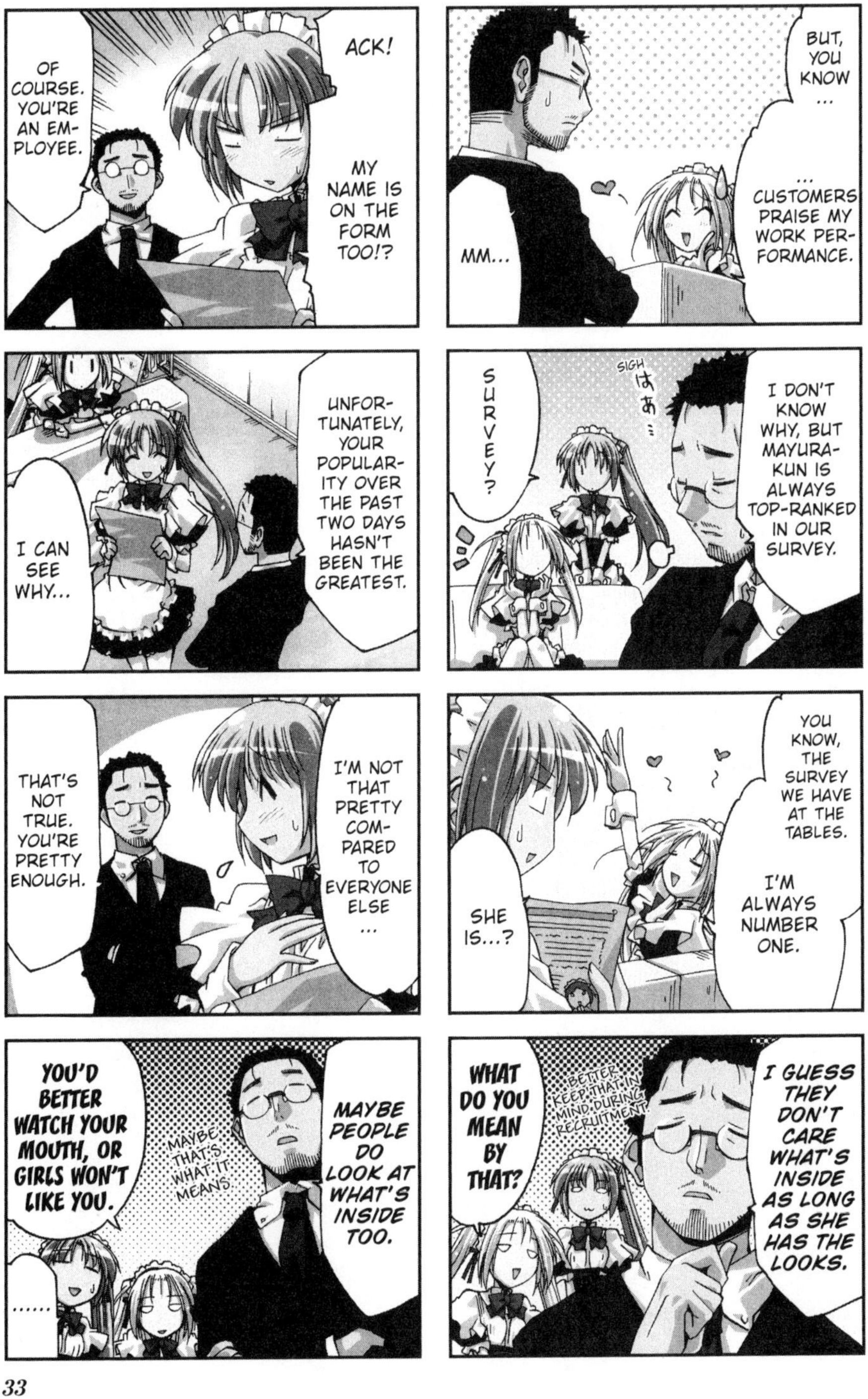

BUT, YOU KNOW ...
... CUSTOMERS PRAISE MY WORK PERFORMANCE.
MM...
I DON'T KNOW WHY, BUT MAYURA-KUN IS ALWAYS TOP-RANKED IN OUR SURVEY.
SIGH はぁ…
SURVEY?
YOU KNOW, THE SURVEY WE HAVE AT THE TABLES.
I'M ALWAYS NUMBER ONE.
SHE IS...?
I GUESS THEY DON'T CARE WHAT'S INSIDE AS LONG AS SHE HAS THE LOOKS.
BETTER KEEP THAT IN MIND DURING RECRUITMENT.
WHAT DO YOU MEAN BY THAT?
ACK!
MY NAME IS ON THE FORM TOO!?
OF COURSE. YOU'RE AN EMPLOYEE.
UNFORTUNATELY, YOUR POPULARITY OVER THE PAST TWO DAYS HASN'T BEEN THE GREATEST.
I CAN SEE WHY...
I'M NOT THAT PRETTY COMPARED TO EVERYONE ELSE ...
THAT'S NOT TRUE. YOU'RE PRETTY ENOUGH.
MAYBE PEOPLE DO LOOK AT WHAT'S INSIDE TOO.
MAYBE THAT'S WHAT IT MEANS.
YOU'D BETTER WATCH YOUR MOUTH, OR GIRLS WON'T LIKE YOU.
......

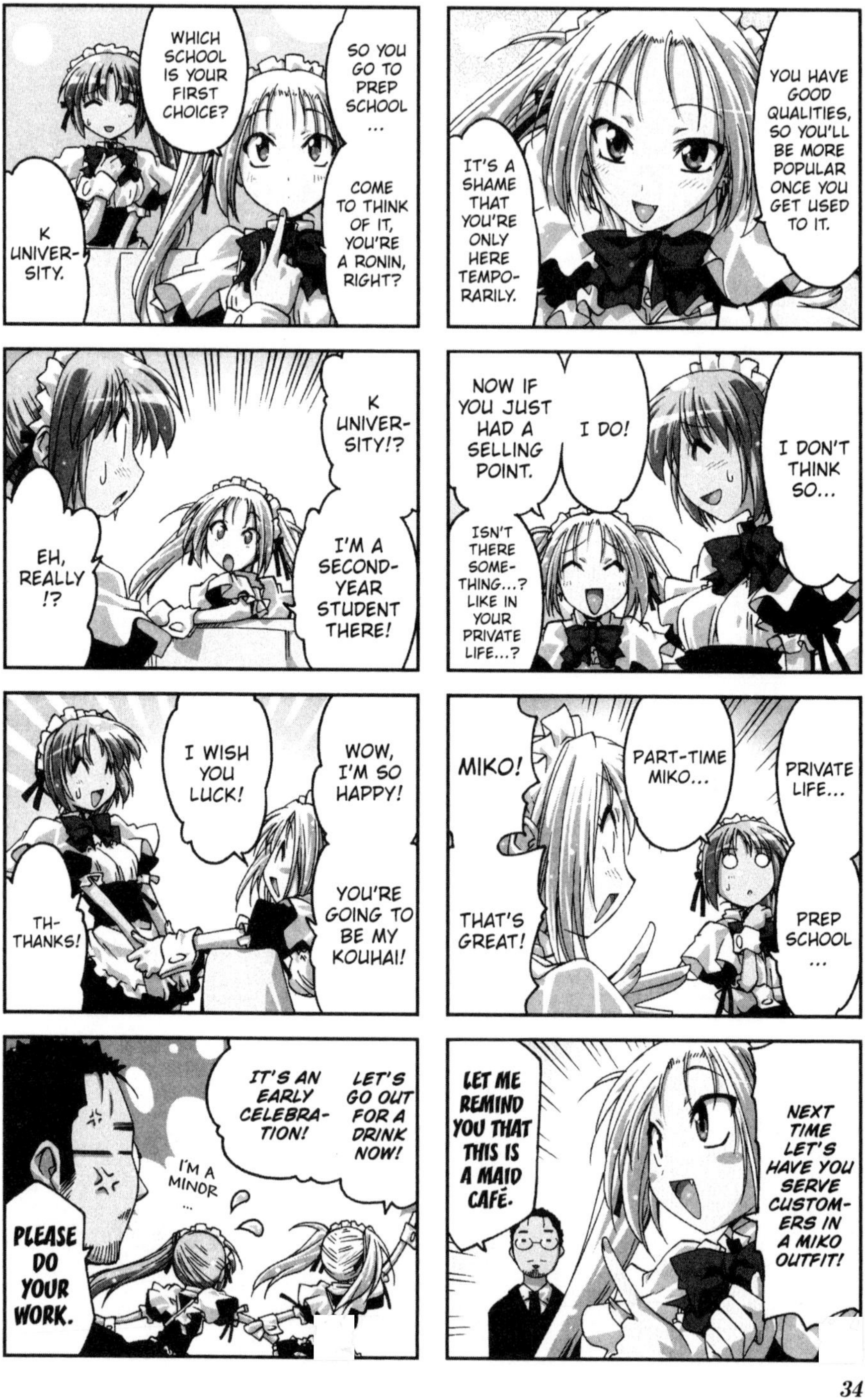
YOU HAVE GOOD QUALITIES, SO YOU'LL BE MORE POPULAR ONCE YOU GET USED TO IT.
IT'S A SHAME THAT YOU'RE ONLY HERE TEMPO-RARILY.
I DON'T THINK SO...
I DO!
NOW IF YOU JUST HAD A SELLING POINT.
ISN'T THERE SOME-THING...? LIKE IN YOUR PRIVATE LIFE...?
PRIVATE LIFE...
PART-TIME MIKO...
MIKO!
PREP SCHOOL ...
THAT'S GREAT!
NEXT TIME LET'S HAVE YOU SERVE CUSTOM-ERS IN A MIKO OUTFIT!
LET ME REMIND YOU THAT THIS IS A MAID CAFÉ.
SO YOU GO TO PREP SCHOOL ...
WHICH SCHOOL IS YOUR FIRST CHOICE?
COME TO THINK OF IT, YOU'RE A RONIN, RIGHT?
K UNIVER-SITY.
K UNIVER-SITY!?
I'M A SECOND-YEAR STUDENT THERE!
EH, REALLY !?
WOW, I'M SO HAPPY!
I WISH YOU LUCK!
YOU'RE GOING TO BE MY KOUHAI!
TH-THANKS!
LET'S GO OUT FOR A DRINK NOW!
IT'S AN EARLY CELEBRA-TION!
I'M A MINOR ...
PLEASE DO YOUR WORK.

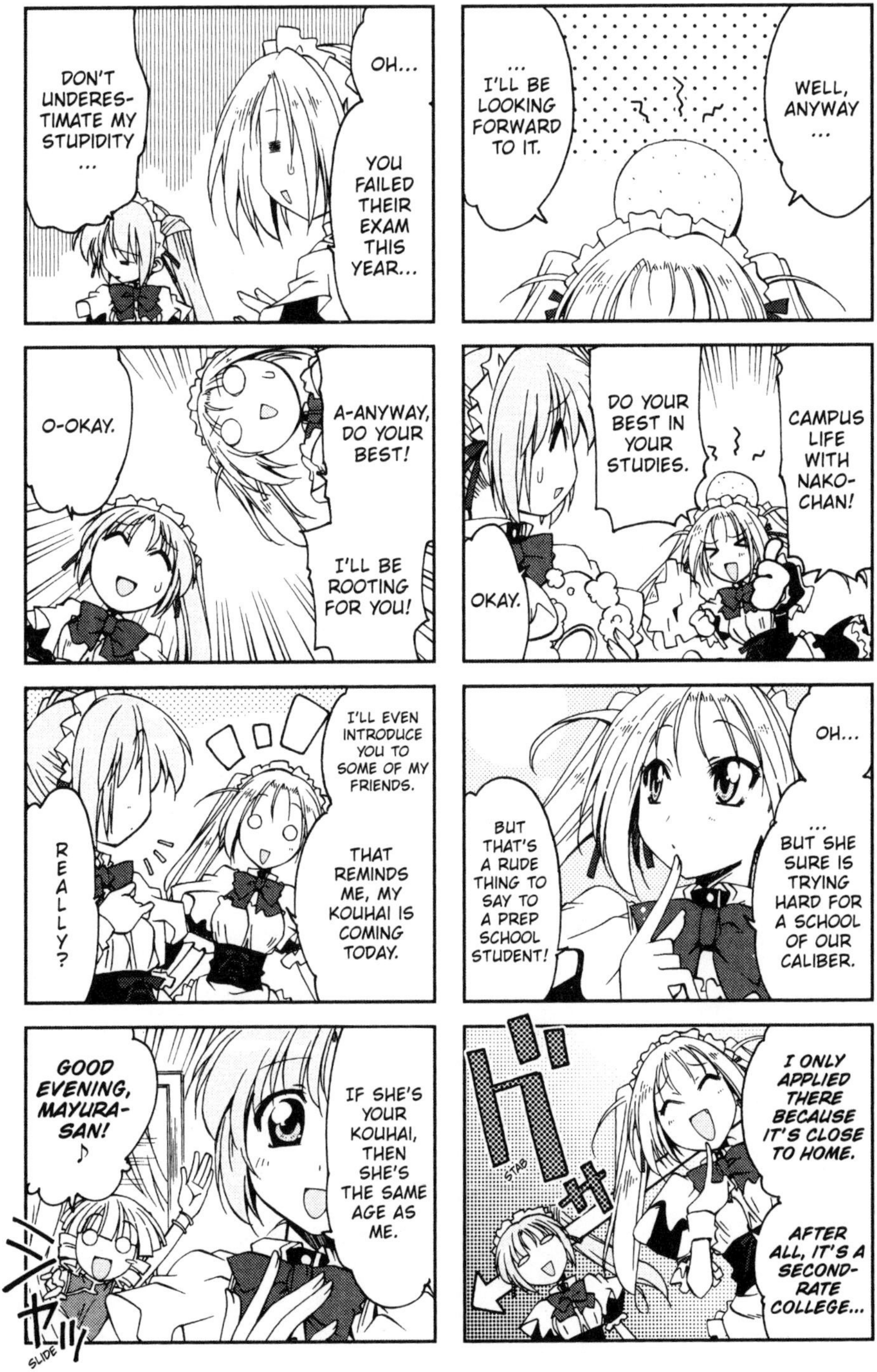
WELL, ANYWAY...
...I'LL BE LOOKING FORWARD TO IT.
CAMPUS LIFE WITH NAKO-CHAN!
DO YOUR BEST IN YOUR STUDIES.
OKAY.
OH...
...BUT SHE SURE IS TRYING HARD FOR A SCHOOL OF OUR CALIBER.
BUT THAT'S A RUDE THING TO SAY TO A PREP SCHOOL STUDENT!
I ONLY APPLIED THERE BECAUSE IT'S CLOSE TO HOME.
AFTER ALL, IT'S A SECOND-RATE COLLEGE...
STAB
OH...
YOU FAILED THEIR EXAM THIS YEAR...
DON'T UNDERESTIMATE MY STUPIDITY...
A-ANYWAY, DO YOUR BEST!
I'LL BE ROOTING FOR YOU!
O-OKAY.
I'LL EVEN INTRODUCE YOU TO SOME OF MY FRIENDS.
THAT REMINDS ME, MY KOUHAI IS COMING TODAY.
REALLY?
IF SHE'S YOUR KOUHAI, THEN SHE'S THE SAME AGE AS ME.
GOOD EVENING, MAYURA-SAN! ♪
SLIDE

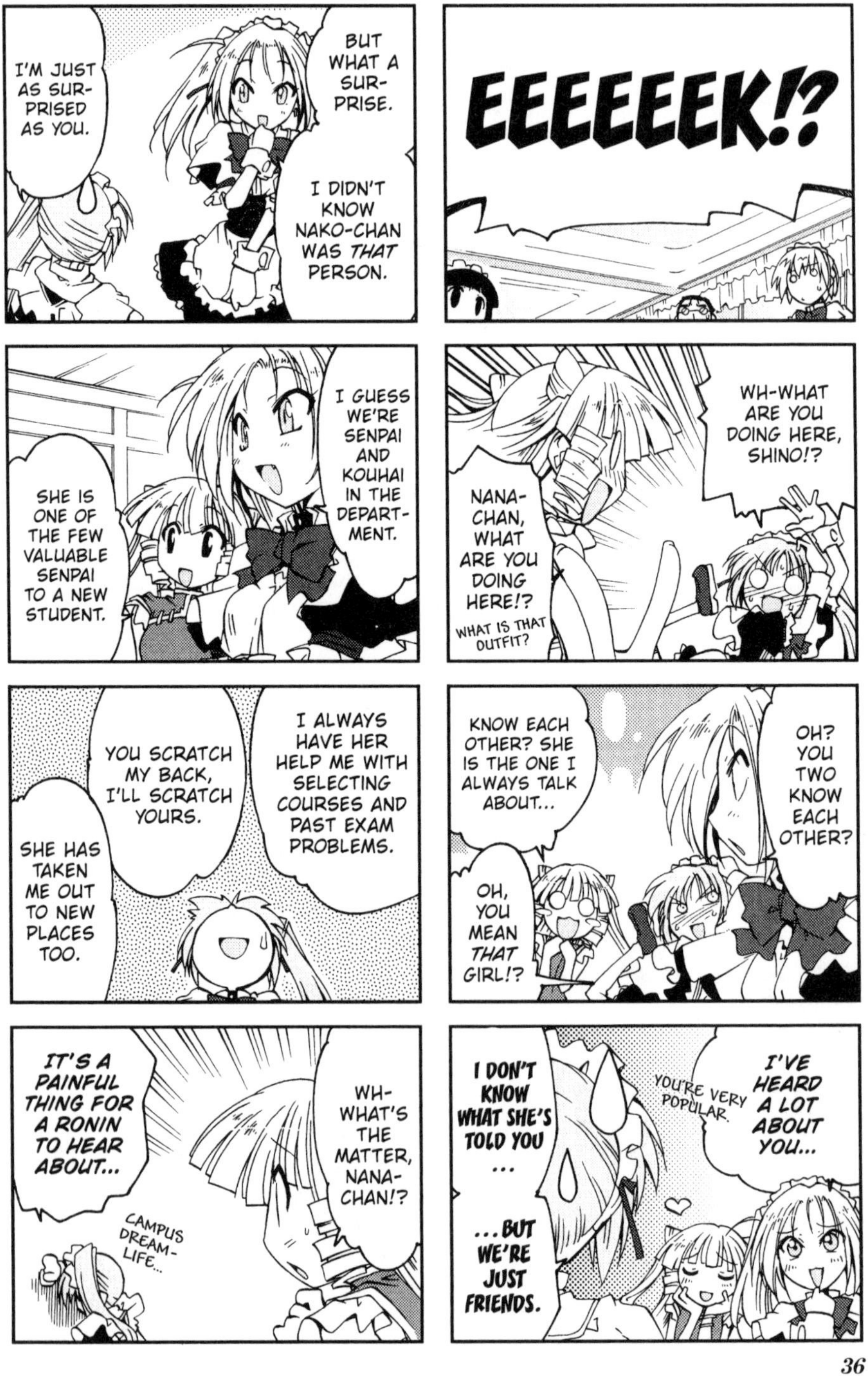
EEEEEEK!?
WH-WHAT ARE YOU DOING HERE, SHINO!?
NANA-CHAN, WHAT ARE YOU DOING HERE!?
WHAT IS THAT OUTFIT?
OH? YOU TWO KNOW EACH OTHER?
KNOW EACH OTHER? SHE IS THE ONE I ALWAYS TALK ABOUT...
OH, YOU MEAN *THAT* GIRL!?
*I'VE HEARD A LOT ABOUT YOU...*
YOU'RE VERY POPULAR.
**I DON'T KNOW WHAT SHE'S TOLD YOU ...**
**...BUT WE'RE JUST FRIENDS.**
BUT WHAT A SURPRISE.
I DIDN'T KNOW NAKO-CHAN WAS *THAT* PERSON.
I'M JUST AS SURPRISED AS YOU.
I GUESS WE'RE SENPAI AND KOUHAI IN THE DEPARTMENT.
SHE IS ONE OF THE FEW VALUABLE SENPAI TO A NEW STUDENT.
I ALWAYS HAVE HER HELP ME WITH SELECTING COURSES AND PAST EXAM PROBLEMS.
YOU SCRATCH MY BACK, I'LL SCRATCH YOURS.
SHE HAS TAKEN ME OUT TO NEW PLACES TOO.
WH-WHAT'S THE MATTER, NANA-CHAN!?
*IT'S A PAINFUL THING FOR A RONIN TO HEAR ABOUT...*
CAMPUS DREAM-LIFE...

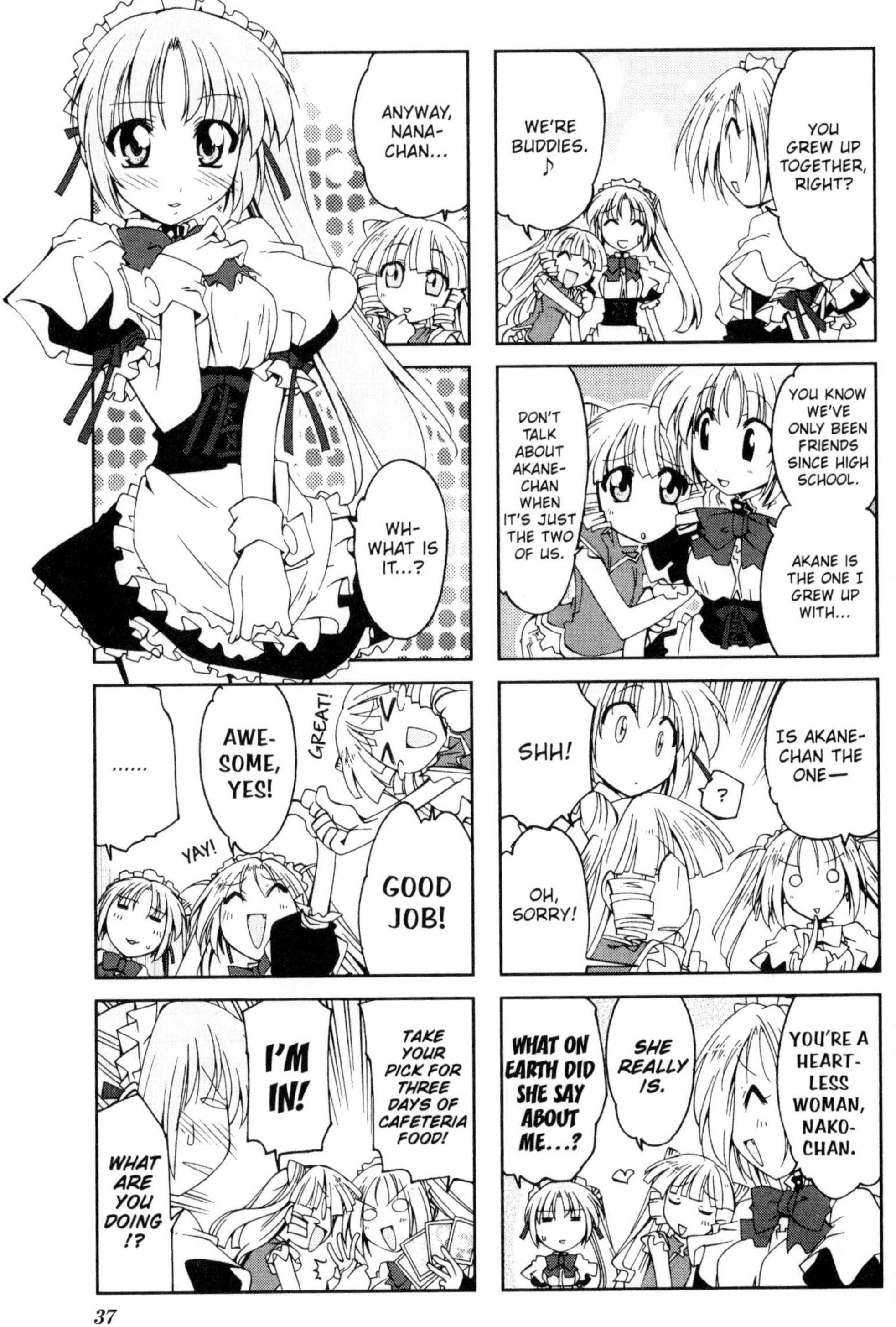
YOU GREW UP TOGETHER, RIGHT?
WE'RE BUDDIES. ♪
YOU KNOW WE'VE ONLY BEEN FRIENDS SINCE HIGH SCHOOL.
AKANE IS THE ONE I GREW UP WITH...
DON'T TALK ABOUT AKANE-CHAN WHEN IT'S JUST THE TWO OF US.
IS AKANE-CHAN THE ONE—
?
SHH!
OH, SORRY!
YOU'RE A HEART-LESS WOMAN, NAKO-CHAN.
SHE REALLY IS.
WHAT ON EARTH DID SHE SAY ABOUT ME...?
ANYWAY, NANA-CHAN...
WH-WHAT IS IT...?
GREAT!
GOOD JOB!
AWE-SOME, YES!
YAY!
......
TAKE YOUR PICK FOR THREE DAYS OF CAFETERIA FOOD!
I'M IN!
WHAT ARE YOU DOING!?

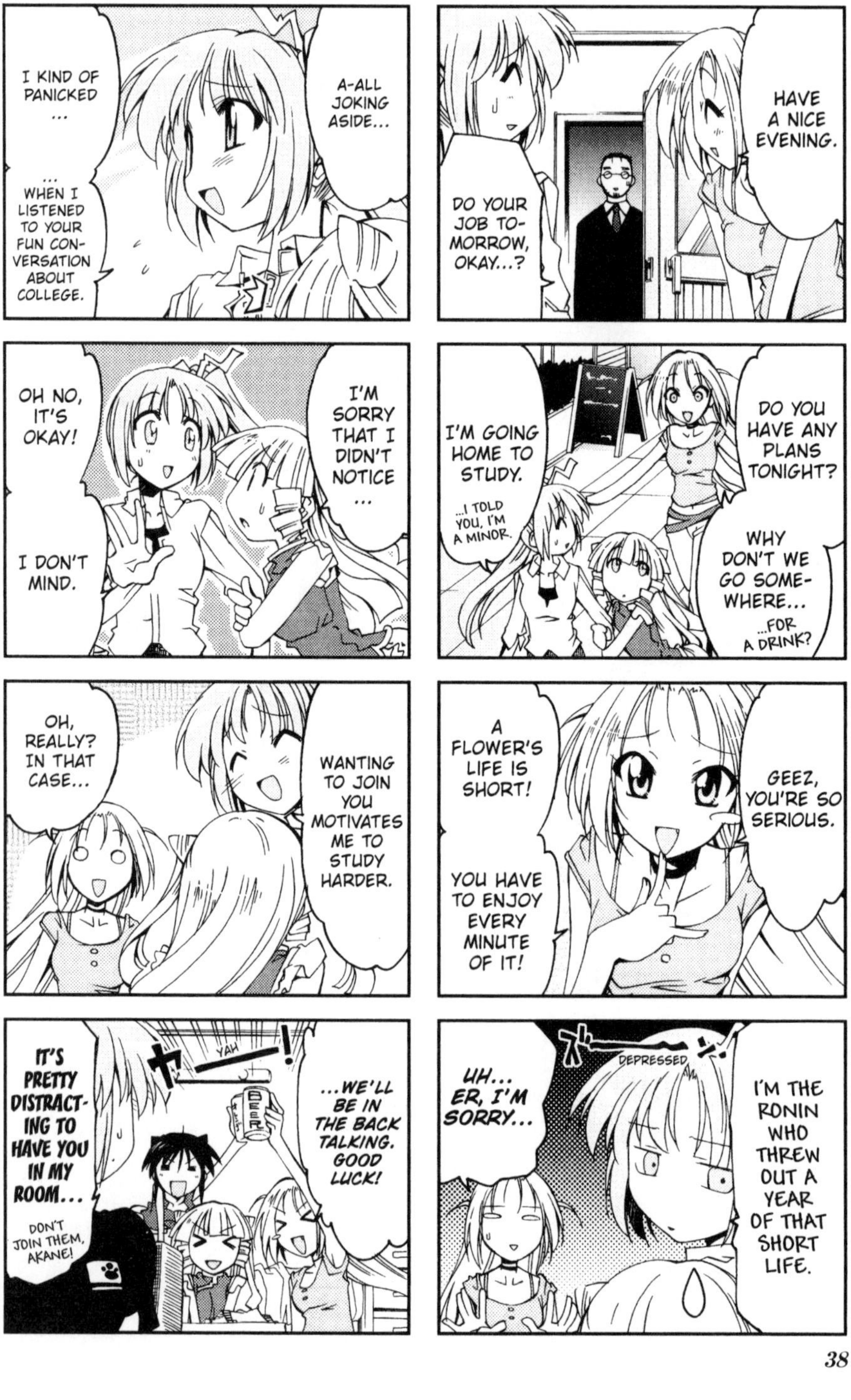
HAVE A NICE EVENING.
DO YOUR JOB TO-MORROW, OKAY...?
DO YOU HAVE ANY PLANS TONIGHT?
WHY DON'T WE GO SOME-WHERE...
...FOR A DRINK?
I'M GOING HOME TO STUDY.
...I TOLD YOU, I'M A MINOR.
GEEZ, YOU'RE SO SERIOUS.
A FLOWER'S LIFE IS SHORT!
YOU HAVE TO ENJOY EVERY MINUTE OF IT!
DEPRESSED
I'M THE RONIN WHO THREW OUT A YEAR OF THAT SHORT LIFE.
UH... ER, I'M SORRY...
A-ALL JOKING ASIDE...
I KIND OF PANICKED ...
... WHEN I LISTENED TO YOUR FUN CON-VERSATION ABOUT COLLEGE.
I'M SORRY THAT I DIDN'T NOTICE ...
OH NO, IT'S OKAY!
I DON'T MIND.
WANTING TO JOIN YOU MOTIVATES ME TO STUDY HARDER.
OH, REALLY? IN THAT CASE...
YAH
...WE'LL BE IN THE BACK TALKING. GOOD LUCK!
BEER
IT'S PRETTY DISTRACT-ING TO HAVE YOU IN MY ROOM...
DON'T JOIN THEM, AKANE!

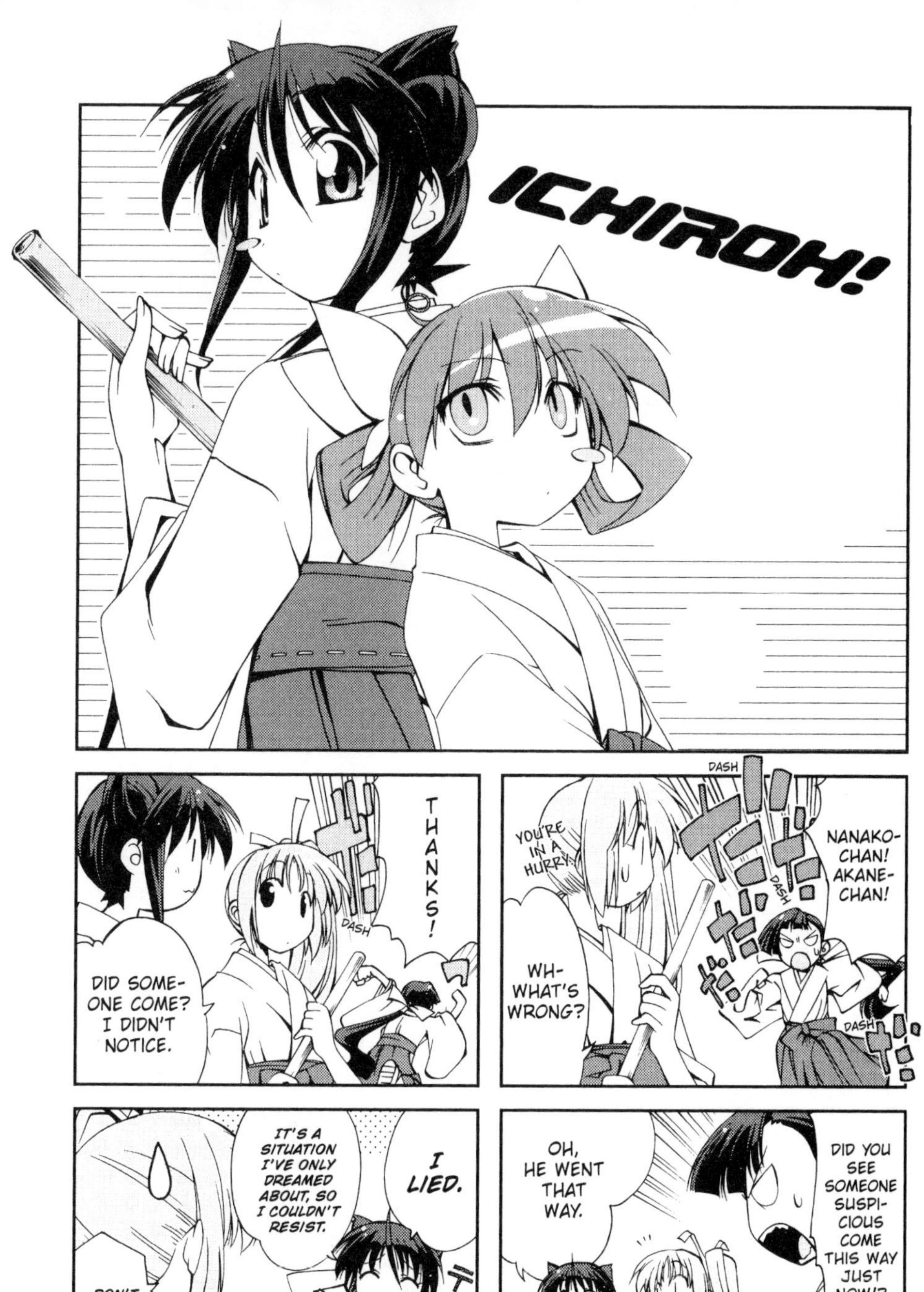
ICHIROH!
DASH
NANAKO-CHAN! AKANE-CHAN!
DASH
YOU'RE IN A HURRY.
WH- WHAT'S WRONG?
DASH
THANKS!
DASH
DID SOME-ONE COME? I DIDN'T NOTICE.
DID YOU SEE SOMEONE SUSPICIOUS COME THIS WAY JUST NOW!?
OH, HE WENT THAT WAY.
I LIED.
IT'S A SITUATION I'VE ONLY DREAMED ABOUT, SO I COULDN'T RESIST.
TEE HEE
DON'T MAKE UP NONSENSE LIKE THAT.

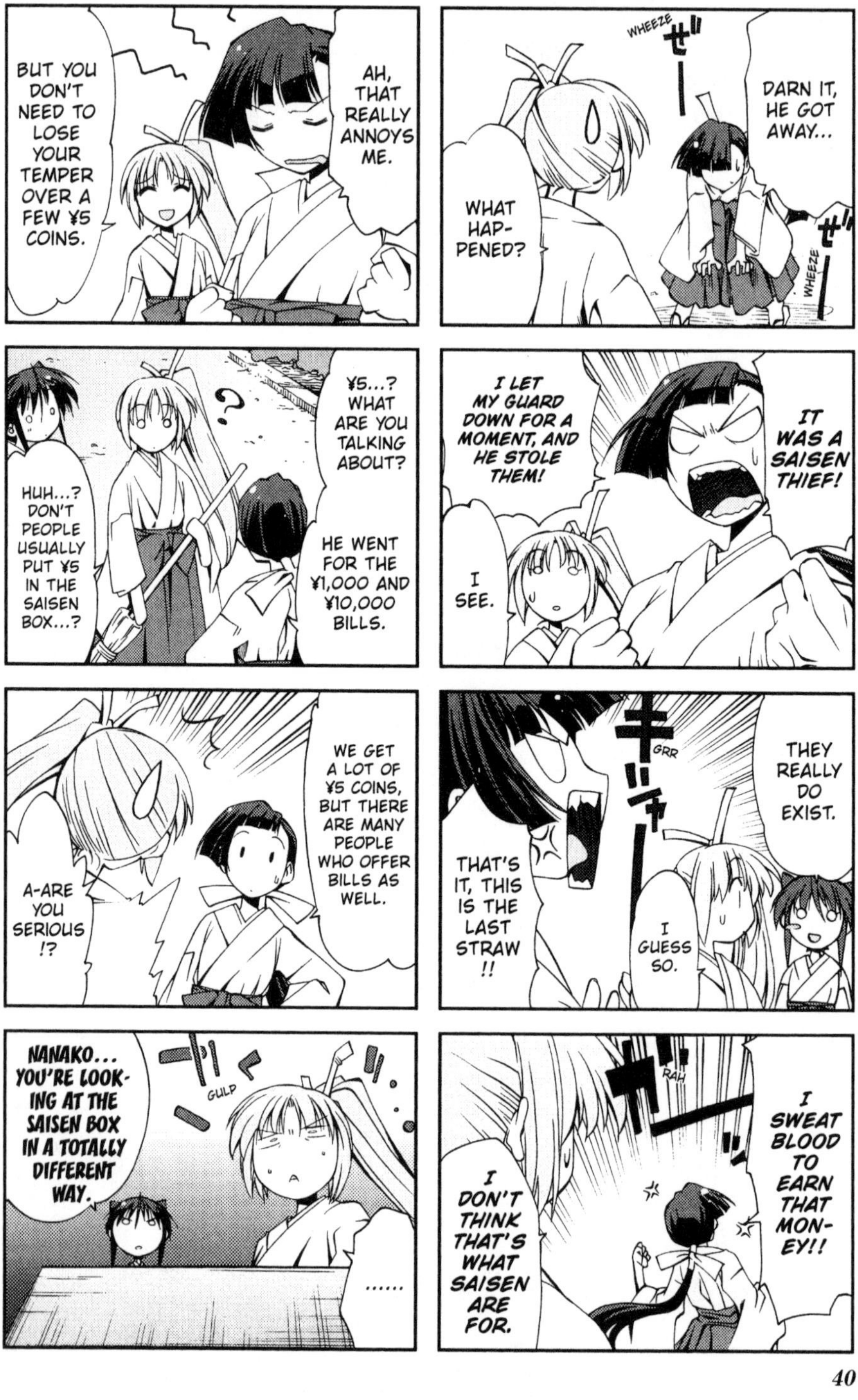
WHEEZE
DARN IT, HE GOT AWAY...
WHAT HAP-PENED?
WHEEZE
IT WAS A SAISEN THIEF!
I LET MY GUARD DOWN FOR A MOMENT, AND HE STOLE THEM!
I SEE.
THEY REALLY DO EXIST.
GRR
THAT'S IT, THIS IS THE LAST STRAW!!
I GUESS SO.
RAH
I SWEAT BLOOD TO EARN THAT MON-EY!!
I DON'T THINK THAT'S WHAT SAISEN ARE FOR.
AH, THAT REALLY ANNOYS ME.
BUT YOU DON'T NEED TO LOSE YOUR TEMPER OVER A FEW ¥5 COINS.
¥5...? WHAT ARE YOU TALKING ABOUT?
HE WENT FOR THE ¥1,000 AND ¥10,000 BILLS.
HUH...? DON'T PEOPLE USUALLY PUT ¥5 IN THE SAISEN BOX...?
WE GET A LOT OF ¥5 COINS, BUT THERE ARE MANY PEOPLE WHO OFFER BILLS AS WELL.
A-ARE YOU SERIOUS!?
NANAKO... YOU'RE LOOK-ING AT THE SAISEN BOX IN A TOTALLY DIFFERENT WAY.
GULP
......

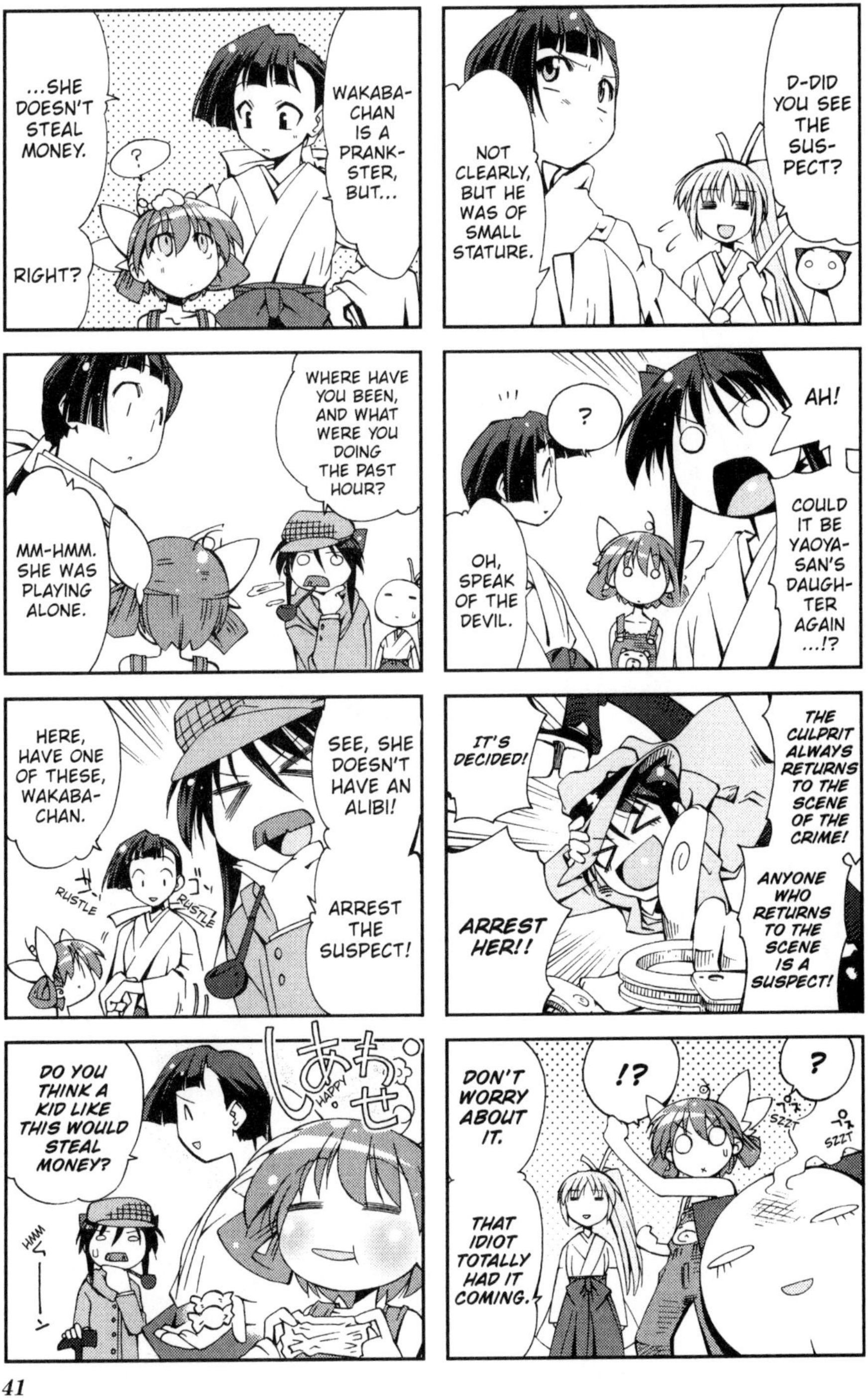
D-DID YOU SEE THE SUSPECT?
NOT CLEARLY, BUT HE WAS OF SMALL STATURE.
WAKABA-CHAN IS A PRANKSTER, BUT...
...SHE DOESN'T STEAL MONEY.
?
RIGHT?
AH!
?
COULD IT BE YAOYA-SAN'S DAUGHTER AGAIN ...!?
OH, SPEAK OF THE DEVIL.
WHERE HAVE YOU BEEN, AND WHAT WERE YOU DOING THE PAST HOUR?
MM-HMM. SHE WAS PLAYING ALONE.
THE CULPRIT ALWAYS RETURNS TO THE SCENE OF THE CRIME!
IT'S DECIDED!
ANYONE WHO RETURNS TO THE SCENE IS A SUSPECT!
ARREST HER!!
SEE, SHE DOESN'T HAVE AN ALIBI!
ARREST THE SUSPECT!
HERE, HAVE ONE OF THESE, WAKABA-CHAN.
RUSTLE
RUSTLE
?
!?
SZZT
SZZT
DON'T WORRY ABOUT IT.
THAT IDIOT TOTALLY HAD IT COMING.
HAPPY
DO YOU THINK A KID LIKE THIS WOULD STEAL MONEY?
HMM

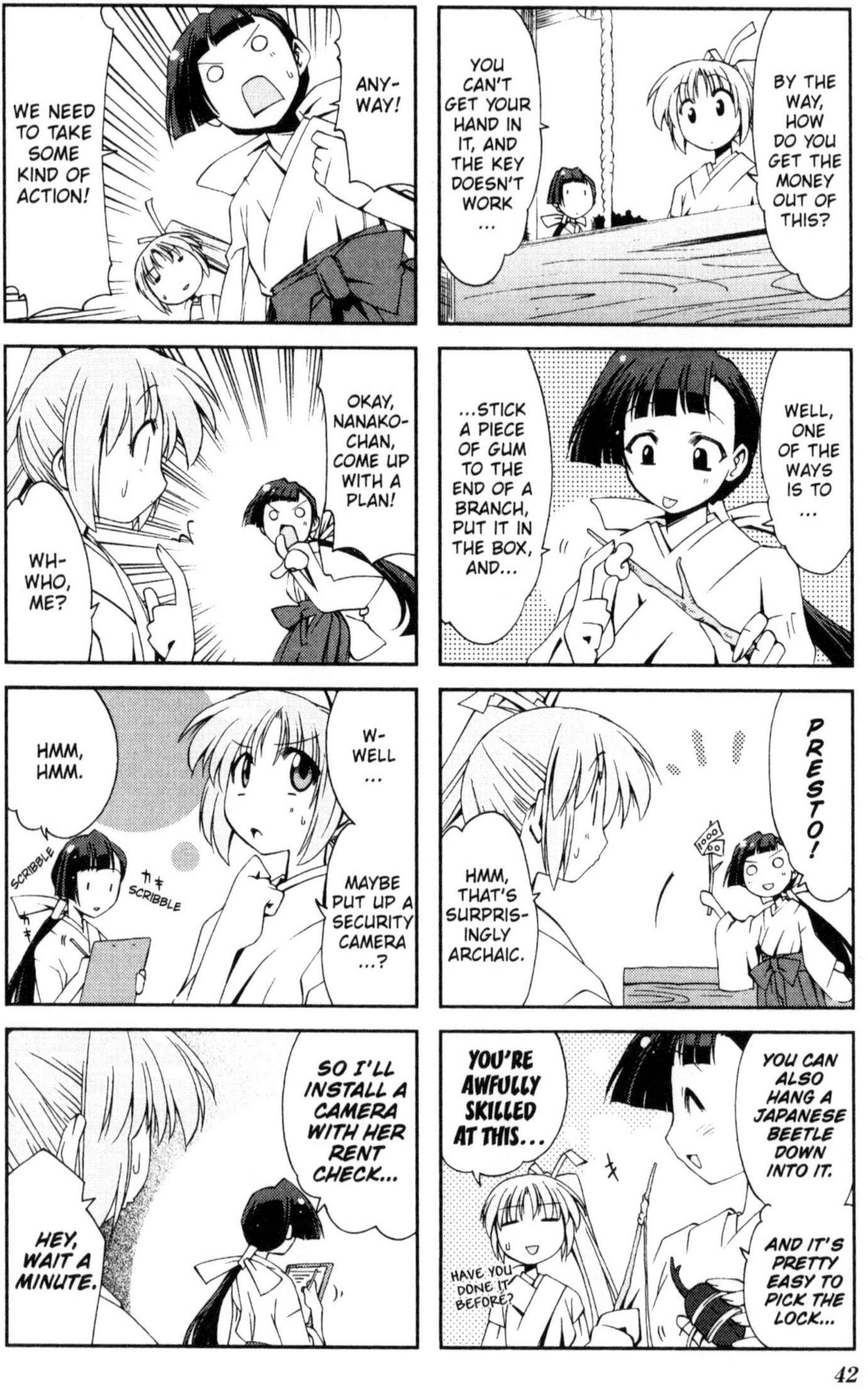
BY THE WAY, HOW DO YOU GET THE MONEY OUT OF THIS?
YOU CAN'T GET YOUR HAND IN IT, AND THE KEY DOESN'T WORK ...
ANY-WAY!
WE NEED TO TAKE SOME KIND OF ACTION!
WELL, ONE OF THE WAYS IS TO ...
...STICK A PIECE OF GUM TO THE END OF A BRANCH, PUT IT IN THE BOX, AND...
OKAY, NANAKO-CHAN, COME UP WITH A PLAN!
WH-WHO, ME?
PRESTO!
HMM, THAT'S SURPRIS-INGLY ARCHAIC.
W-WELL ...
MAYBE PUT UP A SECURITY CAMERA ...?
HMM, HMM.
SCRIBBLE
SCRIBBLE
YOU CAN ALSO HANG A JAPANESE BEETLE DOWN INTO IT.
AND IT'S PRETTY EASY TO PICK THE LOCK...
YOU'RE AWFULLY SKILLED AT THIS...
HAVE YOU DONE IT BEFORE?
SO I'LL INSTALL A CAMERA WITH HER RENT CHECK...
HEY, WAIT A MINUTE.

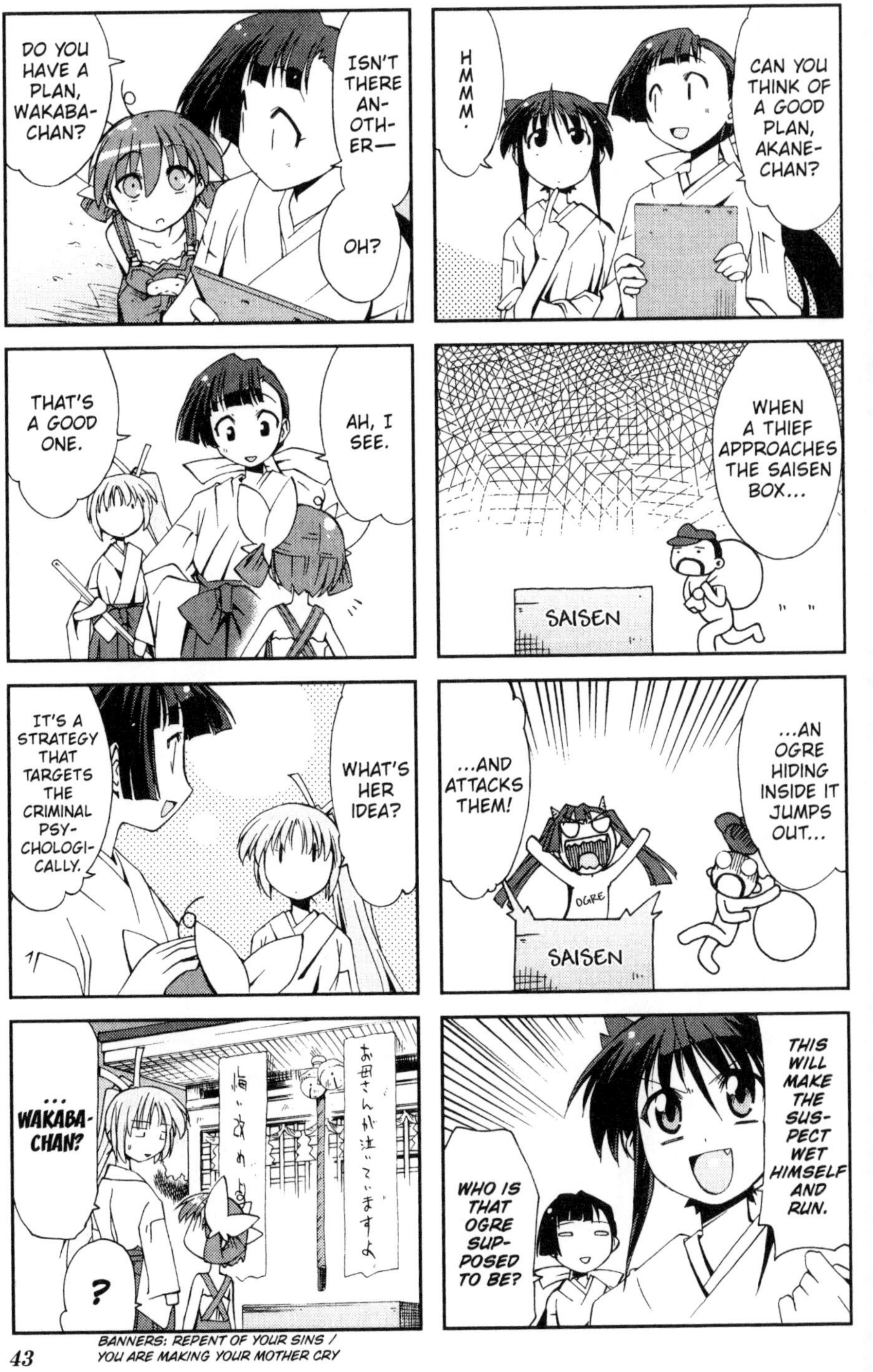
CAN YOU THINK OF A GOOD PLAN, AKANE-CHAN?
HMMM.
ISN'T THERE AN-OTHER—
DO YOU HAVE A PLAN, WAKABA-CHAN?
OH?
WHEN A THIEF APPROACHES THE SAISEN BOX...
SAISEN
AH, I SEE.
THAT'S A GOOD ONE.
...AN OGRE HIDING INSIDE IT JUMPS OUT...
...AND ATTACKS THEM!
OGRE
SAISEN
WHAT'S HER IDEA?
IT'S A STRATEGY THAT TARGETS THE CRIMINAL PSY-CHOLOGI-CALLY.
THIS WILL MAKE THE SUS-PECT WET HIMSELF AND RUN.
WHO IS THAT OGRE SUP-POSED TO BE?
お母さんが泣いていますよ
悔い改めよ
...WAKABA-CHAN?
?

BANNERS: REPENT OF YOUR SINS / YOU ARE MAKING YOUR MOTHER CRY

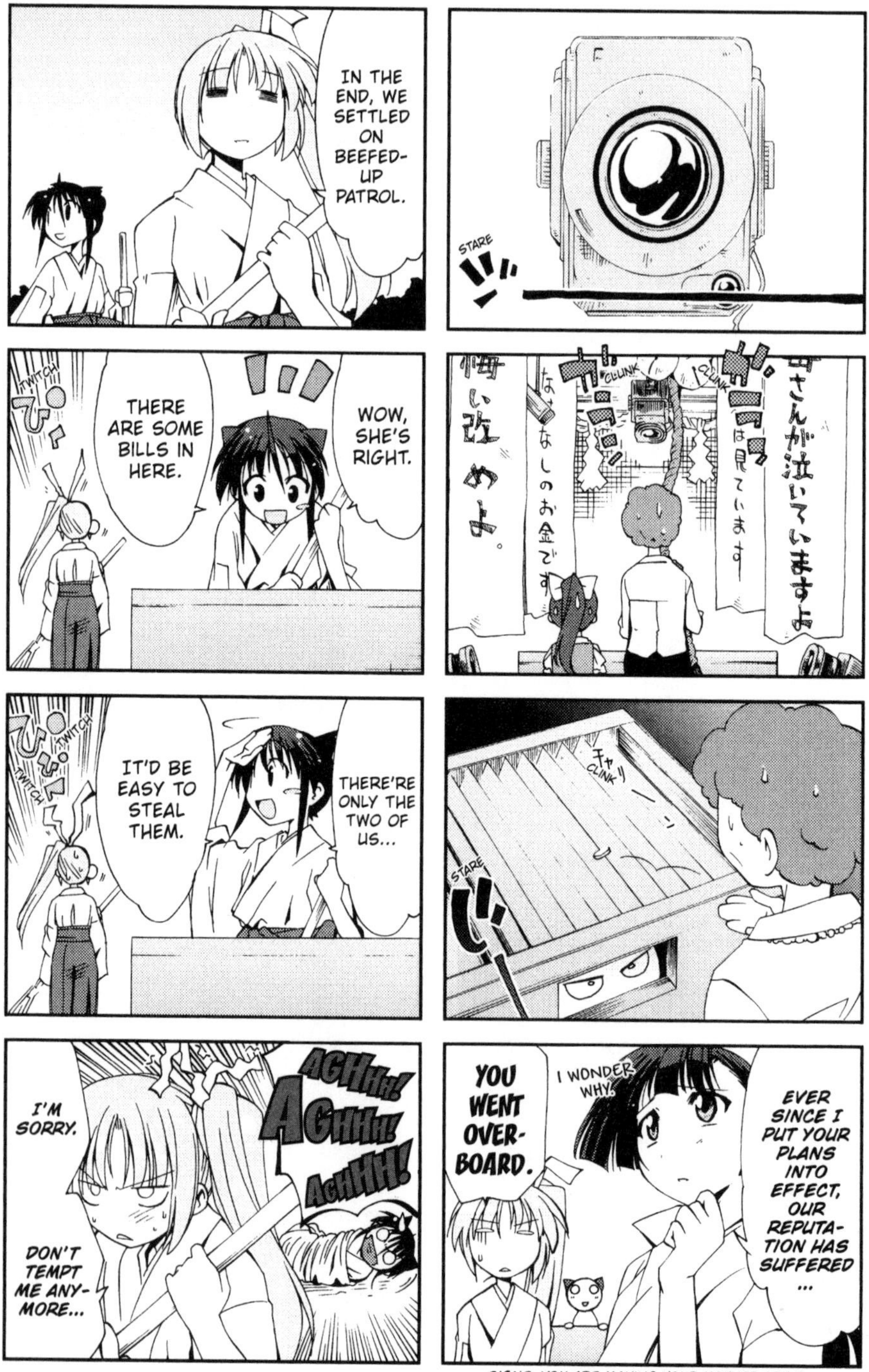
STARE
CLINK
CLINK
は見ています
さんが泣いていますよ
なしのお金です
悔い改めよ。
CLINK
STARE
EVER SINCE I PUT YOUR PLANS INTO EFFECT, OUR REPUTATION HAS SUFFERED...
I WONDER WHY.
YOU WENT OVERBOARD.
IN THE END, WE SETTLED ON BEEFED-UP PATROL.
TWITCH
WOW, SHE'S RIGHT.
THERE ARE SOME BILLS IN HERE.
TWITCH
TWITCH
THERE'RE ONLY THE TWO OF US...
IT'D BE EASY TO STEAL THEM.
AGHHH! AGHHH! AGHHH!
I'M SORRY.
DON'T TEMPT ME ANYMORE...

SIGNS: YOU ARE MAKING YOUR MOTHER CRY / -IS WATCHING YOU / -IS WHAT LITTLE MONEY WE HAVE / -PENT OF YOUR SINS.

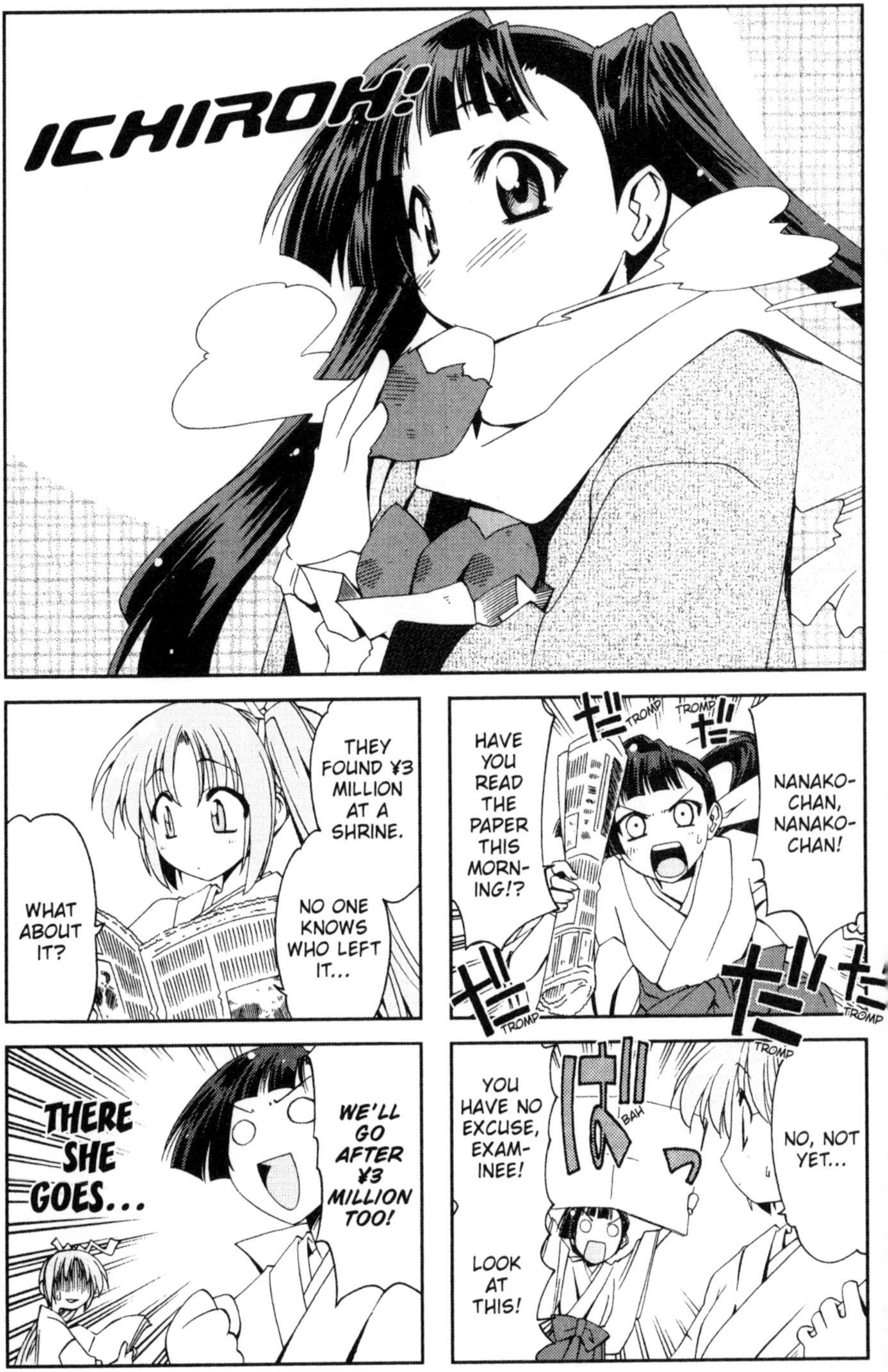
ICHIROH!
TROMP
TROMP
NANAKO-CHAN, NANAKO-CHAN!
HAVE YOU READ THE PAPER THIS MORNING!?
TROMP
TROMP
TROMP
THEY FOUND ¥3 MILLION AT A SHRINE.
NO ONE KNOWS WHO LEFT IT...
WHAT ABOUT IT?
NO, NOT YET...
YOU HAVE NO EXCUSE, EXAMINEE!
BAH
LOOK AT THIS!
WE'LL GO AFTER ¥3 MILLION TOO!
THERE SHE GOES...

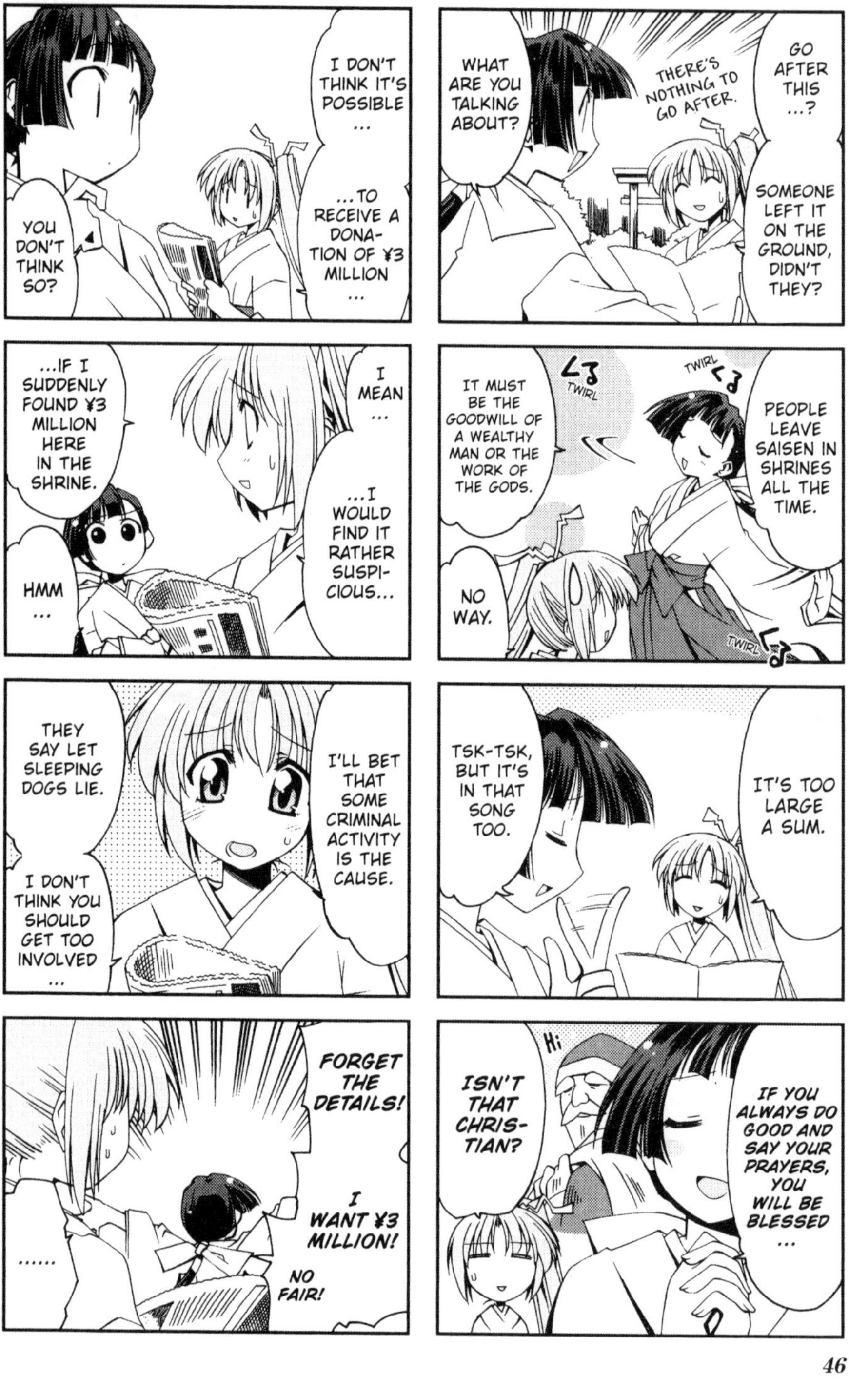
GO AFTER THIS ...?
SOMEONE LEFT IT ON THE GROUND, DIDN'T THEY?
THERE'S NOTHING TO GO AFTER.
WHAT ARE YOU TALKING ABOUT?
PEOPLE LEAVE SAISEN IN SHRINES ALL THE TIME.
TWIRL くる
TWIRL くる
IT MUST BE THE GOODWILL OF A WEALTHY MAN OR THE WORK OF THE GODS.
NO WAY.
TWIRL くる
IT'S TOO LARGE A SUM.
TSK-TSK, BUT IT'S IN THAT SONG TOO.
IF YOU ALWAYS DO GOOD AND SAY YOUR PRAYERS, YOU WILL BE BLESSED ...
Hi
ISN'T THAT CHRISTIAN?
I DON'T THINK IT'S POSSIBLE ...
...TO RECEIVE A DONATION OF ¥3 MILLION ...
YOU DON'T THINK SO?
I MEAN ...
...I WOULD FIND IT RATHER SUSPICIOUS...
...IF I SUDDENLY FOUND ¥3 MILLION HERE IN THE SHRINE.
HMM ...
I'LL BET THAT SOME CRIMINAL ACTIVITY IS THE CAUSE.
THEY SAY LET SLEEPING DOGS LIE.
I DON'T THINK YOU SHOULD GET TOO INVOLVED ...
FORGET THE DETAILS!
I WANT ¥3 MILLION!
NO FAIR!
......

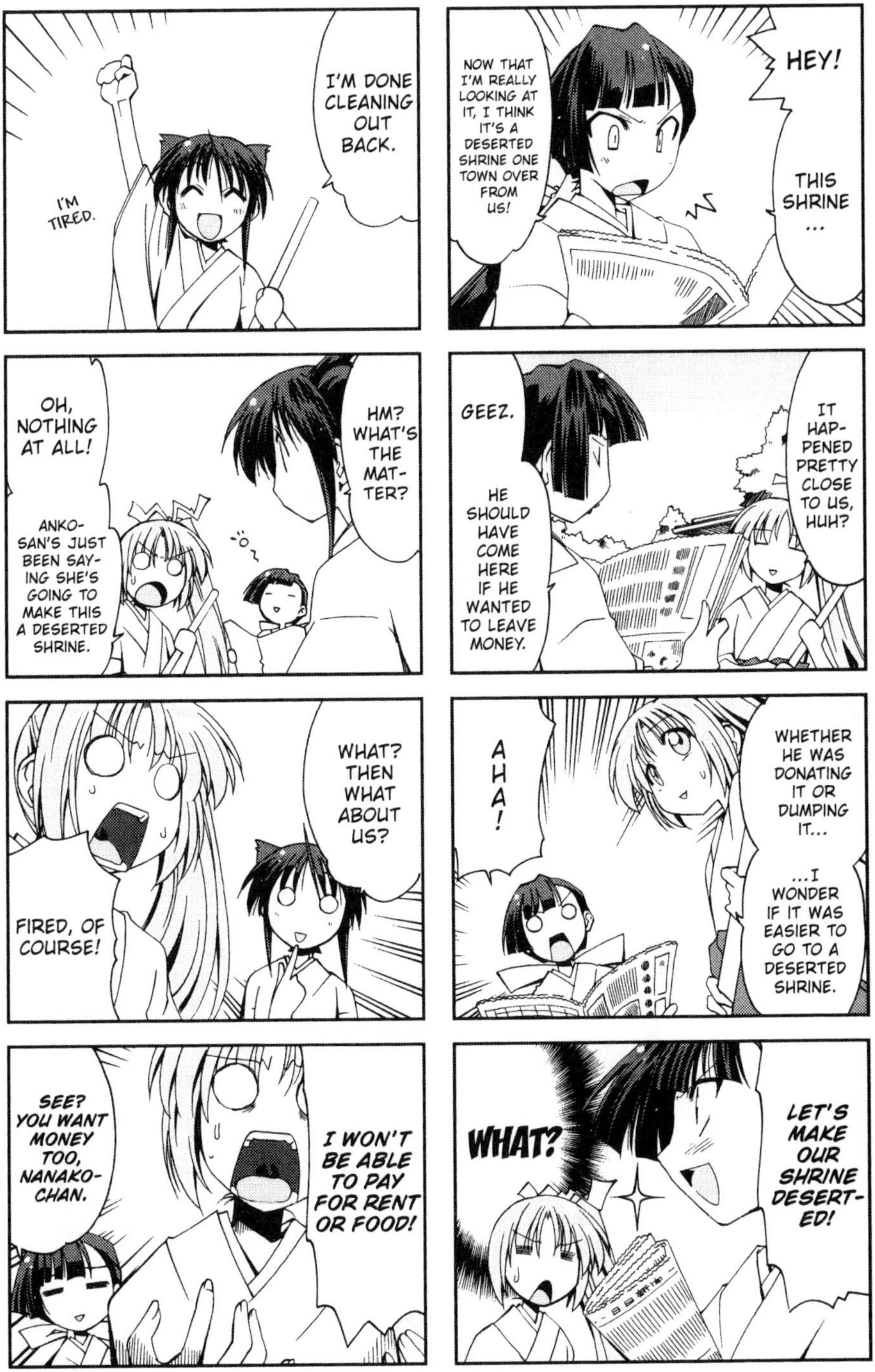
HEY!
THIS SHRINE ...
NOW THAT I'M REALLY LOOKING AT IT, I THINK IT'S A DESERTED SHRINE ONE TOWN OVER FROM US!
I'M DONE CLEANING OUT BACK.
I'M TIRED.
IT HAPPENED PRETTY CLOSE TO US, HUH?
GEEZ.
HE SHOULD HAVE COME HERE IF HE WANTED TO LEAVE MONEY.
HM? WHAT'S THE MATTER?
OH, NOTHING AT ALL!
ANKO-SAN'S JUST BEEN SAYING SHE'S GOING TO MAKE THIS A DESERTED SHRINE.
WHETHER HE WAS DONATING IT OR DUMPING IT...
...I WONDER IF IT WAS EASIER TO GO TO A DESERTED SHRINE.
AHA!
WHAT? THEN WHAT ABOUT US?
FIRED, OF COURSE!
LET'S MAKE OUR SHRINE DESERTED!
WHAT?
I WON'T BE ABLE TO PAY FOR RENT OR FOOD!
SEE? YOU WANT MONEY TOO, NANAKO-CHAN.

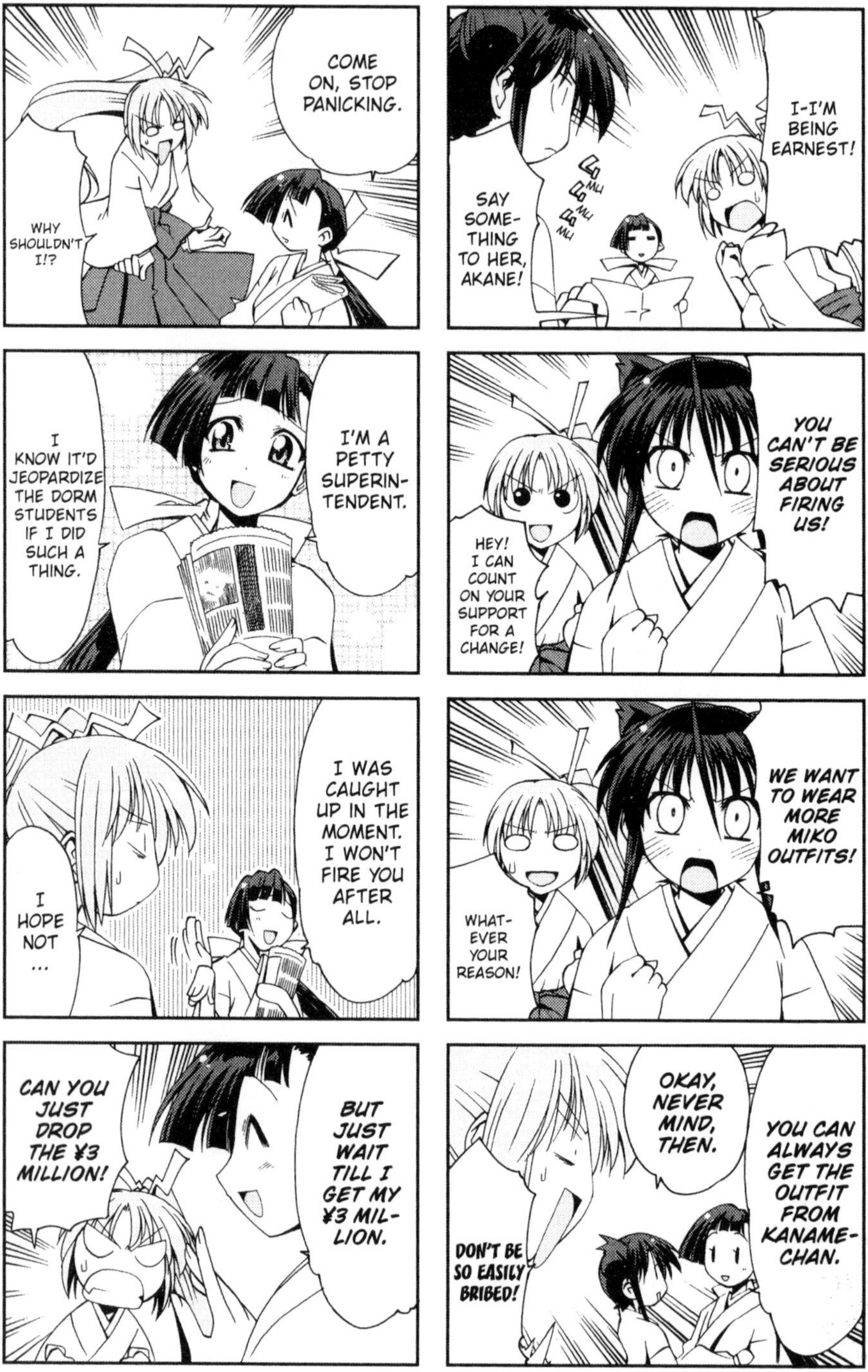
I-I'M BEING EARNEST!
SAY SOMETHING TO HER, AKANE!
MU
MU
MU
MU
YOU CAN'T BE SERIOUS ABOUT FIRING US!
HEY! I CAN COUNT ON YOUR SUPPORT FOR A CHANGE!
WE WANT TO WEAR MORE MIKO OUTFITS!
WHATEVER YOUR REASON!
YOU CAN ALWAYS GET THE OUTFIT FROM KANAME-CHAN.
OKAY, NEVER MIND, THEN.
DON'T BE SO EASILY BRIBED!
COME ON, STOP PANICKING.
WHY SHOULDN'T I!?
I'M A PETTY SUPERINTENDENT.
I KNOW IT'D JEOPARDIZE THE DORM STUDENTS IF I DID SUCH A THING.
I WAS CAUGHT UP IN THE MOMENT. I WON'T FIRE YOU AFTER ALL.
I HOPE NOT ...
BUT JUST WAIT TILL I GET MY ¥3 MILLION.
CAN YOU JUST DROP THE ¥3 MILLION!

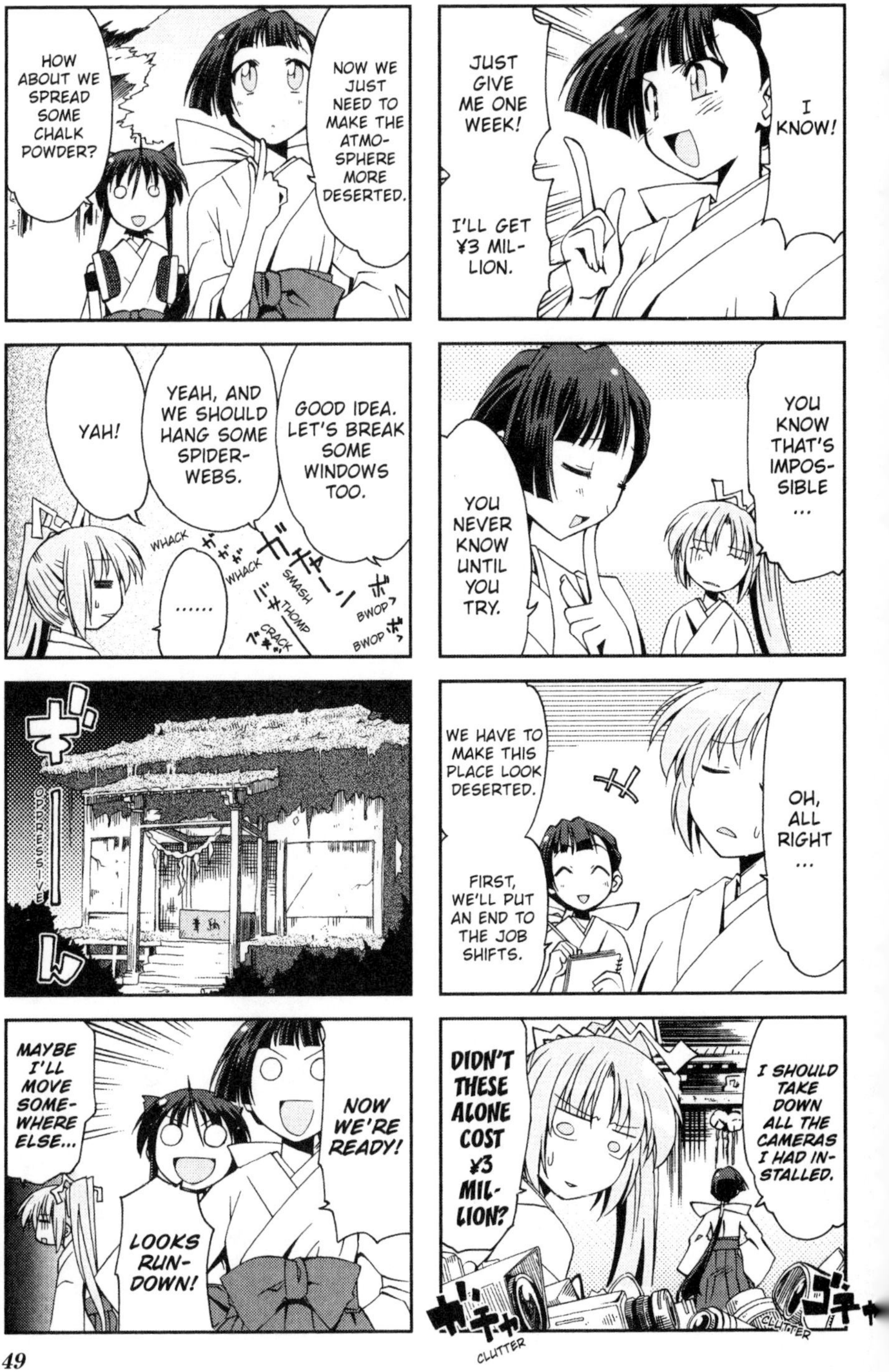
I KNOW!
JUST GIVE ME ONE WEEK!
I'LL GET ¥3 MILLION.
NOW WE JUST NEED TO MAKE THE ATMOSPHERE MORE DESERTED.
HOW ABOUT WE SPREAD SOME CHALK POWDER?
YOU KNOW THAT'S IMPOSSIBLE ...
YOU NEVER KNOW UNTIL YOU TRY.
GOOD IDEA. LET'S BREAK SOME WINDOWS TOO.
YEAH, AND WE SHOULD HANG SOME SPIDERWEBS.
YAH!
BWOP
BWOP
SMASH
THOMP
CRACK
WHACK
WHACK
......
OH, ALL RIGHT ...
WE HAVE TO MAKE THIS PLACE LOOK DESERTED.
FIRST, WE'LL PUT AN END TO THE JOB SHIFTS.
OPPRESSIVE
I SHOULD TAKE DOWN ALL THE CAMERAS I HAD INSTALLED.
DIDN'T THESE ALONE COST ¥3 MILLION?
CLUTTER
CLUTTER
NOW WE'RE READY!
MAYBE I'LL MOVE SOMEWHERE ELSE...
LOOKS RUN-DOWN!

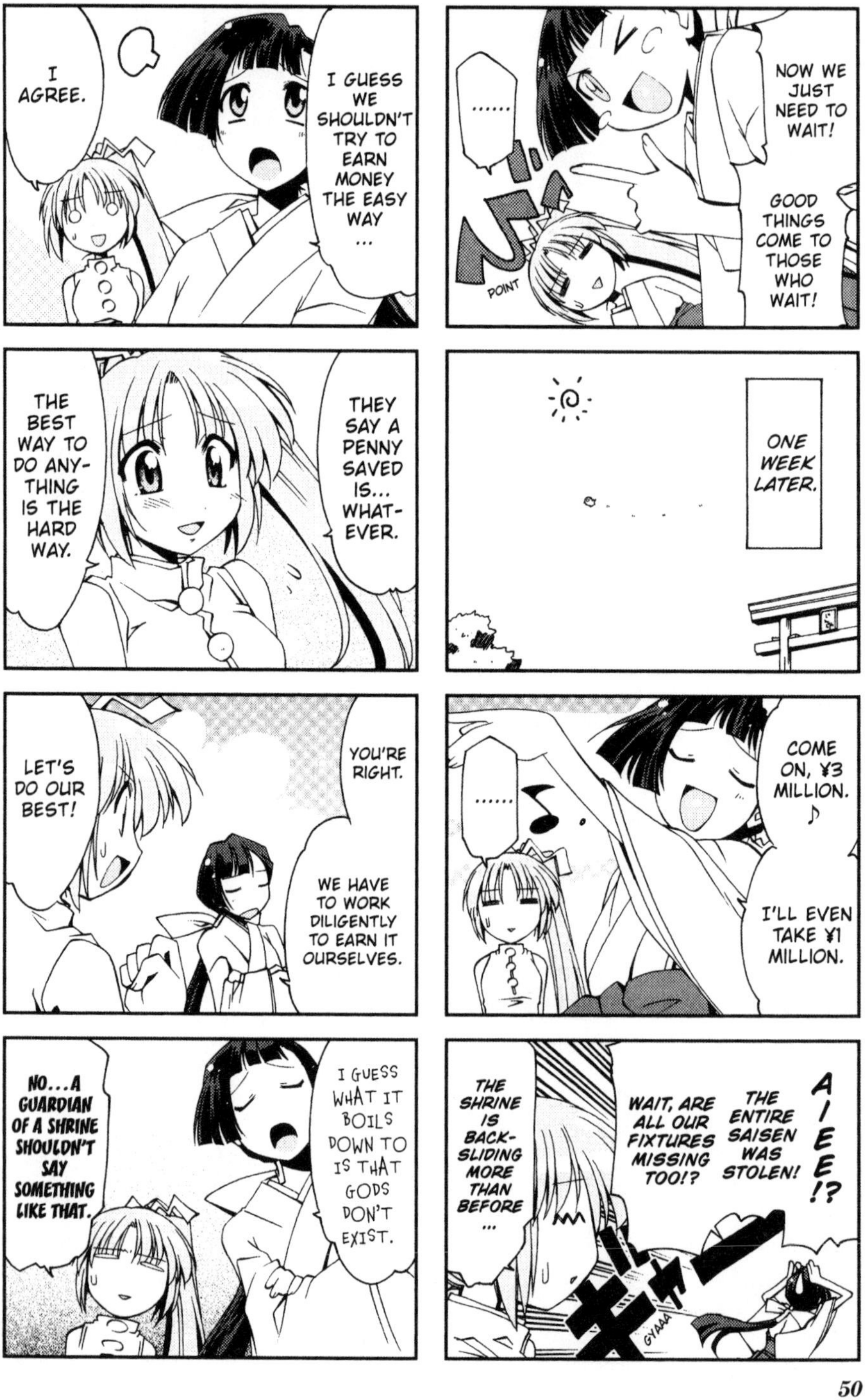
NOW WE JUST NEED TO WAIT!
GOOD THINGS COME TO THOSE WHO WAIT!
......
POINT
ONE WEEK LATER.
COME ON, ¥3 MILLION. ♪
I'LL EVEN TAKE ¥1 MILLION.
......
A I E E !?
THE ENTIRE SAISEN WAS STOLEN!
WAIT, ARE ALL OUR FIXTURES MISSING TOO!?
THE SHRINE IS BACK-SLIDING MORE THAN BEFORE ...
GYAAA
I GUESS WE SHOULDN'T TRY TO EARN MONEY THE EASY WAY ...
I AGREE.
THEY SAY A PENNY SAVED IS... WHAT-EVER.
THE BEST WAY TO DO ANY-THING IS THE HARD WAY.
YOU'RE RIGHT.
WE HAVE TO WORK DILIGENTLY TO EARN IT OURSELVES.
LET'S DO OUR BEST!
I GUESS WHAT IT BOILS DOWN TO IS THAT GODS DON'T EXIST.
NO...A GUARDIAN OF A SHRINE SHOULDN'T SAY SOMETHING LIKE THAT.

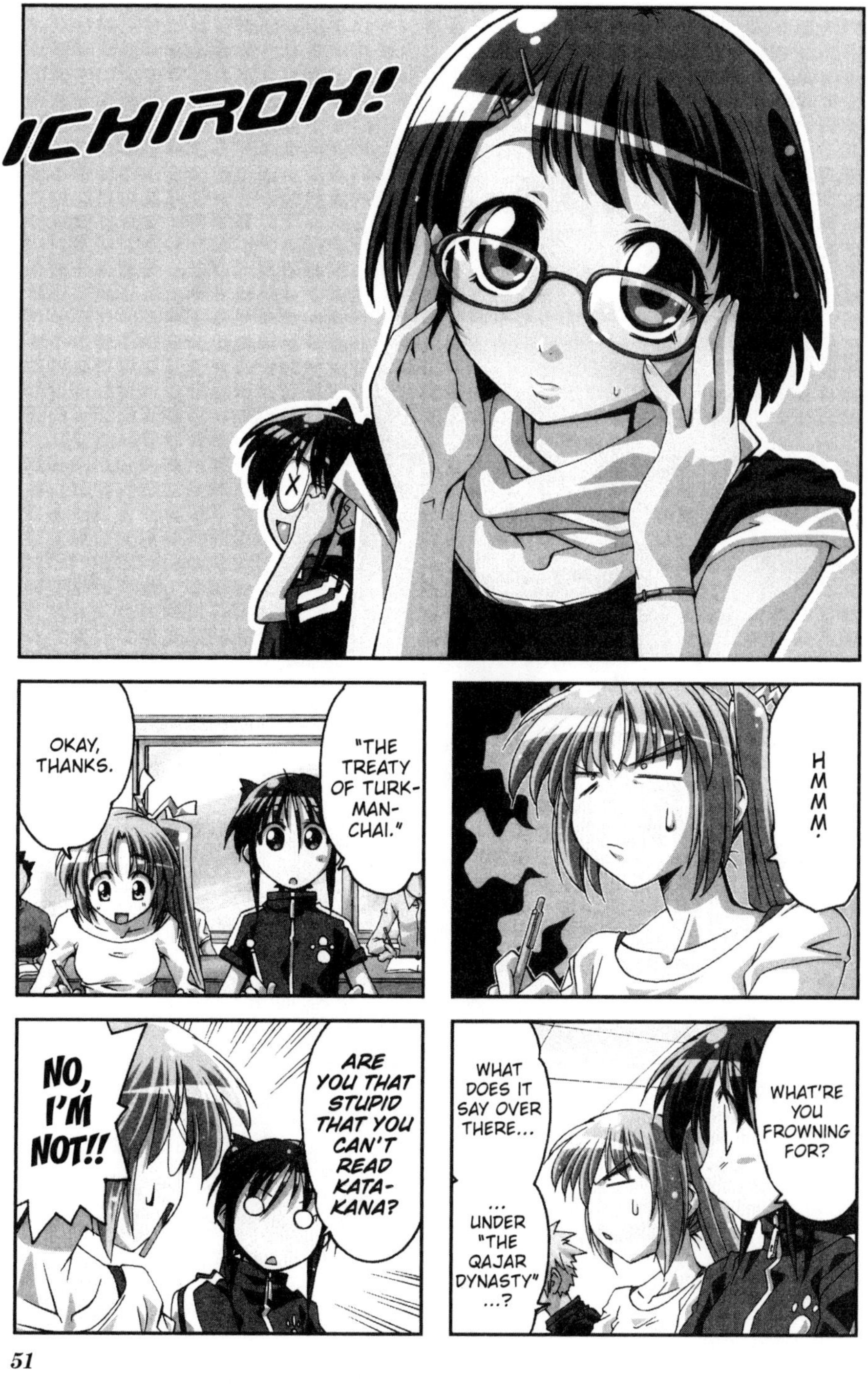
ICHIROH!
HMMM.
"THE TREATY OF TURK-MAN-CHAI."
OKAY, THANKS.
WHAT'RE YOU FROWNING FOR?
WHAT DOES IT SAY OVER THERE...
...UNDER "THE QAJAR DYNASTY"...?
ARE YOU THAT STUPID THAT YOU CAN'T READ KATA-KANA?
NO, I'M NOT!!

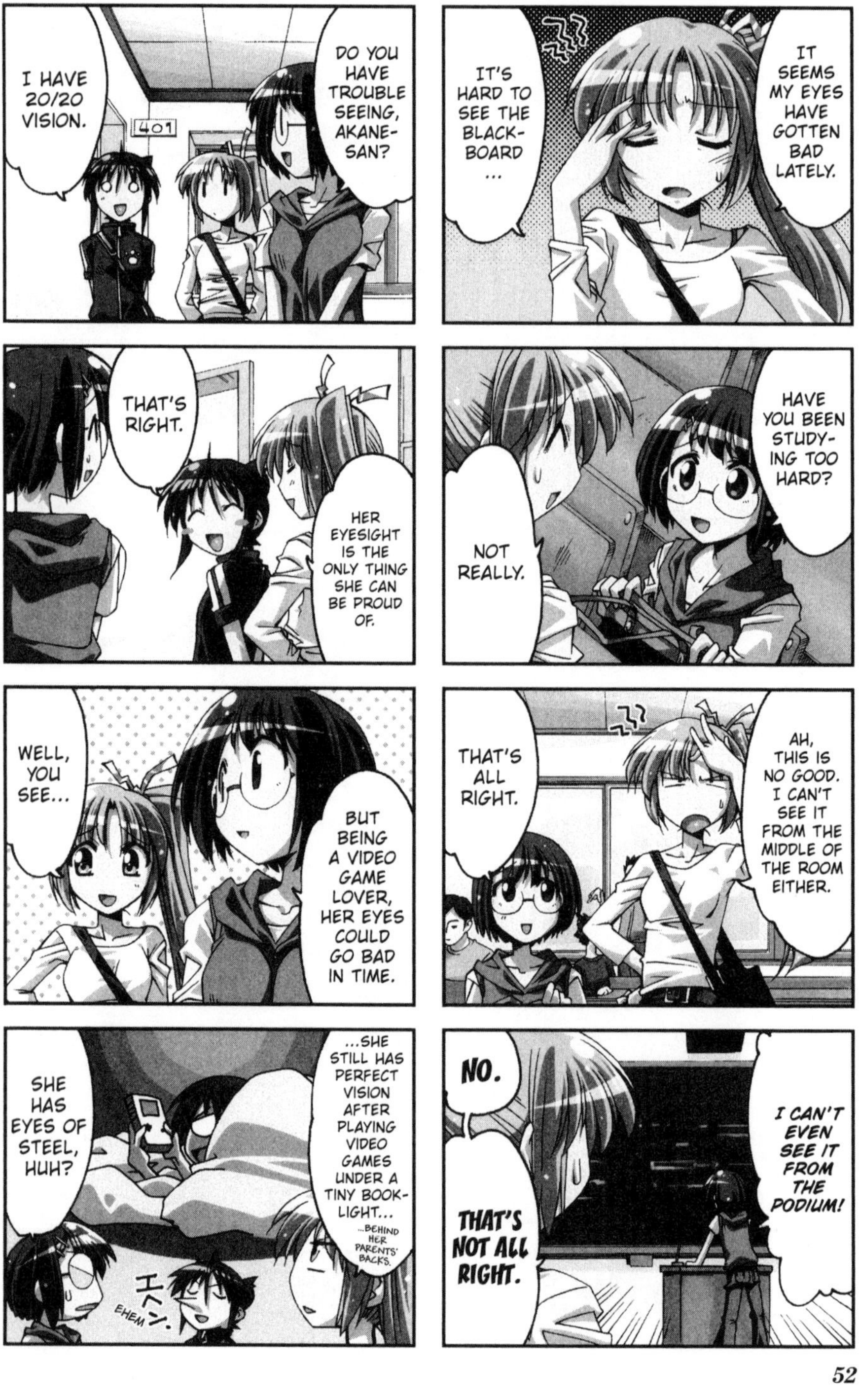
IT SEEMS MY EYES HAVE GOTTEN BAD LATELY.
IT'S HARD TO SEE THE BLACK-BOARD ...
401
DO YOU HAVE TROUBLE SEEING, AKANE-SAN?
I HAVE 20/20 VISION.
HAVE YOU BEEN STUDY-ING TOO HARD?
NOT REALLY.
THAT'S RIGHT.
HER EYESIGHT IS THE ONLY THING SHE CAN BE PROUD OF.
AH, THIS IS NO GOOD. I CAN'T SEE IT FROM THE MIDDLE OF THE ROOM EITHER.
THAT'S ALL RIGHT.
WELL, YOU SEE...
BUT BEING A VIDEO GAME LOVER, HER EYES COULD GO BAD IN TIME.
NO.
THAT'S NOT ALL RIGHT.
I CAN'T EVEN SEE IT FROM THE PODIUM!
...SHE STILL HAS PERFECT VISION AFTER PLAYING VIDEO GAMES UNDER A TINY BOOK-LIGHT...
...BEHIND HER PARENTS' BACKS.
SHE HAS EYES OF STEEL, HUH?
EHEM

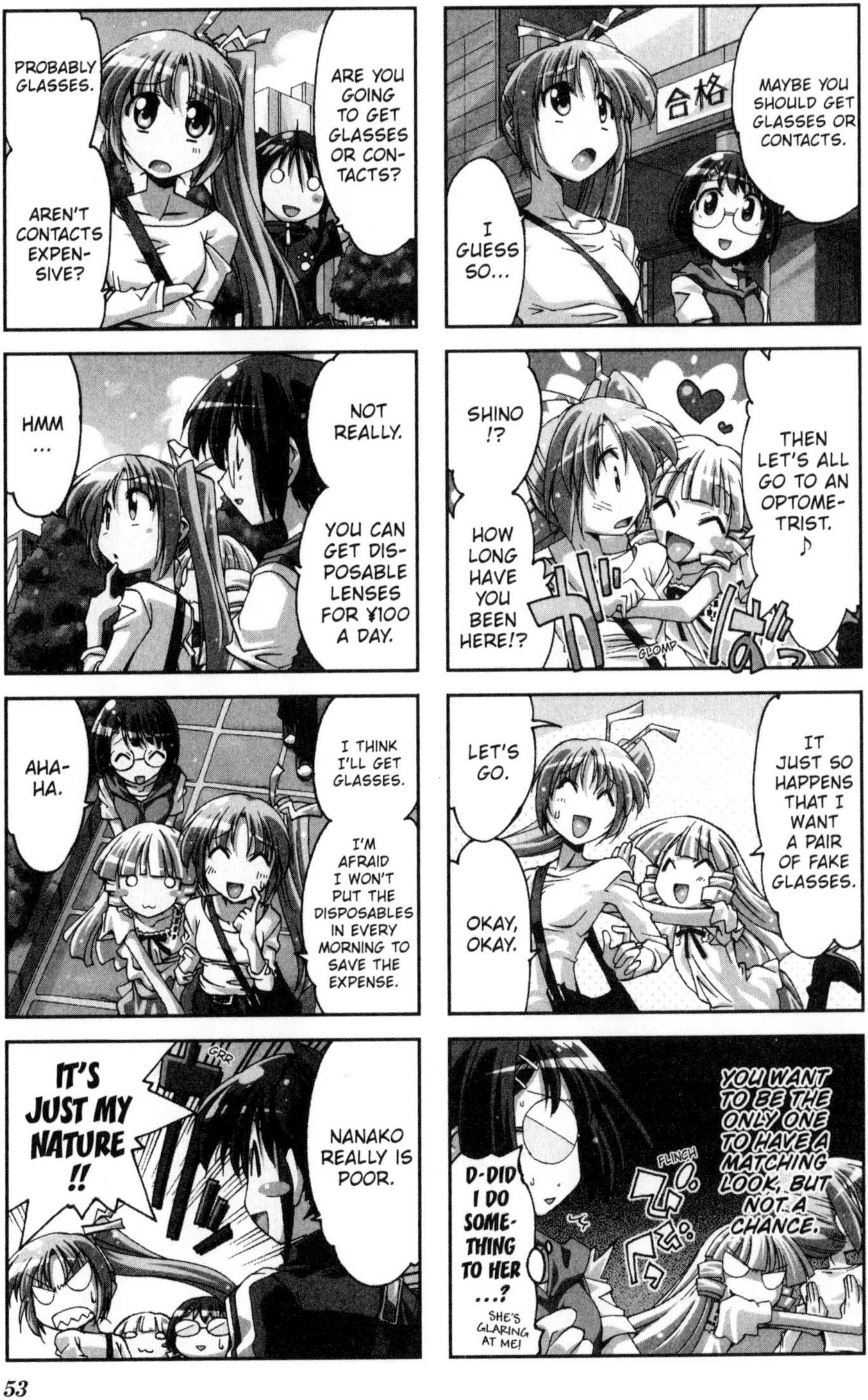
MAYBE YOU SHOULD GET GLASSES OR CONTACTS.
合格
I GUESS SO...
THEN LET'S ALL GO TO AN OPTOME-TRIST. ♪
SHINO !?
HOW LONG HAVE YOU BEEN HERE!?
GLOMP
IT JUST SO HAPPENS THAT I WANT A PAIR OF FAKE GLASSES.
LET'S GO.
OKAY, OKAY.
YOU WANT TO BE THE ONLY ONE TO HAVE A MATCHING LOOK, BUT NOT A CHANCE.
FLINCH
D-DID I DO SOME-THING TO HER ...?
SHE'S GLARING AT ME!
ARE YOU GOING TO GET GLASSES OR CON-TACTS?
PROBABLY GLASSES.
AREN'T CONTACTS EXPEN-SIVE?
NOT REALLY.
YOU CAN GET DIS-POSABLE LENSES FOR ¥100 A DAY.
HMM ...
I THINK I'LL GET GLASSES.
I'M AFRAID I WON'T PUT THE DISPOSABLES IN EVERY MORNING TO SAVE THE EXPENSE.
AHA-HA.
NANAKO REALLY IS POOR.
GRR
IT'S JUST MY NATURE !!

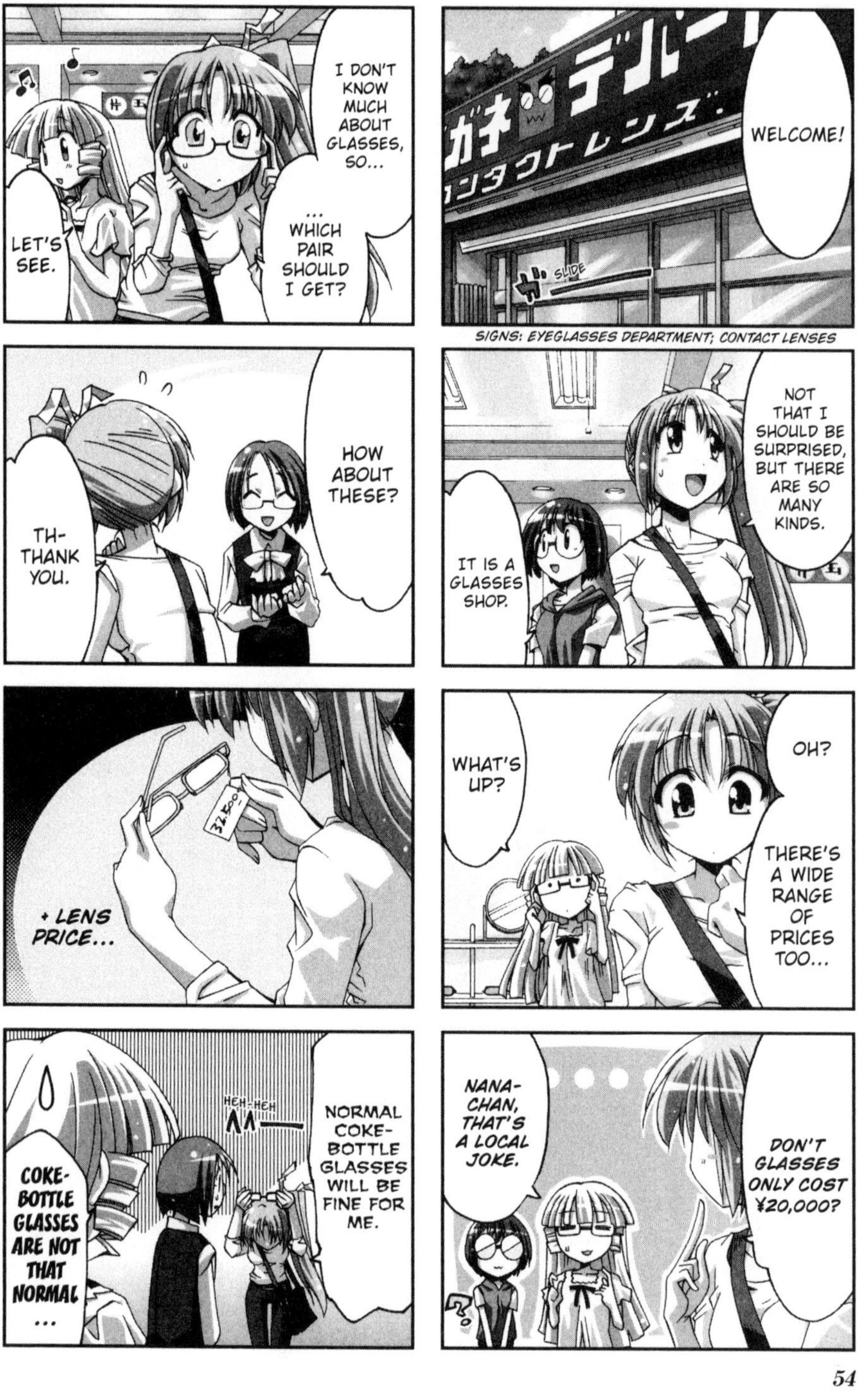
WELCOME!
SLIDE
SIGNS: EYEGLASSES DEPARTMENT; CONTACT LENSES
I DON'T KNOW MUCH ABOUT GLASSES, SO...
... WHICH PAIR SHOULD I GET?
LET'S SEE.
NOT THAT I SHOULD BE SURPRISED, BUT THERE ARE SO MANY KINDS.
IT IS A GLASSES SHOP.
HOW ABOUT THESE?
TH-THANK YOU.
OH?
THERE'S A WIDE RANGE OF PRICES TOO...
WHAT'S UP?
+ LENS PRICE...
DON'T GLASSES ONLY COST ¥20,000?
NANA-CHAN, THAT'S A LOCAL JOKE.
NORMAL COKE-BOTTLE GLASSES WILL BE FINE FOR ME.
HEH-HEH
COKE-BOTTLE GLASSES ARE NOT THAT NORMAL ...

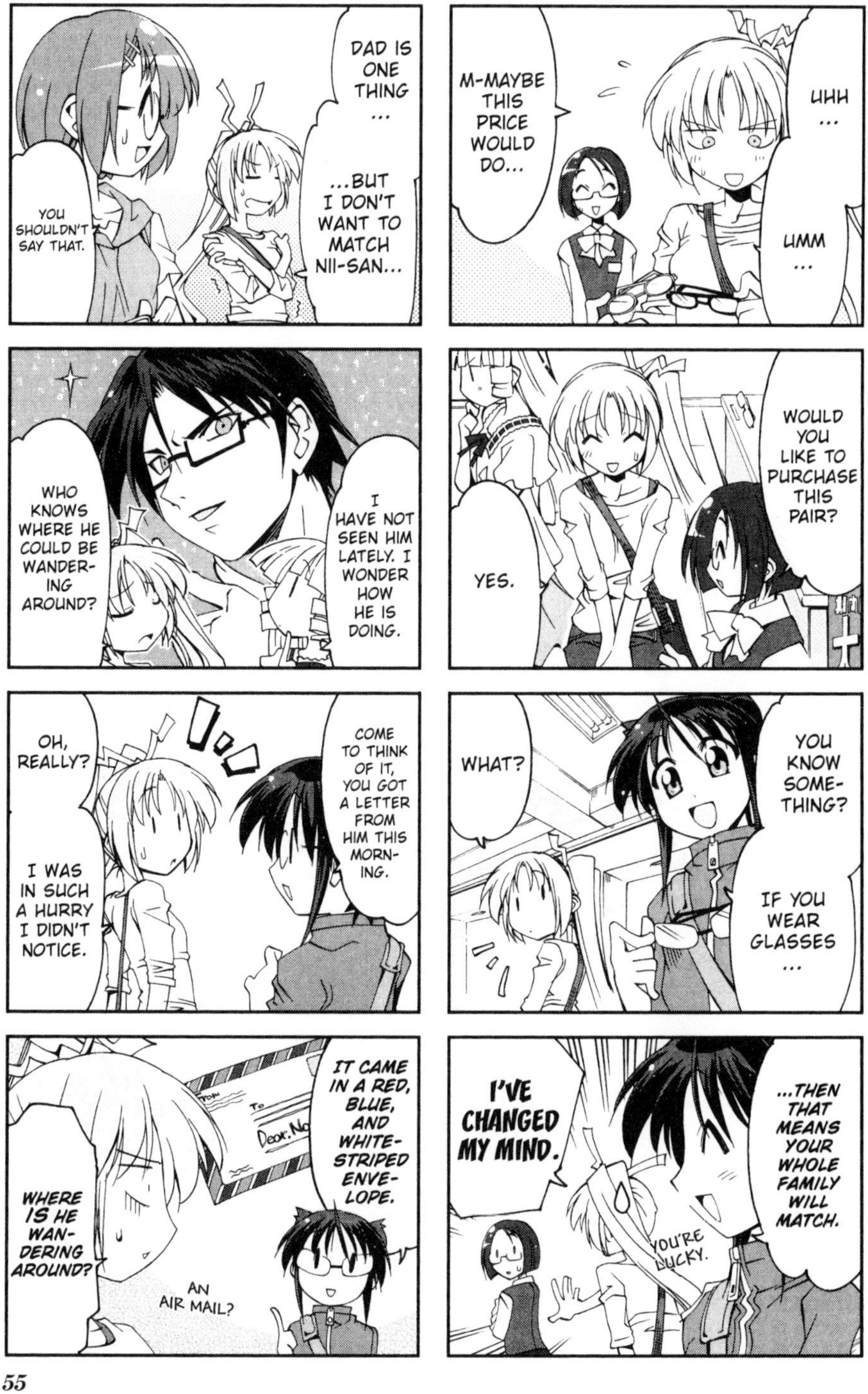
UHH ...
M-MAYBE THIS PRICE WOULD DO...
UMM ...
WOULD YOU LIKE TO PURCHASE THIS PAIR?
YES.
YOU KNOW SOMETHING?
WHAT?
IF YOU WEAR GLASSES ...
...THEN THAT MEANS YOUR WHOLE FAMILY WILL MATCH.
I'VE CHANGED MY MIND.
YOU'RE LUCKY.
DAD IS ONE THING ...
...BUT I DON'T WANT TO MATCH NII-SAN...
YOU SHOULDN'T SAY THAT.
I HAVE NOT SEEN HIM LATELY. I WONDER HOW HE IS DOING.
WHO KNOWS WHERE HE COULD BE WANDERING AROUND?
COME TO THINK OF IT, YOU GOT A LETTER FROM HIM THIS MORNING.
OH, REALLY?
I WAS IN SUCH A HURRY I DIDN'T NOTICE.
IT CAME IN A RED, BLUE, AND WHITE-STRIPED ENVELOPE.
AN AIR MAIL?
WHERE IS HE WANDERING AROUND?

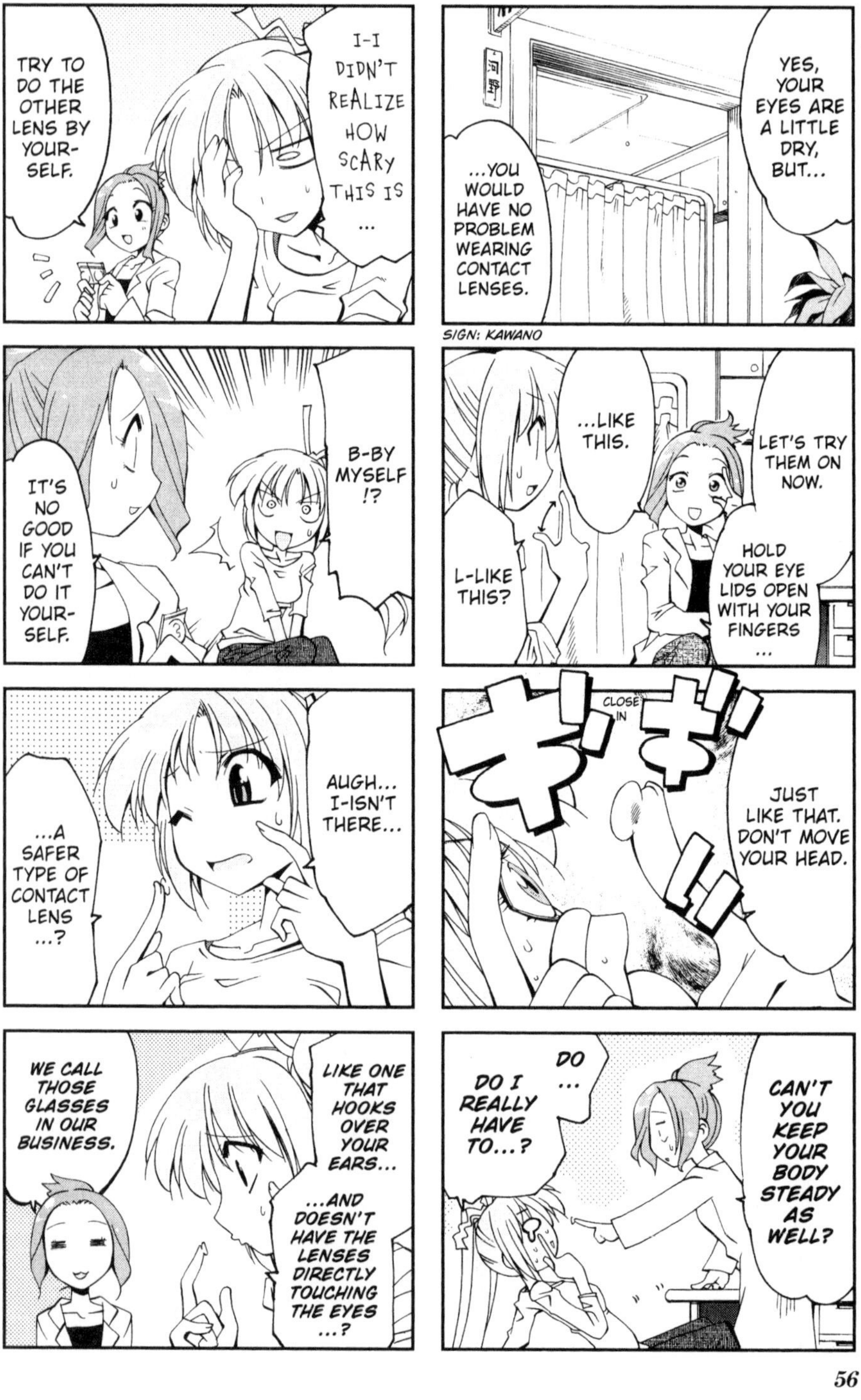
YES, YOUR EYES ARE A LITTLE DRY, BUT...
...YOU WOULD HAVE NO PROBLEM WEARING CONTACT LENSES.
河野
SIGN: KAWANO
LET'S TRY THEM ON NOW.
HOLD YOUR EYE LIDS OPEN WITH YOUR FINGERS ...
...LIKE THIS.
L-LIKE THIS?
CLOSE IN
JUST LIKE THAT. DON'T MOVE YOUR HEAD.
CAN'T YOU KEEP YOUR BODY STEADY AS WELL?
DO ...
DO I REALLY HAVE TO...?
I-I DIDN'T REALIZE HOW SCARY THIS IS ...
TRY TO DO THE OTHER LENS BY YOUR-SELF.
B-BY MYSELF !?
IT'S NO GOOD IF YOU CAN'T DO IT YOUR-SELF.
AUGH... I-ISN'T THERE...
...A SAFER TYPE OF CONTACT LENS ...?
LIKE ONE THAT HOOKS OVER YOUR EARS...
...AND DOESN'T HAVE THE LENSES DIRECTLY TOUCHING THE EYES ...?
WE CALL THOSE GLASSES IN OUR BUSINESS.

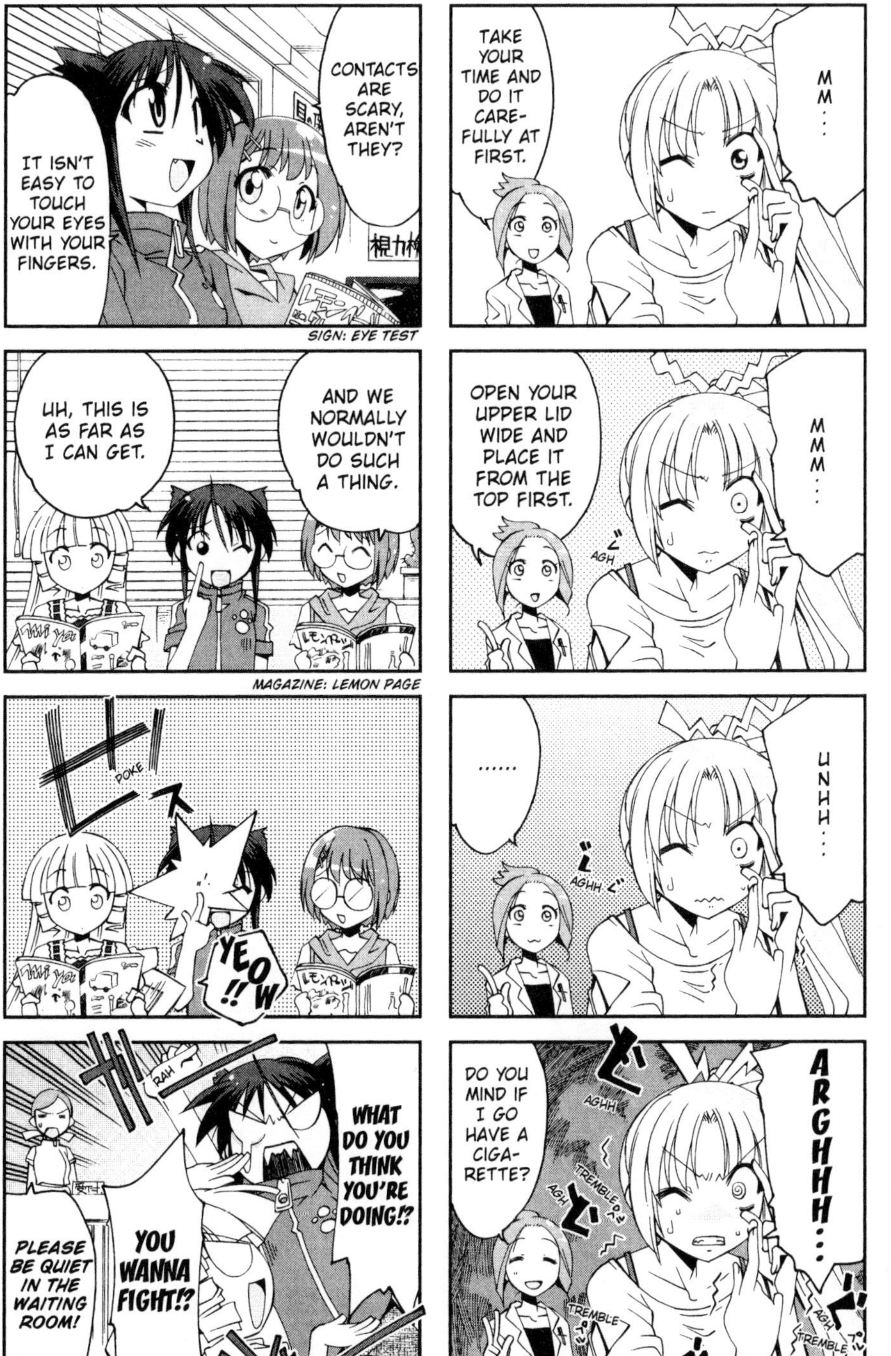
MM...
TAKE YOUR TIME AND DO IT CAREFULLY AT FIRST.
MMM...
OPEN YOUR UPPER LID WIDE AND PLACE IT FROM THE TOP FIRST.
AGH
UNHH...
......
AGHH
ARGHHH...
AGHH
DO YOU MIND IF I GO HAVE A CIGARETTE?
TREMBLE
AGH
AGH
TREMBLE
TREMBLE
CONTACTS ARE SCARY, AREN'T THEY?
IT ISN'T EASY TO TOUCH YOUR EYES WITH YOUR FINGERS.
SIGN: EYE TEST
AND WE NORMALLY WOULDN'T DO SUCH A THING.
UH, THIS IS AS FAR AS I CAN GET.
MAGAZINE: LEMON PAGE
POKE
YEOW!!
RAH~
WHAT DO YOU THINK YOU'RE DOING!?
YOU WANNA FIGHT!?
PLEASE BE QUIET IN THE WAITING ROOM!
GRR

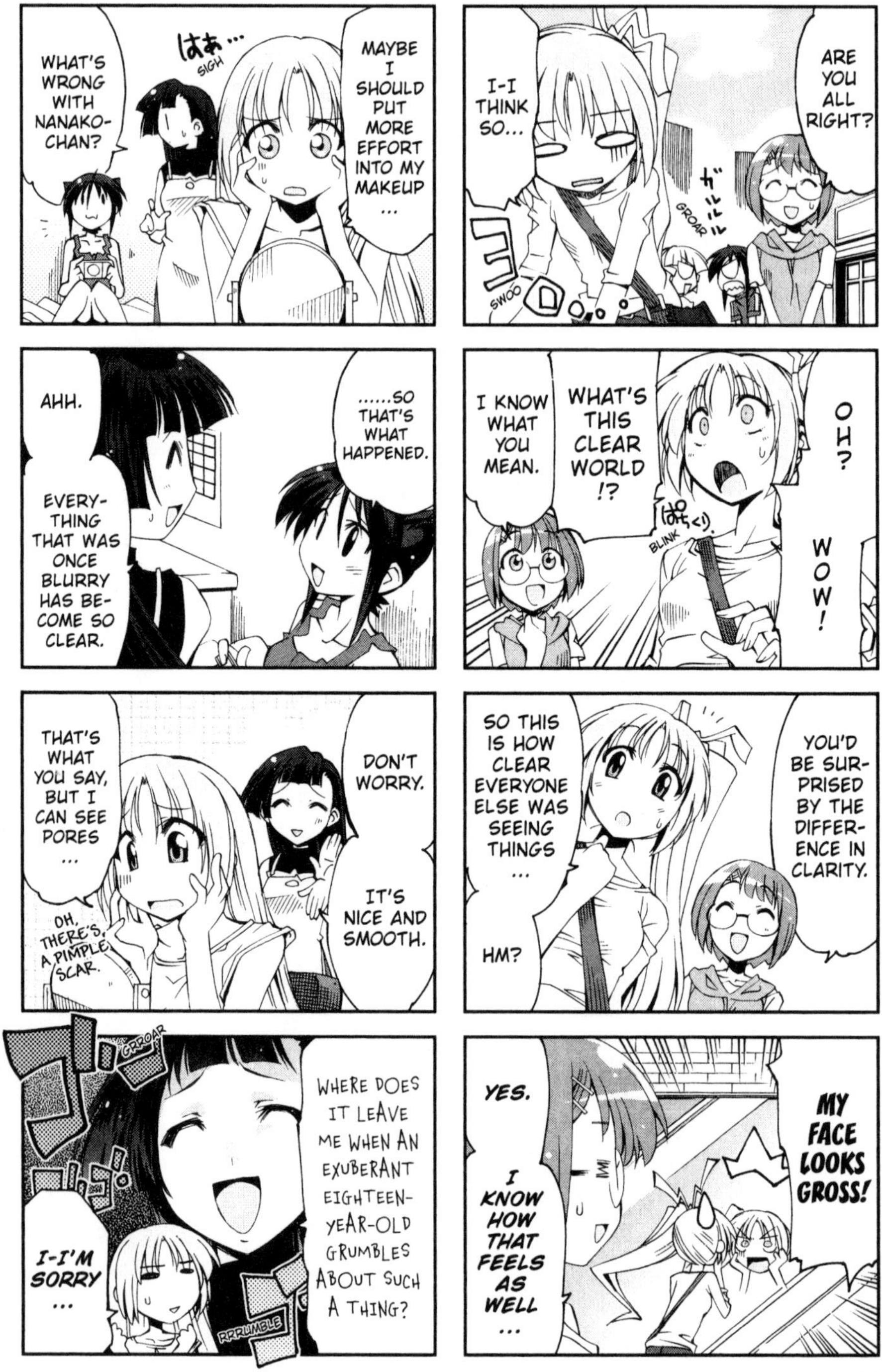
ARE YOU ALL RIGHT?
I-I THINK SO...
ガルル
GROAR
SWOO
OH? WOW!
WHAT'S THIS CLEAR WORLD!?
I KNOW WHAT YOU MEAN.
BLINK
YOU'D BE SURPRISED BY THE DIFFERENCE IN CLARITY.
SO THIS IS HOW CLEAR EVERYONE ELSE WAS SEEING THINGS...
HM?
MY FACE LOOKS GROSS!
YES.
I KNOW HOW THAT FEELS AS WELL...
MAYBE I SHOULD PUT MORE EFFORT INTO MY MAKEUP...
はぁ…
SIGH
WHAT'S WRONG WITH NANAKO-CHAN?
......SO THAT'S WHAT HAPPENED.
AHH.
EVERYTHING THAT WAS ONCE BLURRY HAS BECOME SO CLEAR.
DON'T WORRY.
IT'S NICE AND SMOOTH.
THAT'S WHAT YOU SAY, BUT I CAN SEE PORES...
OH, THERE'S A PIMPLE SCAR.
WHERE DOES IT LEAVE ME WHEN AN EXUBERANT EIGHTEEN-YEAR-OLD GRUMBLES ABOUT SUCH A THING?
GRRROAR
RRRUMBLE
I-I'M SORRY...

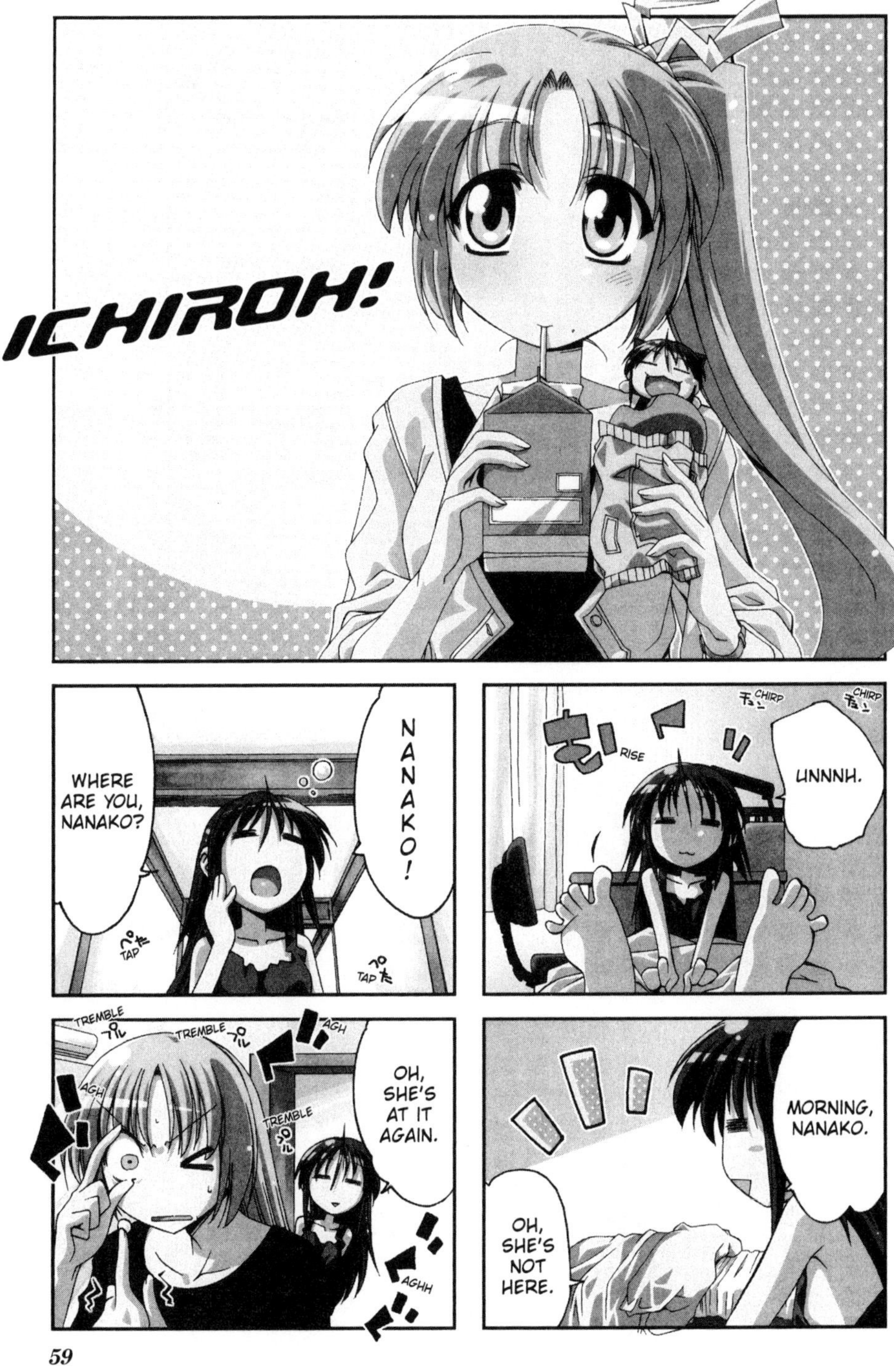
ICHIROH!
CHIRP
CHIRP
RISE
UNNNH.
NANAKO!
WHERE ARE YOU, NANAKO?
TAP
TAP
MORNING, NANAKO.
OH, SHE'S NOT HERE.
TREMBLE
TREMBLE
AGH
AGH
TREMBLE
OH, SHE'S AT IT AGAIN.
AGHH

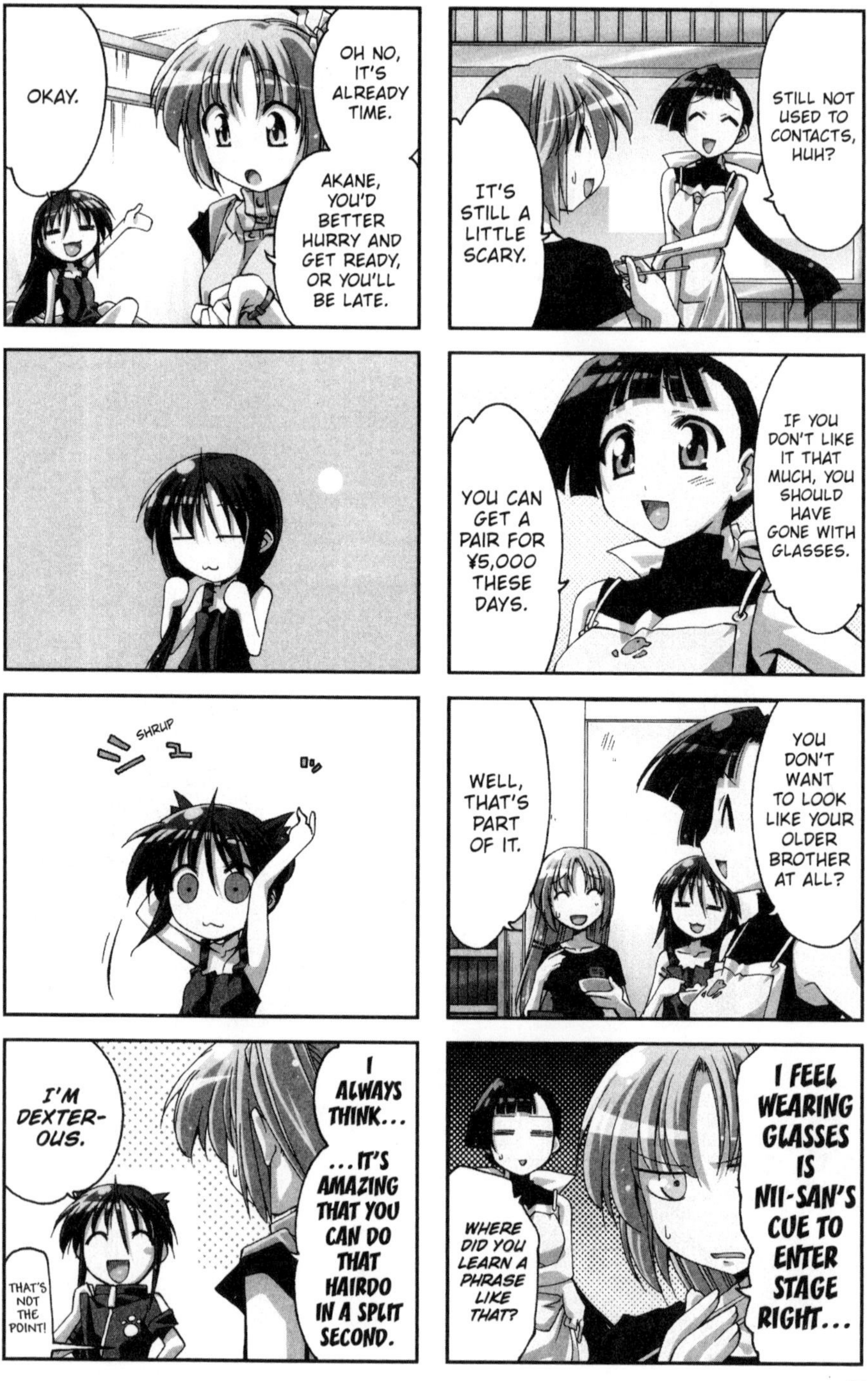
STILL NOT USED TO CONTACTS, HUH?
IT'S STILL A LITTLE SCARY.
OH NO, IT'S ALREADY TIME.
AKANE, YOU'D BETTER HURRY AND GET READY, OR YOU'LL BE LATE.
OKAY.
IF YOU DON'T LIKE IT THAT MUCH, YOU SHOULD HAVE GONE WITH GLASSES.
YOU CAN GET A PAIR FOR ¥5,000 THESE DAYS.
YOU DON'T WANT TO LOOK LIKE YOUR OLDER BROTHER AT ALL?
WELL, THAT'S PART OF IT.
SHRUP
I FEEL WEARING GLASSES IS NII-SAN'S CUE TO ENTER STAGE RIGHT...
WHERE DID YOU LEARN A PHRASE LIKE THAT?
I ALWAYS THINK...
...IT'S AMAZING THAT YOU CAN DO THAT HAIRDO IN A SPLIT SECOND.
I'M DEXTEROUS.
THAT'S NOT THE POINT!

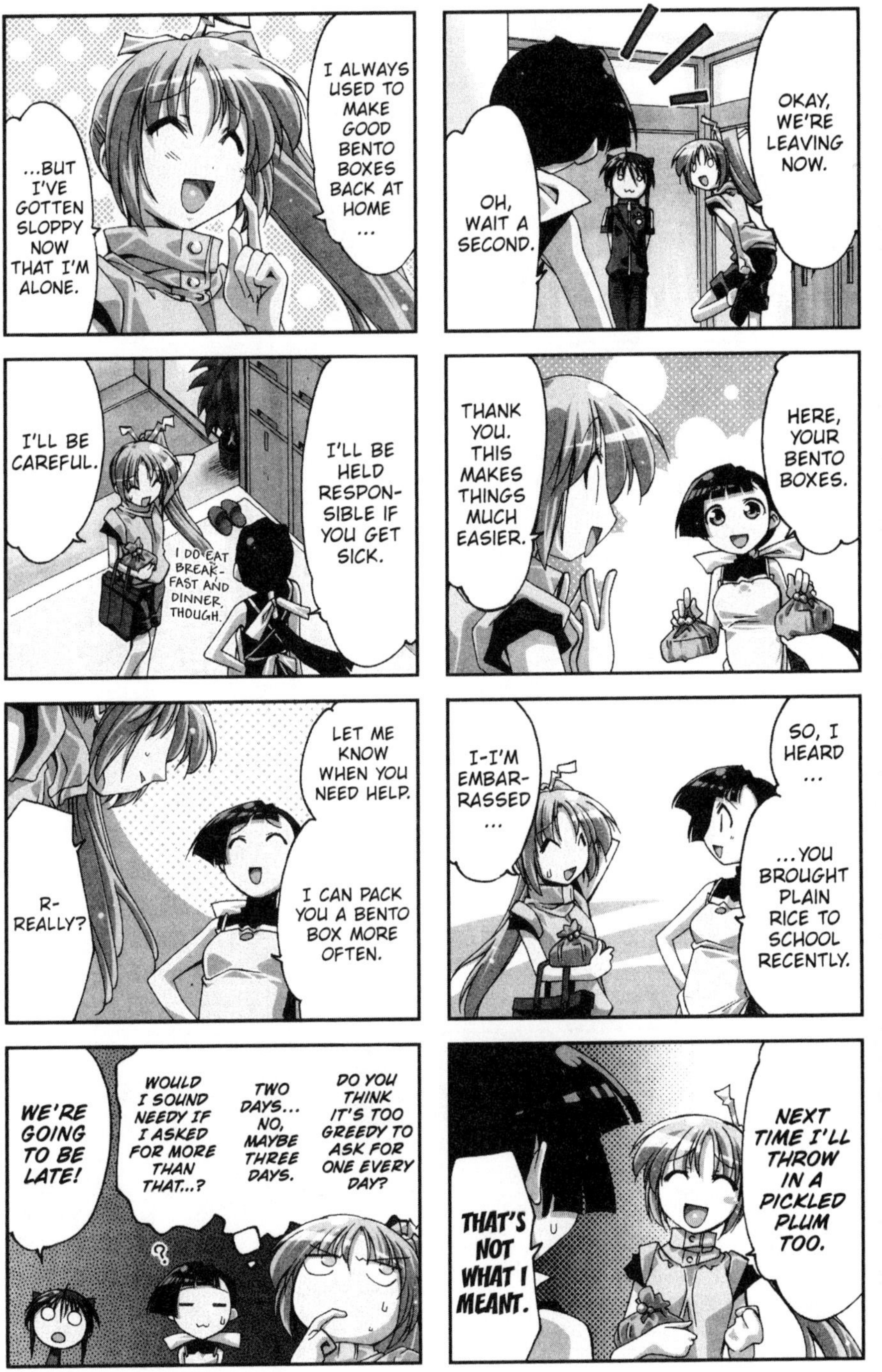
OKAY, WE'RE LEAVING NOW.
OH, WAIT A SECOND.
HERE, YOUR BENTO BOXES.
THANK YOU. THIS MAKES THINGS MUCH EASIER.
SO, I HEARD ...
...YOU BROUGHT PLAIN RICE TO SCHOOL RECENTLY.
I-I'M EMBARRASSED ...
NEXT TIME I'LL THROW IN A PICKLED PLUM TOO.
THAT'S NOT WHAT I MEANT.
I ALWAYS USED TO MAKE GOOD BENTO BOXES BACK AT HOME ...
...BUT I'VE GOTTEN SLOPPY NOW THAT I'M ALONE.
I'LL BE HELD RESPONSIBLE IF YOU GET SICK.
I'LL BE CAREFUL.
I DO EAT BREAKFAST AND DINNER, THOUGH.
LET ME KNOW WHEN YOU NEED HELP.
I CAN PACK YOU A BENTO BOX MORE OFTEN.
R-REALLY?
DO YOU THINK IT'S TOO GREEDY TO ASK FOR ONE EVERY DAY?
TWO DAYS... NO, MAYBE THREE DAYS.
WOULD I SOUND NEEDY IF I ASKED FOR MORE THAN THAT...?
WE'RE GOING TO BE LATE!

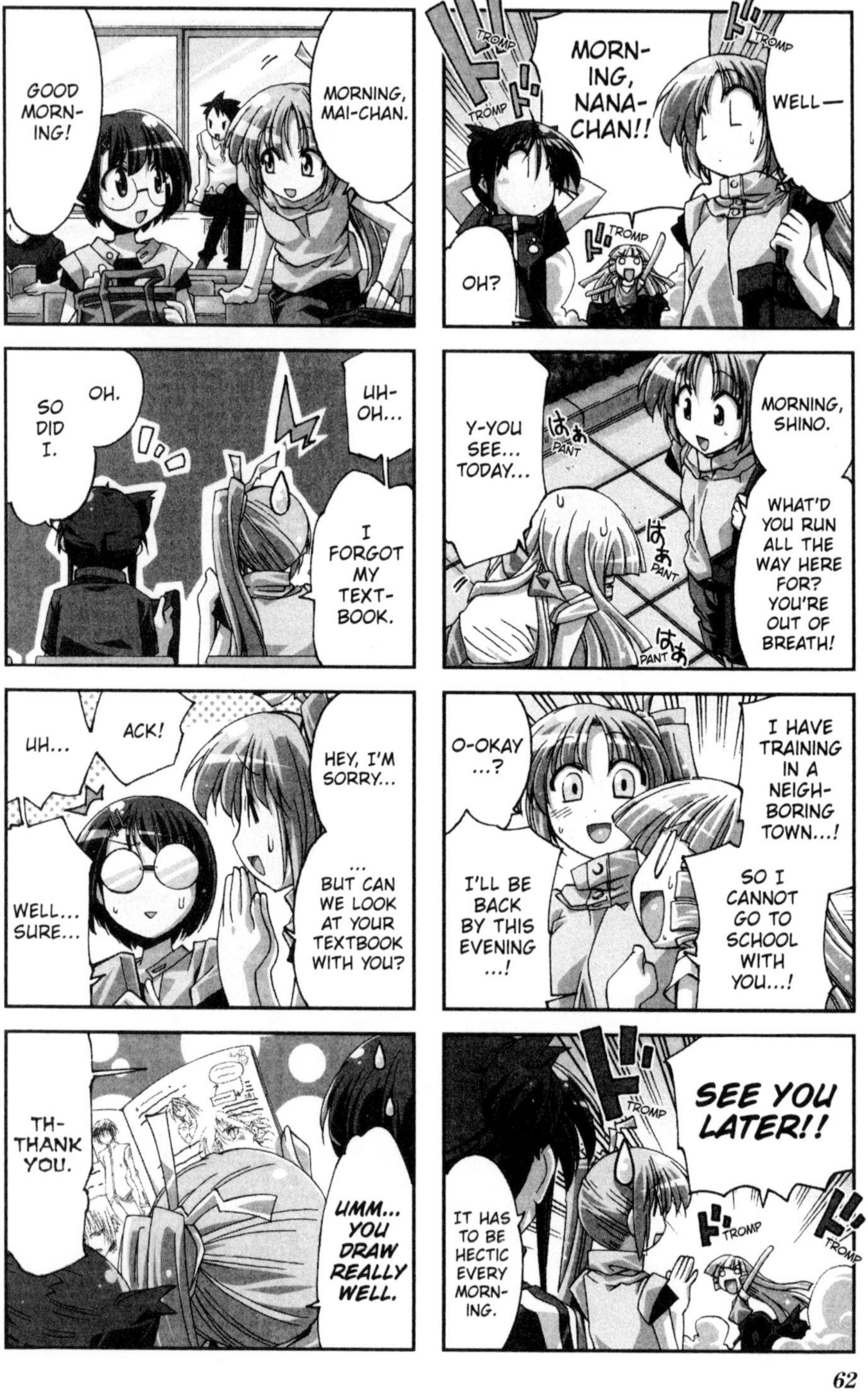
ドッ TROMP
WELL—
MORN-ING, NANA-CHAN!!
ドッ TROMP
ドッ TROMP
ドッ TROMP
OH?
MORNING, SHINO.
WHAT'D YOU RUN ALL THE WAY HERE FOR? YOU'RE OUT OF BREATH!
Y-YOU SEE... TODAY...
はぁ PANT
はぁ PANT
はぁ PANT
I HAVE TRAINING IN A NEIGH-BORING TOWN...!
SO I CANNOT GO TO SCHOOL WITH YOU...!
O-OKAY ...?
I'LL BE BACK BY THIS EVENING ...!
SEE YOU LATER!!
ドッ TROMP
ドッ TROMP
ドッ TROMP
IT HAS TO BE HECTIC EVERY MORN-ING.
MORNING, MAI-CHAN.
GOOD MORN-ING!
UH-OH...
I FORGOT MY TEXT-BOOK.
OH.
SO DID I.
HEY, I'M SORRY...
... BUT CAN WE LOOK AT YOUR TEXTBOOK WITH YOU?
ACK!
UH...
WELL... SURE...
UMM... YOU DRAW REALLY WELL.
TH-THANK YOU.

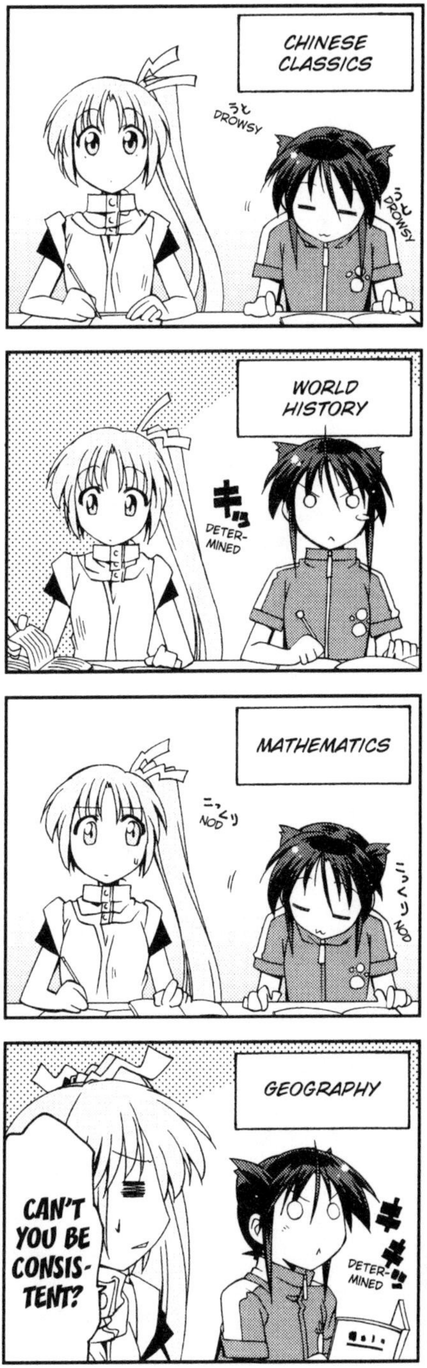
CHINESE CLASSICS
うと DROWSY
うと DROWSY
WORLD HISTORY
キッ DETERMINED
MATHEMATICS
こっくり NOD
こっくり NOD
GEOGRAPHY
キキッ DETERMINED
CAN'T YOU BE CONSISTENT?

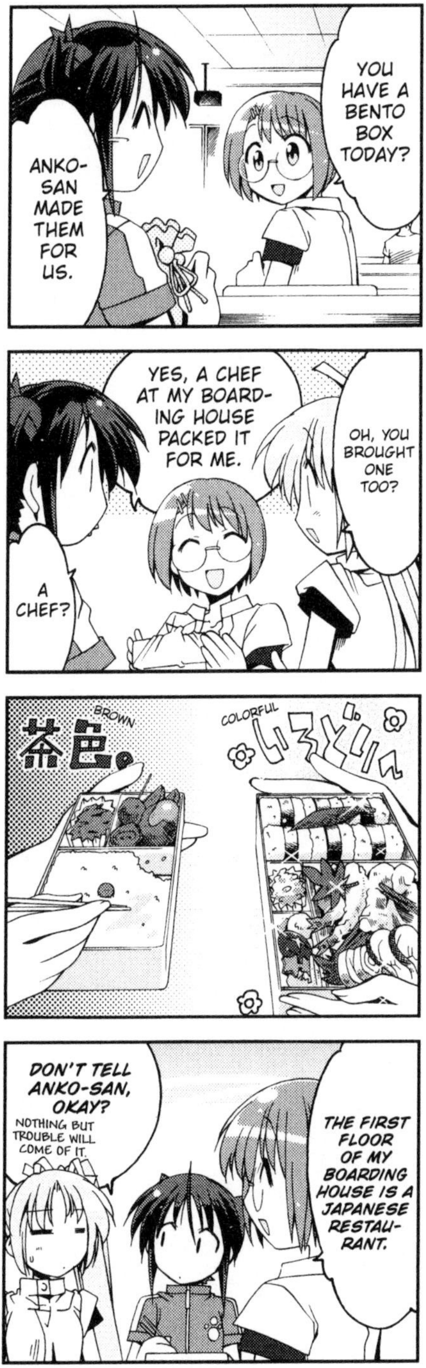
YOU HAVE A BENTO BOX TODAY?
ANKO-SAN MADE THEM FOR US.
OH, YOU BROUGHT ONE TOO?
YES, A CHEF AT MY BOARDING HOUSE PACKED IT FOR ME.
A CHEF?
COLORFUL いろどりん
茶色 BROWN
THE FIRST FLOOR OF MY BOARDING HOUSE IS A JAPANESE RESTAURANT.
DON'T TELL ANKO-SAN, OKAY?
NOTHING BUT TROUBLE WILL COME OF IT.

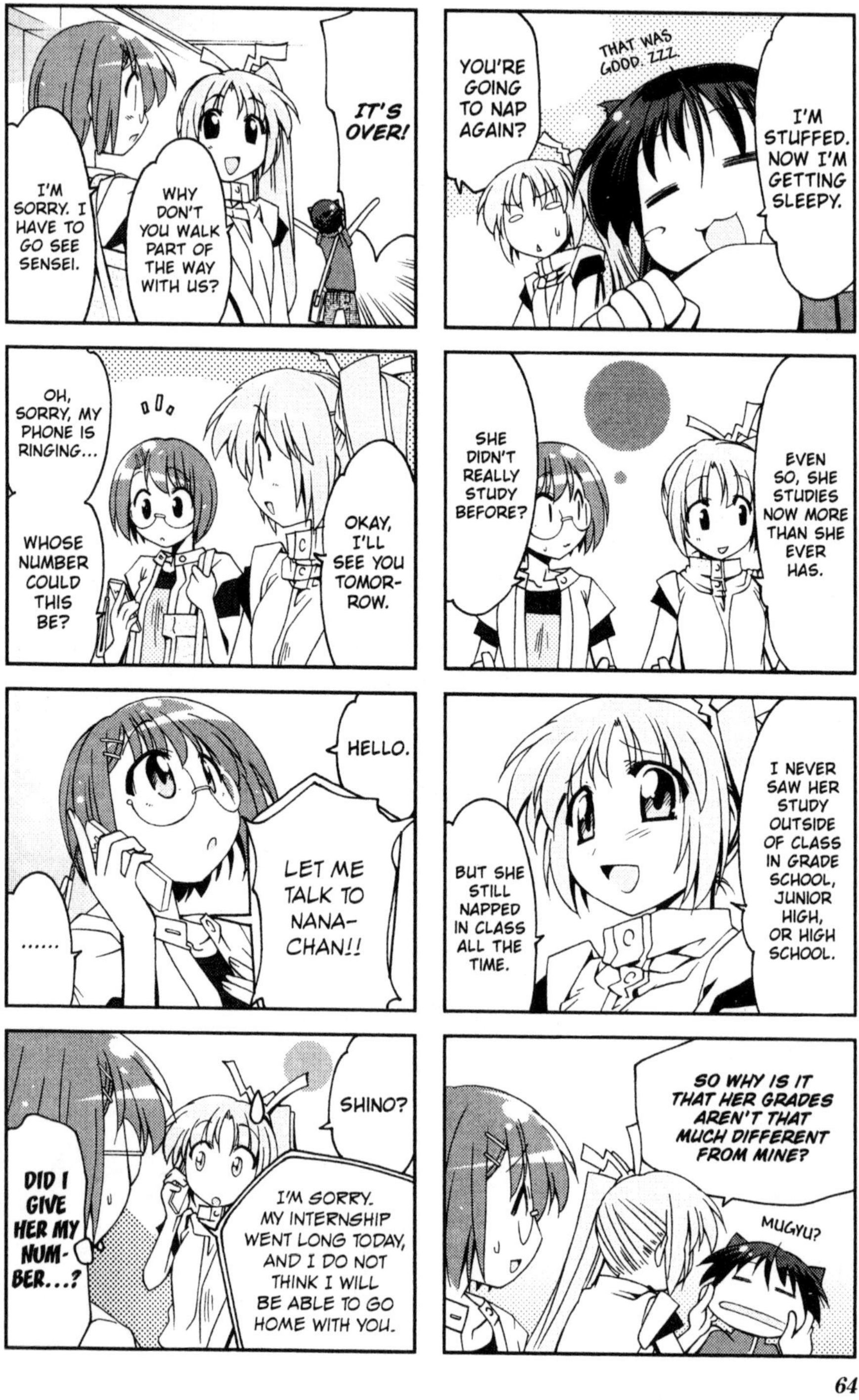
I'M STUFFED. NOW I'M GETTING SLEEPY.
THAT WAS GOOD. ZZZ.
YOU'RE GOING TO NAP AGAIN?
EVEN SO, SHE STUDIES NOW MORE THAN SHE EVER HAS.
SHE DIDN'T REALLY STUDY BEFORE?
I NEVER SAW HER STUDY OUTSIDE OF CLASS IN GRADE SCHOOL, JUNIOR HIGH, OR HIGH SCHOOL.
BUT SHE STILL NAPPED IN CLASS ALL THE TIME.
SO WHY IS IT THAT HER GRADES AREN'T THAT MUCH DIFFERENT FROM MINE?
MUGYU?
IT'S OVER!
WHY DON'T YOU WALK PART OF THE WAY WITH US?
I'M SORRY. I HAVE TO GO SEE SENSEI.
OKAY, I'LL SEE YOU TOMORROW.
OH, SORRY, MY PHONE IS RINGING...
WHOSE NUMBER COULD THIS BE?
HELLO.
LET ME TALK TO NANA-CHAN!!
......
SHINO?
I'M SORRY. MY INTERNSHIP WENT LONG TODAY, AND I DO NOT THINK I WILL BE ABLE TO GO HOME WITH YOU.
DID I GIVE HER MY NUMBER...?

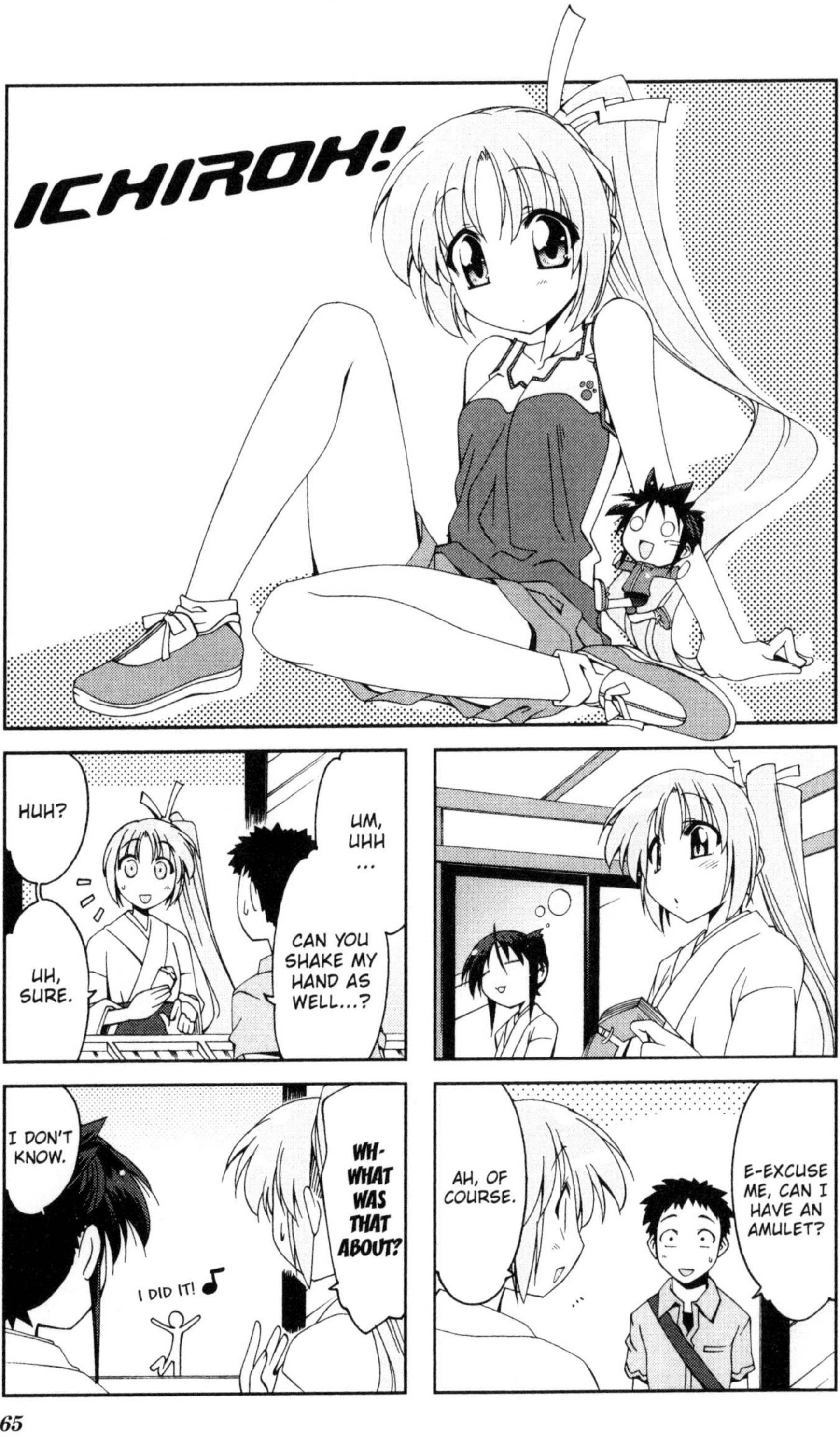
ICHIROH!
UM, UHH ...
CAN YOU SHAKE MY HAND AS WELL...?
HUH?
UH, SURE.
E-EXCUSE ME, CAN I HAVE AN AMULET?
AH, OF COURSE.
...
WH-WHAT WAS THAT ABOUT?
I DON'T KNOW.
I DID IT! ♪

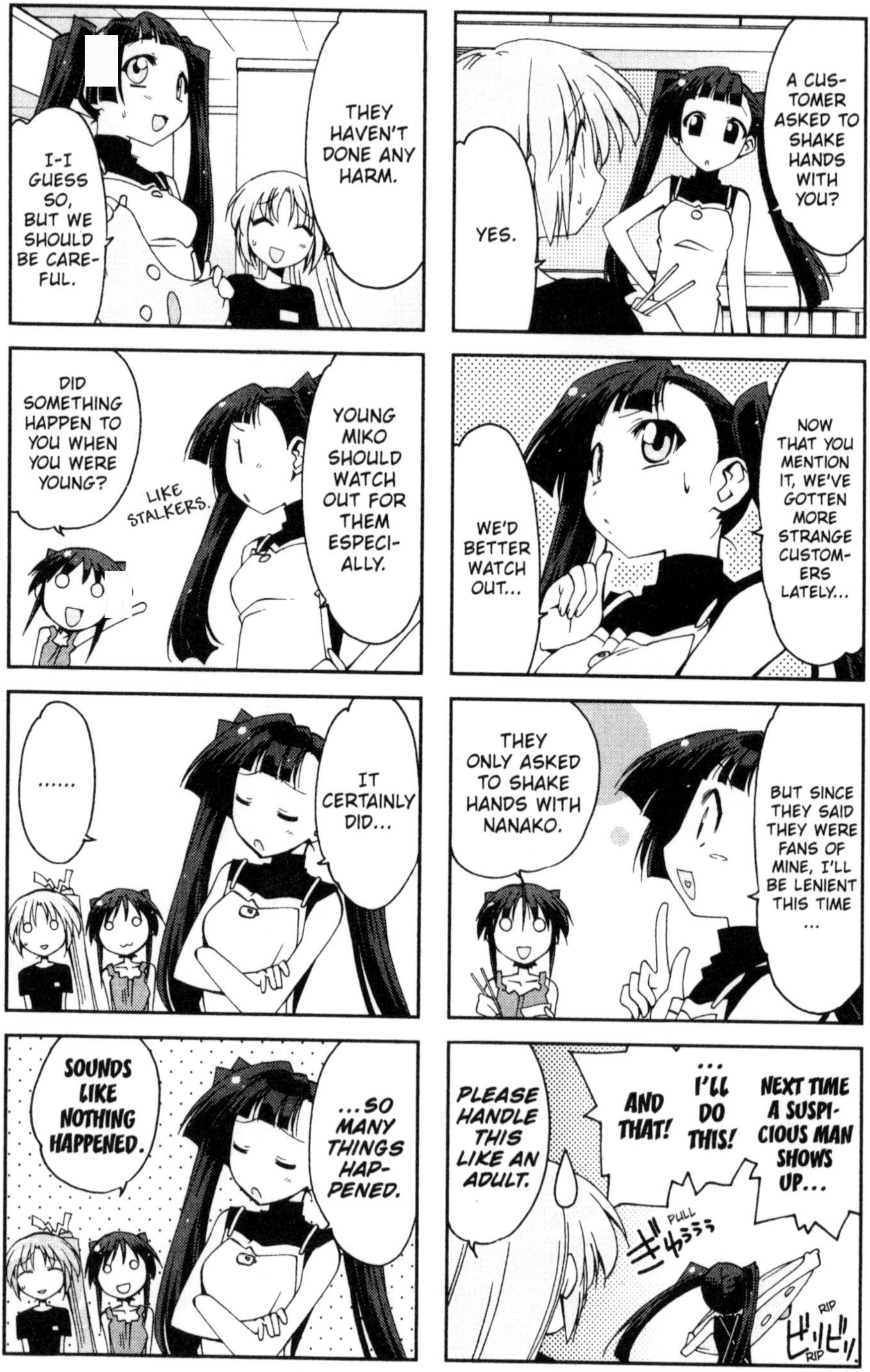
A CUSTOMER ASKED TO SHAKE HANDS WITH YOU?
YES.
THEY HAVEN'T DONE ANY HARM.
I-I GUESS SO, BUT WE SHOULD BE CAREFUL.
NOW THAT YOU MENTION IT, WE'VE GOTTEN MORE STRANGE CUSTOMERS LATELY...
WE'D BETTER WATCH OUT...
YOUNG MIKO SHOULD WATCH OUT FOR THEM ESPECIALLY.
LIKE STALKERS.
DID SOMETHING HAPPEN TO YOU WHEN YOU WERE YOUNG?
BUT SINCE THEY SAID THEY WERE FANS OF MINE, I'LL BE LENIENT THIS TIME ...
THEY ONLY ASKED TO SHAKE HANDS WITH NANAKO.
IT CERTAINLY DID...
......
NEXT TIME A SUSPICIOUS MAN SHOWS UP...
...I'LL DO THIS!
AND THAT!
PLEASE HANDLE THIS LIKE AN ADULT.
PULL
RIP
RIP
...SO MANY THINGS HAPPENED.
SOUNDS LIKE NOTHING HAPPENED.

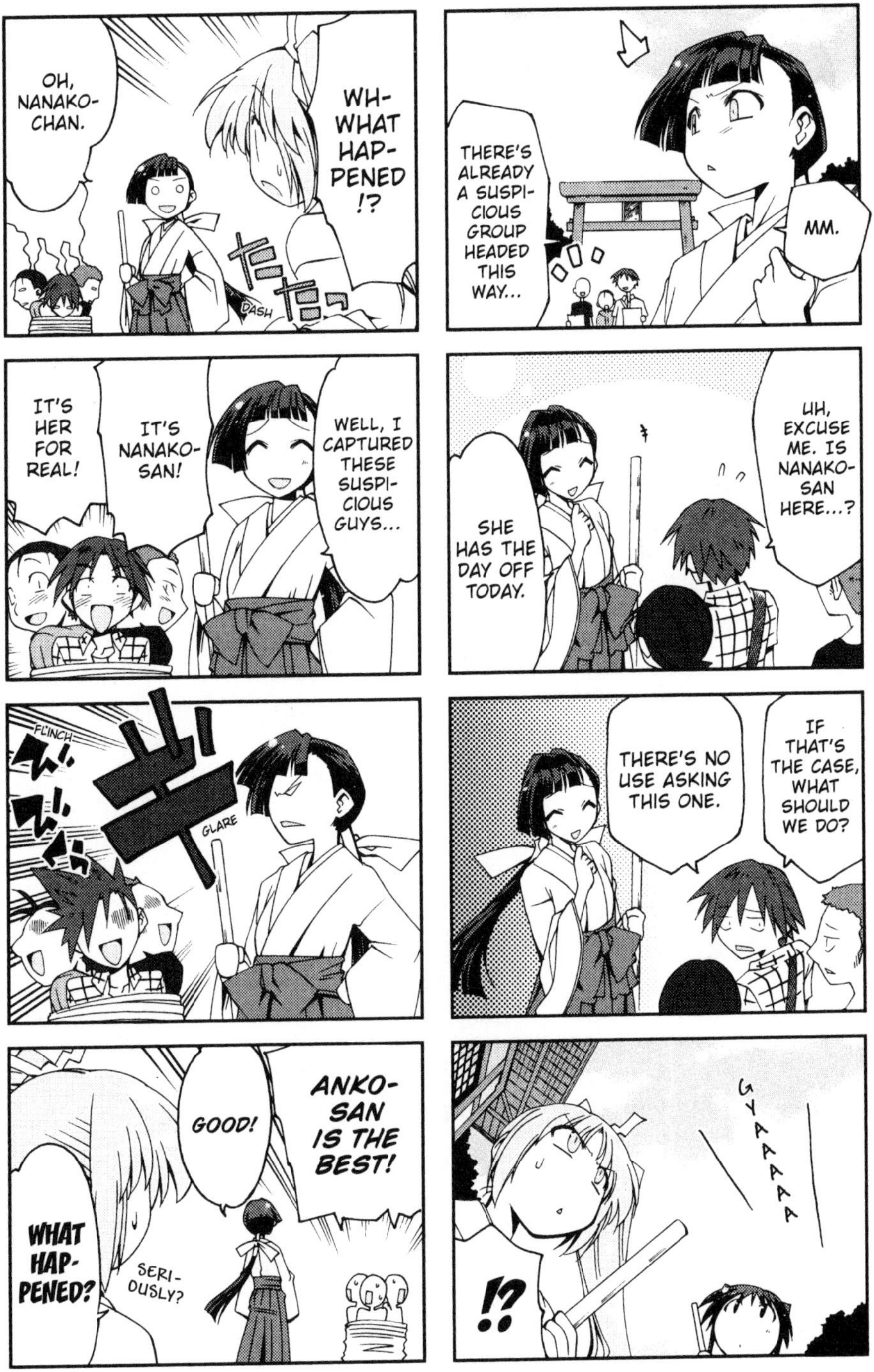
MM.
THERE'S ALREADY A SUSPI-CIOUS GROUP HEADED THIS WAY...
UH, EXCUSE ME. IS NANAKO-SAN HERE...?
SHE HAS THE DAY OFF TODAY.
IF THAT'S THE CASE, WHAT SHOULD WE DO?
THERE'S NO USE ASKING THIS ONE.
GYAAAAA
!?
WH-WHAT HAP-PENED!?
DASH
OH, NANAKO-CHAN.
WELL, I CAPTURED THESE SUSPI-CIOUS GUYS...
IT'S NANAKO-SAN!
IT'S HER FOR REAL!
GLARE
FLINCH
ANKO-SAN IS THE BEST!
GOOD!
SERI-OUSLY?
WHAT HAP-PENED?

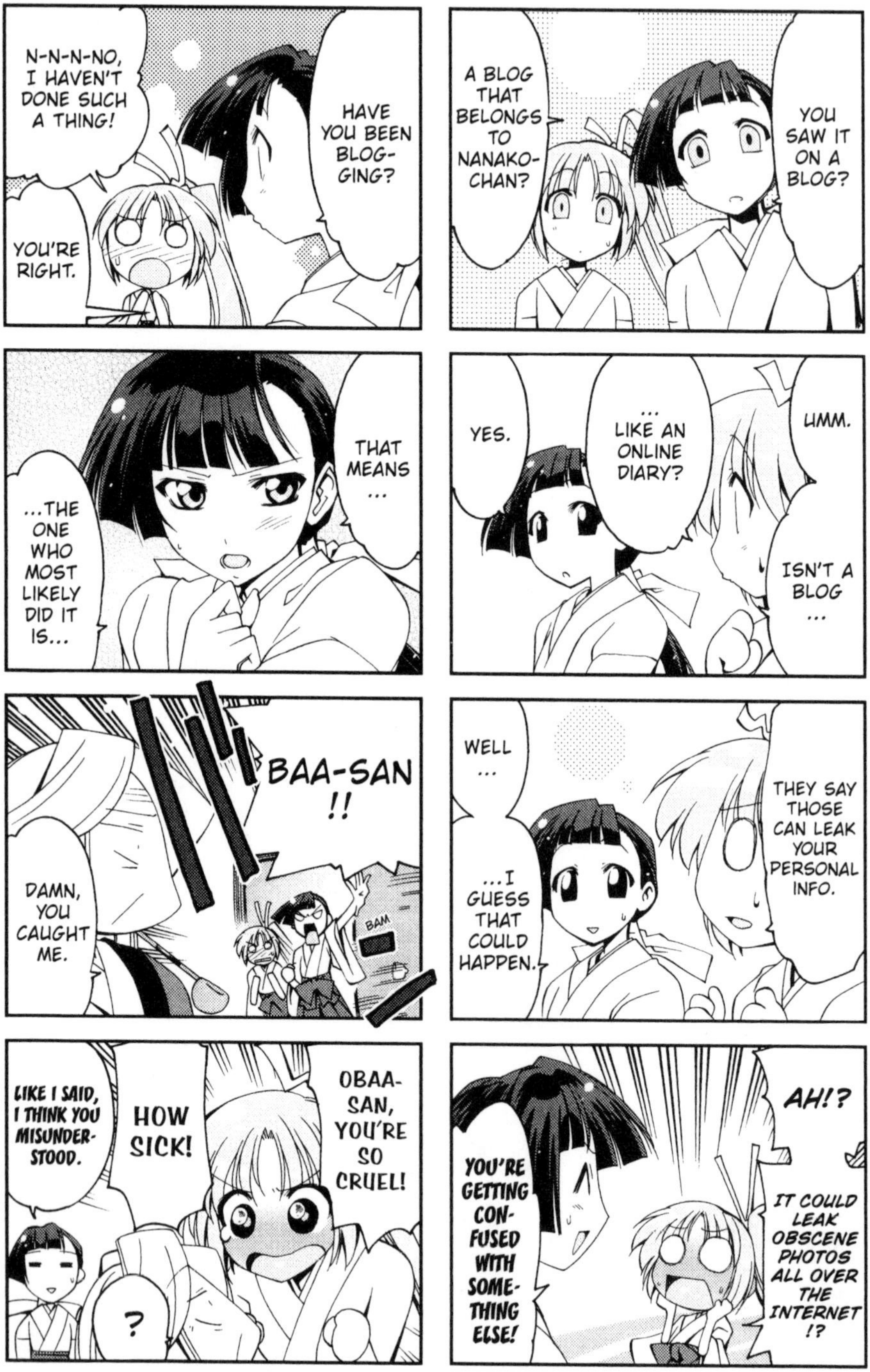

YOU SAW IT ON A BLOG?
A BLOG THAT BELONGS TO NANAKO-CHAN?
UMM.
ISN'T A BLOG ...
... LIKE AN ONLINE DIARY?
YES.
THEY SAY THOSE CAN LEAK YOUR PERSONAL INFO.
WELL ...
...I GUESS THAT COULD HAPPEN.
AH!?
IT COULD LEAK OBSCENE PHOTOS ALL OVER THE INTERNET!?
YOU'RE GETTING CON-FUSED WITH SOME-THING ELSE!
HAVE YOU BEEN BLOG-GING?
N-N-N-NO, I HAVEN'T DONE SUCH A THING!
YOU'RE RIGHT.
THAT MEANS ...
...THE ONE WHO MOST LIKELY DID IT IS...
BAA-SAN !!
BAM
DAMN, YOU CAUGHT ME.
OBAA-SAN, YOU'RE SO CRUEL!
HOW SICK!
LIKE I SAID, I THINK YOU MISUNDER-STOOD.
?

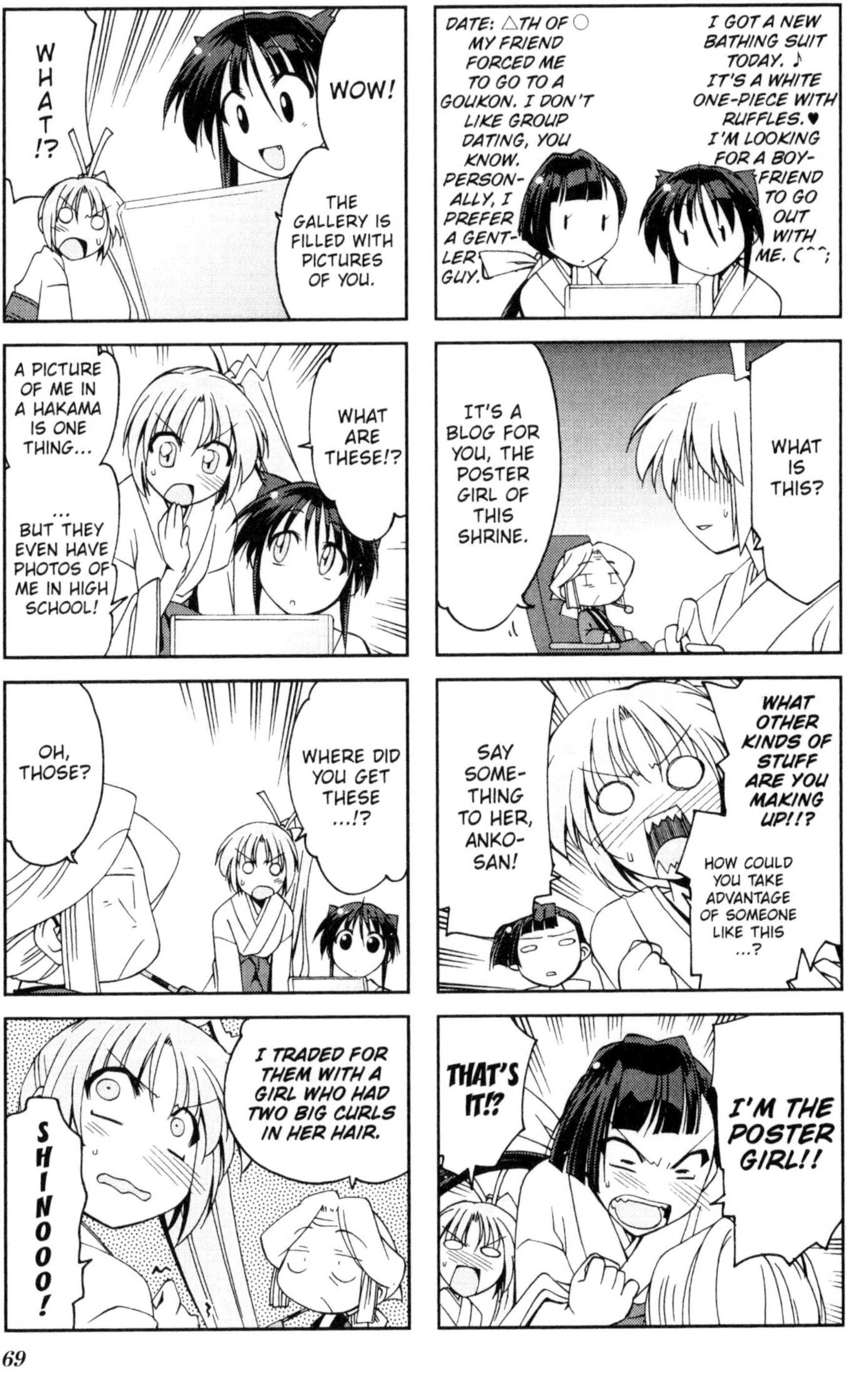
I GOT A NEW BATHING SUIT TODAY. ♪ IT'S A WHITE ONE-PIECE WITH RUFFLES. ♥ I'M LOOKING FOR A BOYFRIEND TO GO OUT WITH ME. (^^;
DATE: △TH OF ○ MY FRIEND FORCED ME TO GO TO A GOUKON. I DON'T LIKE GROUP DATING, YOU KNOW. PERSONALLY, I PREFER A GENTLER GUY.
WHAT IS THIS?
IT'S A BLOG FOR YOU, THE POSTER GIRL OF THIS SHRINE.
WHAT OTHER KINDS OF STUFF ARE YOU MAKING UP!!?
HOW COULD YOU TAKE ADVANTAGE OF SOMEONE LIKE THIS ...?
SAY SOMETHING TO HER, ANKO-SAN!
I'M THE POSTER GIRL!!
THAT'S IT!?
WOW!
THE GALLERY IS FILLED WITH PICTURES OF YOU.
WHAT!?
WHAT ARE THESE!?
A PICTURE OF ME IN A HAKAMA IS ONE THING...
... BUT THEY EVEN HAVE PHOTOS OF ME IN HIGH SCHOOL!
WHERE DID YOU GET THESE ...!?
OH, THOSE?
I TRADED FOR THEM WITH A GIRL WHO HAD TWO BIG CURLS IN HER HAIR.
SHINOOOO!

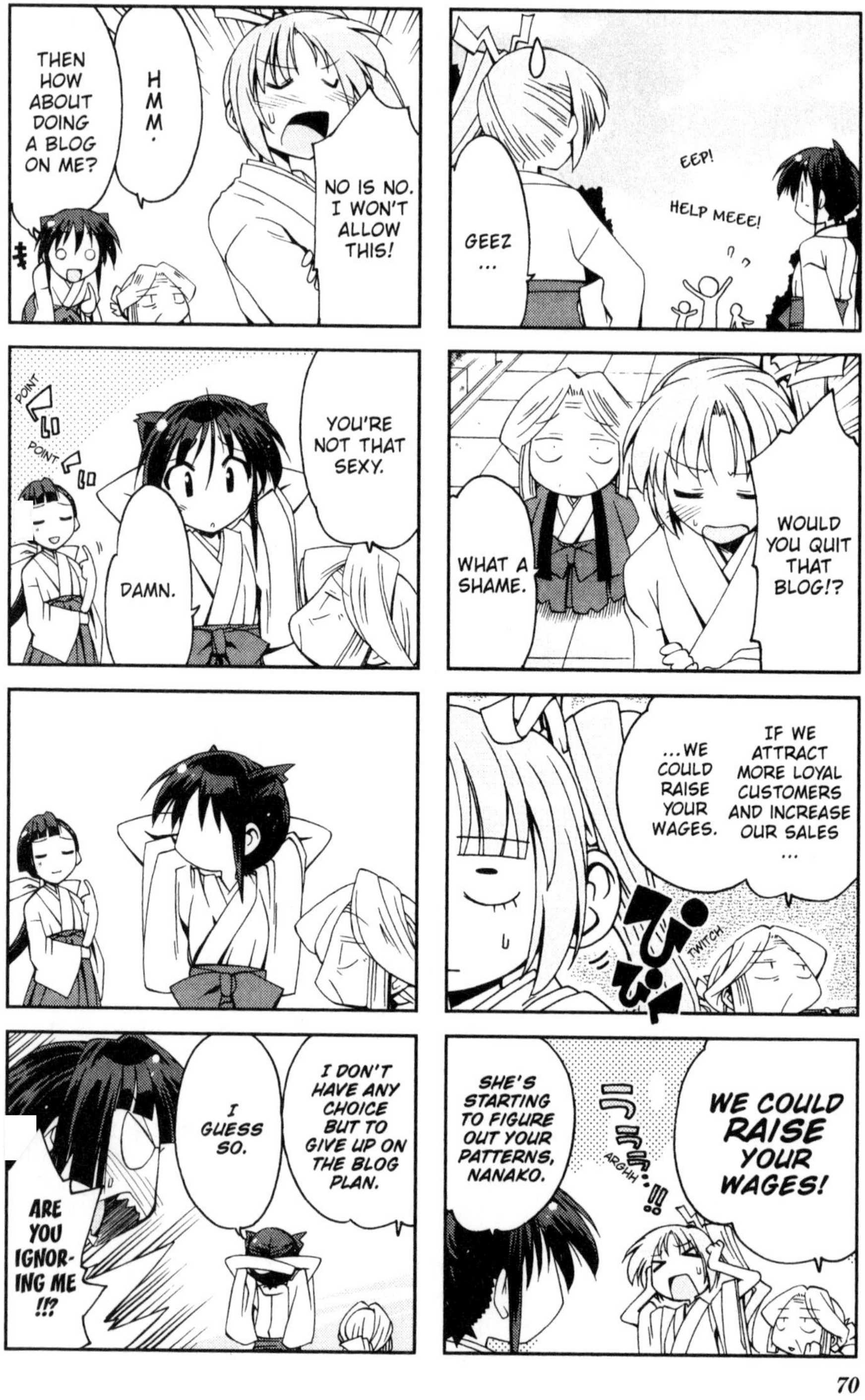
EEP!
HELP MEEE!
GEEZ ...
WOULD YOU QUIT THAT BLOG!?
WHAT A SHAME.
IF WE ATTRACT MORE LOYAL CUSTOMERS AND INCREASE OUR SALES ...
...WE COULD RAISE YOUR WAGES.
TWITCH
WE COULD RAISE YOUR WAGES!
ARGHH..!!
SHE'S STARTING TO FIGURE OUT YOUR PATTERNS, NANAKO.
HMM.
THEN HOW ABOUT DOING A BLOG ON ME?
NO IS NO. I WON'T ALLOW THIS!
POINT
POINT
YOU'RE NOT THAT SEXY.
DAMN.
I DON'T HAVE ANY CHOICE BUT TO GIVE UP ON THE BLOG PLAN.
I GUESS SO.
ARE YOU IGNOR-ING ME !!?

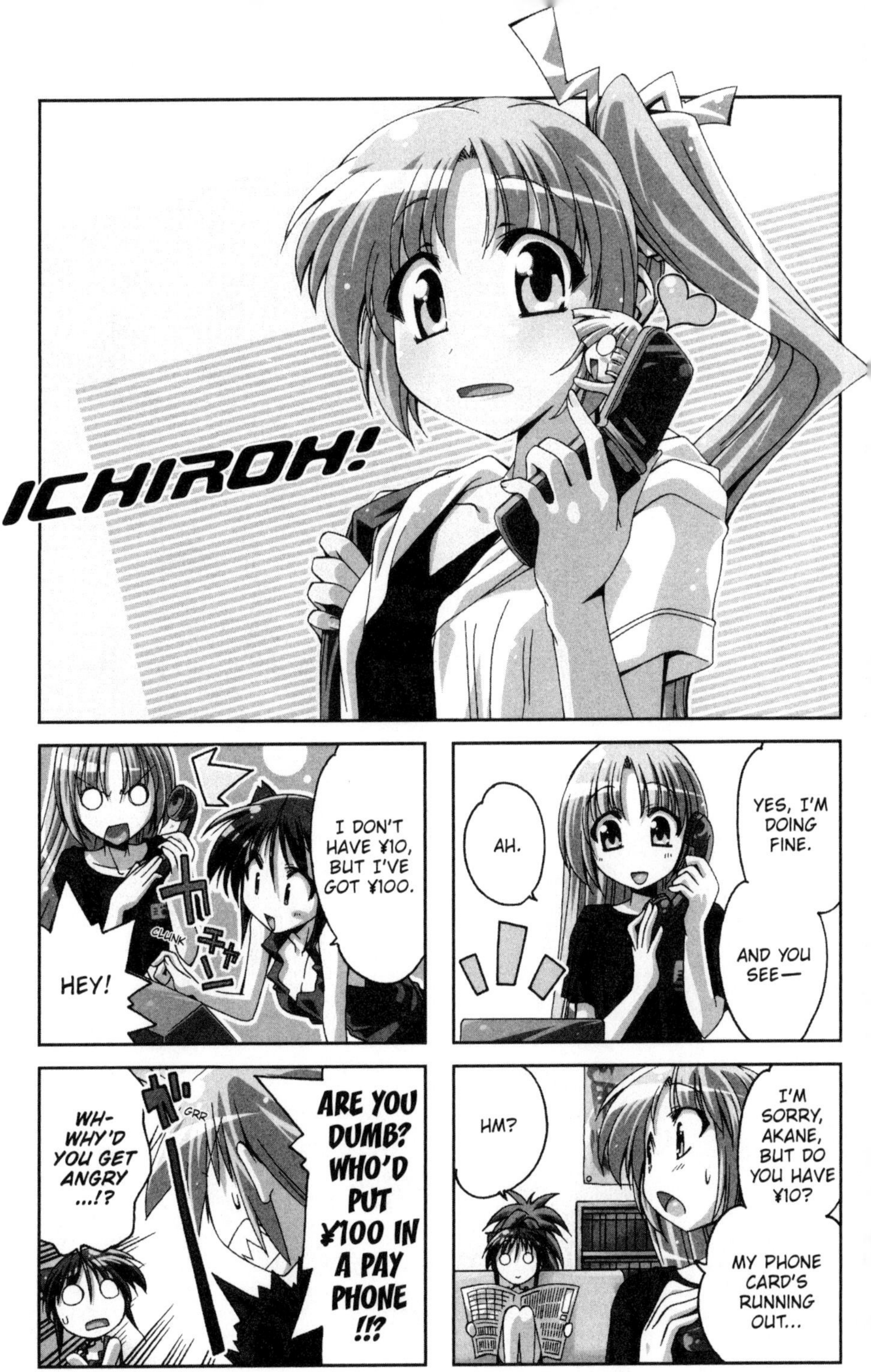
ICHIROH!
YES, I'M DOING FINE.
AH.
AND YOU SEE—
I DON'T HAVE ¥10, BUT I'VE GOT ¥100.
CLUNK
HEY!
I'M SORRY, AKANE, BUT DO YOU HAVE ¥10?
MY PHONE CARD'S RUNNING OUT...
HM?
ARE YOU DUMB? WHO'D PUT ¥100 IN A PAY PHONE !!?
GRR
WH- WHY'D YOU GET ANGRY ...!?

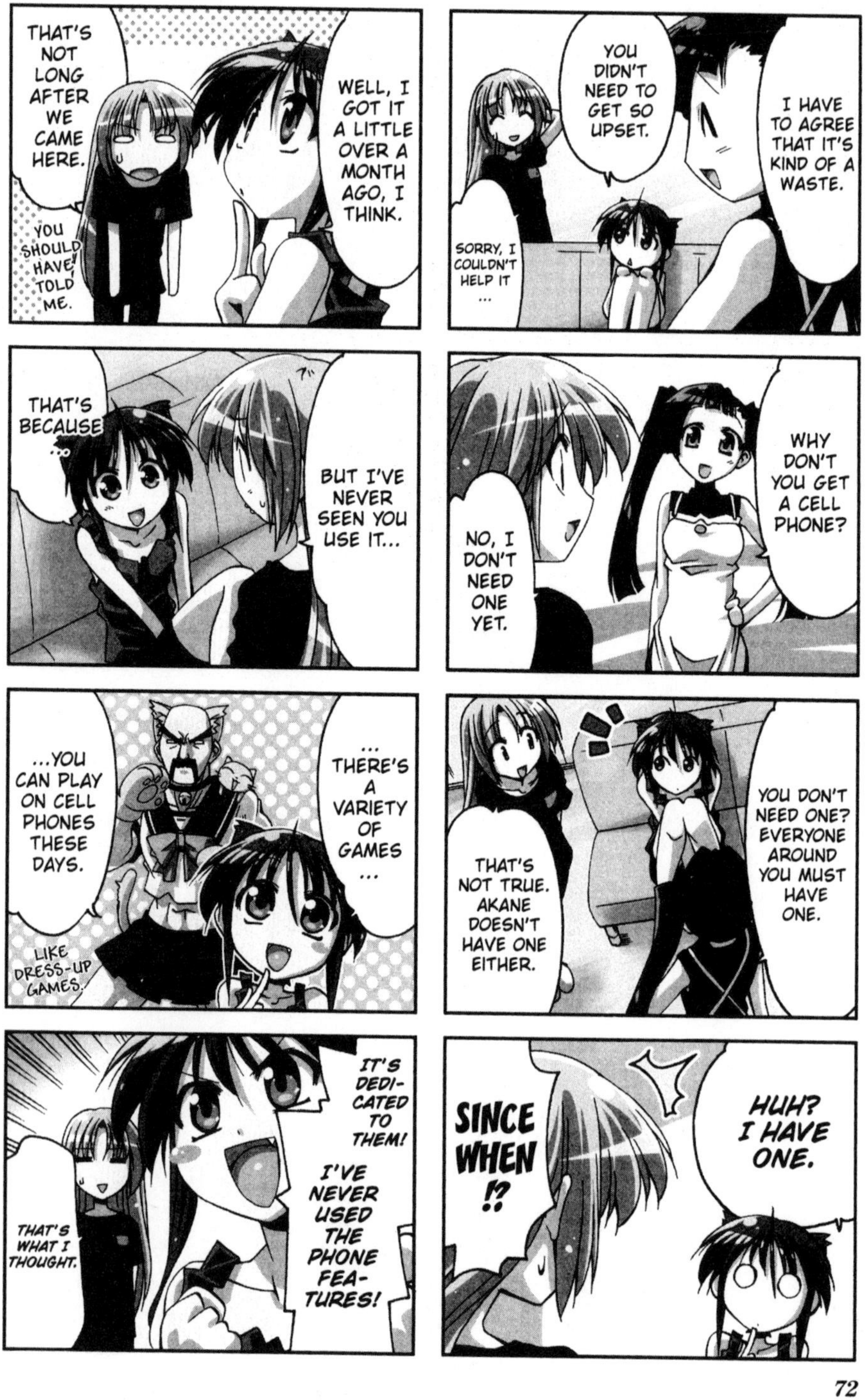
I HAVE TO AGREE THAT IT'S KIND OF A WASTE.
YOU DIDN'T NEED TO GET SO UPSET.
SORRY, I COULDN'T HELP IT ...
WHY DON'T YOU GET A CELL PHONE?
NO, I DON'T NEED ONE YET.
YOU DON'T NEED ONE? EVERYONE AROUND YOU MUST HAVE ONE.
THAT'S NOT TRUE. AKANE DOESN'T HAVE ONE EITHER.
HUH? I HAVE ONE.
SINCE WHEN !?
WELL, I GOT IT A LITTLE OVER A MONTH AGO, I THINK.
THAT'S NOT LONG AFTER WE CAME HERE.
YOU SHOULD HAVE TOLD ME.
BUT I'VE NEVER SEEN YOU USE IT...
THAT'S BECAUSE ...
... THERE'S A VARIETY OF GAMES ...
...YOU CAN PLAY ON CELL PHONES THESE DAYS.
LIKE DRESS-UP GAMES.
IT'S DEDICATED TO THEM!
I'VE NEVER USED THE PHONE FEATURES!
THAT'S WHAT I THOUGHT.

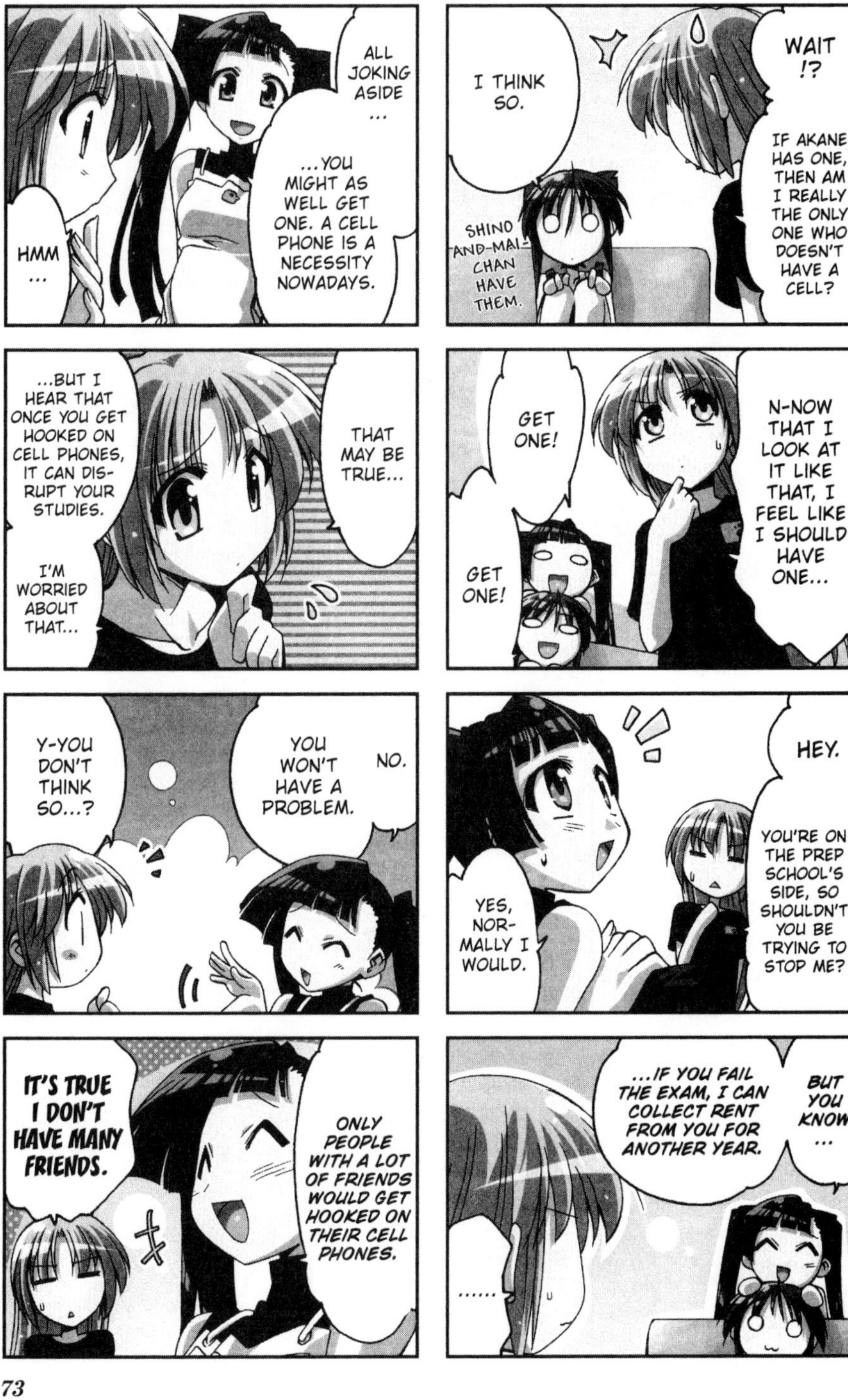
WAIT !?
IF AKANE HAS ONE, THEN AM I REALLY THE ONLY ONE WHO DOESN'T HAVE A CELL?
I THINK SO.
SHINO AND MAI-CHAN HAVE THEM.
ALL JOKING ASIDE ...
...YOU MIGHT AS WELL GET ONE. A CELL PHONE IS A NECESSITY NOWADAYS.
HMM ...
N-NOW THAT I LOOK AT IT LIKE THAT, I FEEL LIKE I SHOULD HAVE ONE...
GET ONE!
GET ONE!
THAT MAY BE TRUE...
...BUT I HEAR THAT ONCE YOU GET HOOKED ON CELL PHONES, IT CAN DISRUPT YOUR STUDIES.
I'M WORRIED ABOUT THAT...
HEY.
YOU'RE ON THE PREP SCHOOL'S SIDE, SO SHOULDN'T YOU BE TRYING TO STOP ME?
YES, NORMALLY I WOULD.
NO.
YOU WON'T HAVE A PROBLEM.
Y-YOU DON'T THINK SO...?
BUT YOU KNOW ...
...IF YOU FAIL THE EXAM, I CAN COLLECT RENT FROM YOU FOR ANOTHER YEAR.
......
ONLY PEOPLE WITH A LOT OF FRIENDS WOULD GET HOOKED ON THEIR CELL PHONES.
IT'S TRUE I DON'T HAVE MANY FRIENDS.

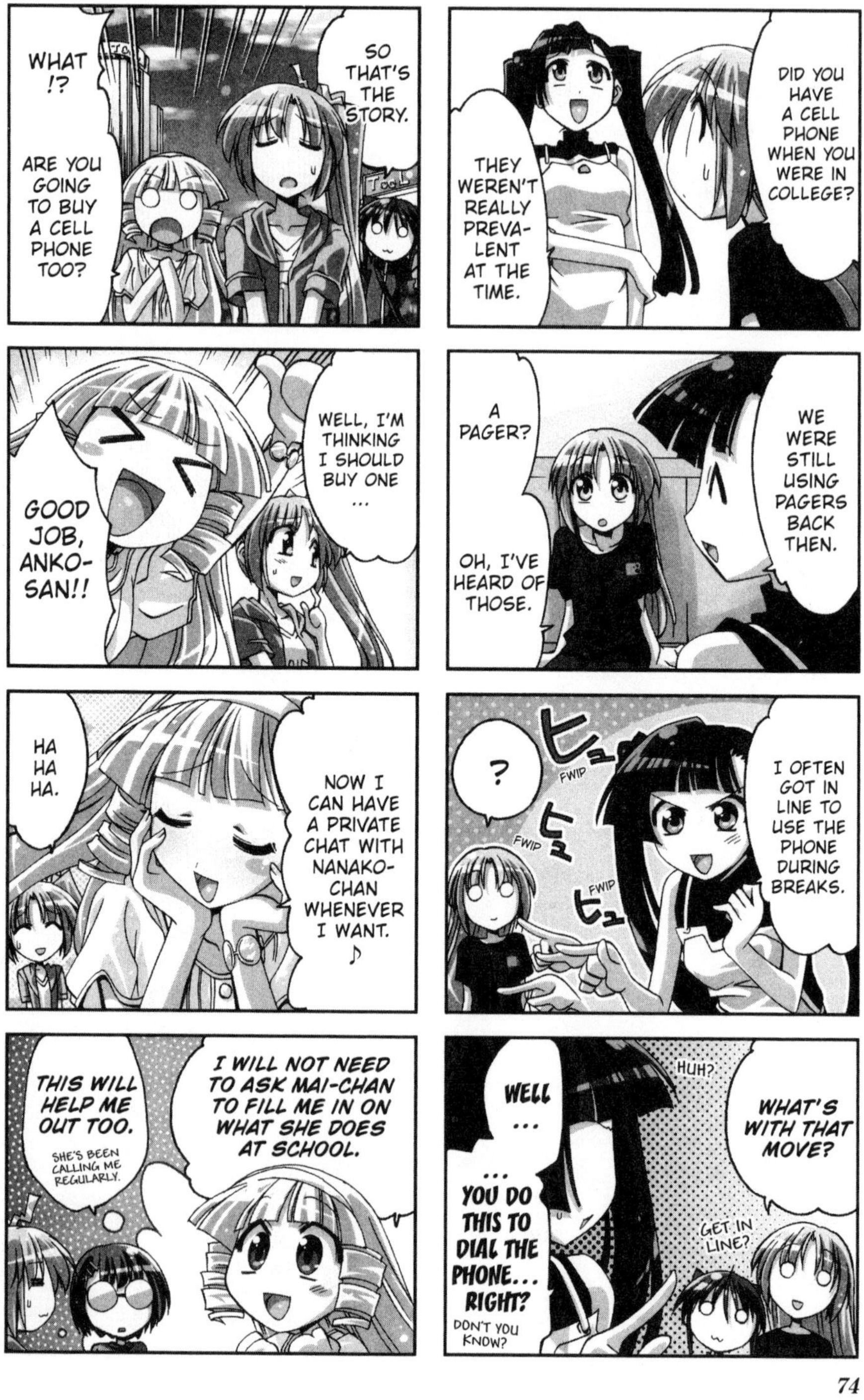
DID YOU HAVE A CELL PHONE WHEN YOU WERE IN COLLEGE?
THEY WEREN'T REALLY PREVA-LENT AT THE TIME.
WE WERE STILL USING PAGERS BACK THEN.
A PAGER?
OH, I'VE HEARD OF THOSE.
I OFTEN GOT IN LINE TO USE THE PHONE DURING BREAKS.
?
FWIP
FWIP
FWIP
WHAT'S WITH THAT MOVE?
HUH?
WELL ...
... YOU DO THIS TO DIAL THE PHONE... RIGHT?
DON'T YOU KNOW?
GET IN LINE?
SO THAT'S THE STORY.
WHAT !?
ARE YOU GOING TO BUY A CELL PHONE TOO?
WELL, I'M THINKING I SHOULD BUY ONE ...
GOOD JOB, ANKO-SAN!!
NOW I CAN HAVE A PRIVATE CHAT WITH NANAKO-CHAN WHENEVER I WANT. ♪
HA HA HA.
I WILL NOT NEED TO ASK MAI-CHAN TO FILL ME IN ON WHAT SHE DOES AT SCHOOL.
THIS WILL HELP ME OUT TOO.
SHE'S BEEN CALLING ME REGULARLY.

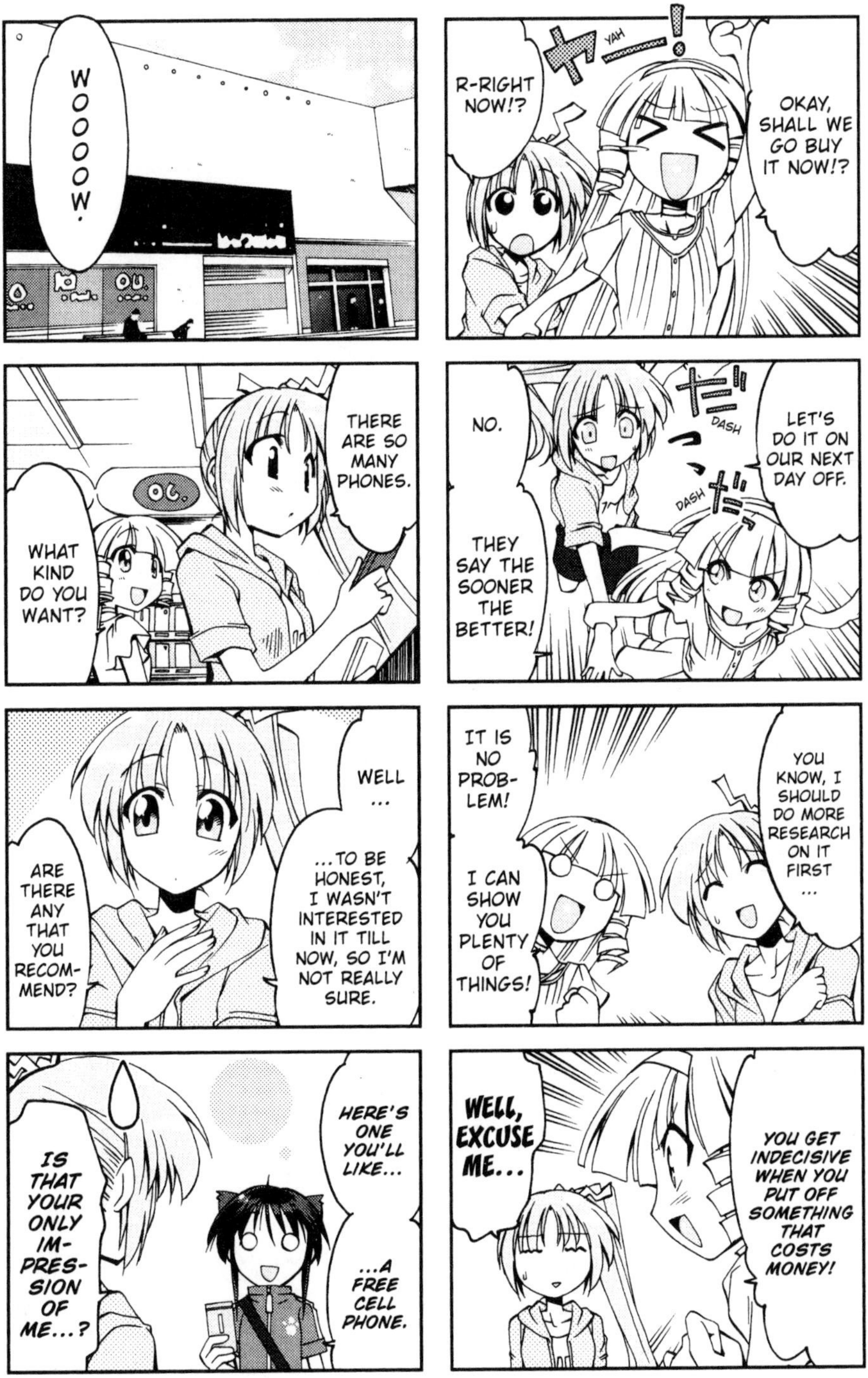
OKAY, SHALL WE GO BUY IT NOW!?
YAH
R-RIGHT NOW!?
LET'S DO IT ON OUR NEXT DAY OFF.
DASH
DASH
NO.
THEY SAY THE SOONER THE BETTER!
YOU KNOW, I SHOULD DO MORE RESEARCH ON IT FIRST ...
IT IS NO PROBLEM!
I CAN SHOW YOU PLENTY OF THINGS!
YOU GET INDECISIVE WHEN YOU PUT OFF SOMETHING THAT COSTS MONEY!
WELL, EXCUSE ME...
WOOOOOW.
THERE ARE SO MANY PHONES.
WHAT KIND DO YOU WANT?
WELL ...
...TO BE HONEST, I WASN'T INTERESTED IN IT TILL NOW, SO I'M NOT REALLY SURE.
ARE THERE ANY THAT YOU RECOMMEND?
HERE'S ONE YOU'LL LIKE...
...A FREE CELL PHONE.
IS THAT YOUR ONLY IMPRESSION OF ME...?

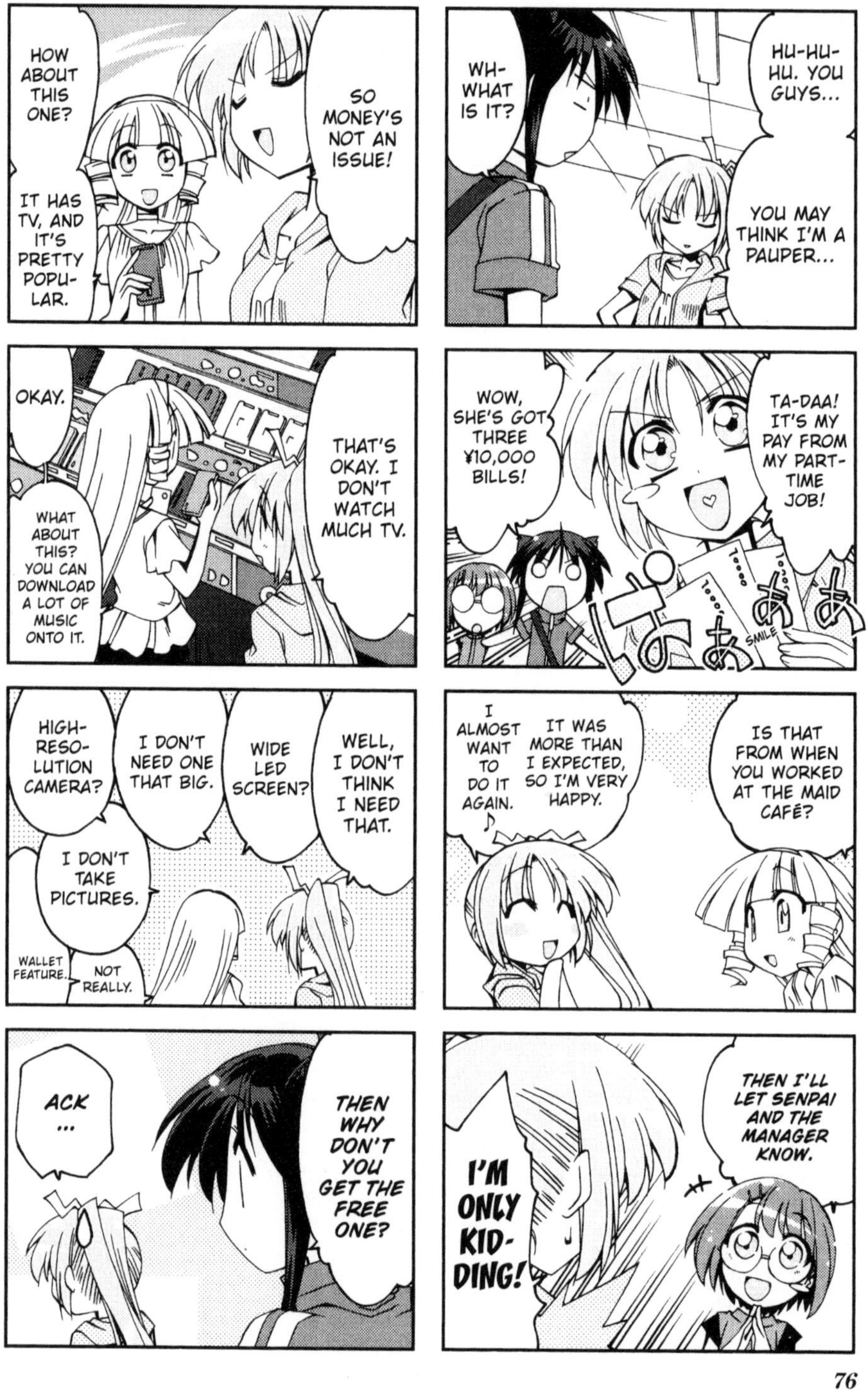
HU-HU-HU. YOU GUYS...
WH-WHAT IS IT?
YOU MAY THINK I'M A PAUPER...
SO MONEY'S NOT AN ISSUE!
HOW ABOUT THIS ONE?
IT HAS TV, AND IT'S PRETTY POPULAR.
TA-DAA! IT'S MY PAY FROM MY PART-TIME JOB!
WOW, SHE'S GOT THREE ¥10,000 BILLS!
SMILE
THAT'S OKAY. I DON'T WATCH MUCH TV.
OKAY.
WHAT ABOUT THIS? YOU CAN DOWNLOAD A LOT OF MUSIC ONTO IT.
IS THAT FROM WHEN YOU WORKED AT THE MAID CAFÉ?
IT WAS MORE THAN I EXPECTED, SO I'M VERY HAPPY.
I ALMOST WANT TO DO IT AGAIN. ♪
WELL, I DON'T THINK I NEED THAT.
WIDE LED SCREEN?
I DON'T NEED ONE THAT BIG.
HIGH-RESOLUTION CAMERA?
I DON'T TAKE PICTURES.
NOT REALLY.
WALLET FEATURE.
THEN I'LL LET SENPAI AND THE MANAGER KNOW.
I'M ONLY KIDDING!
THEN WHY DON'T YOU GET THE FREE ONE?
ACK...

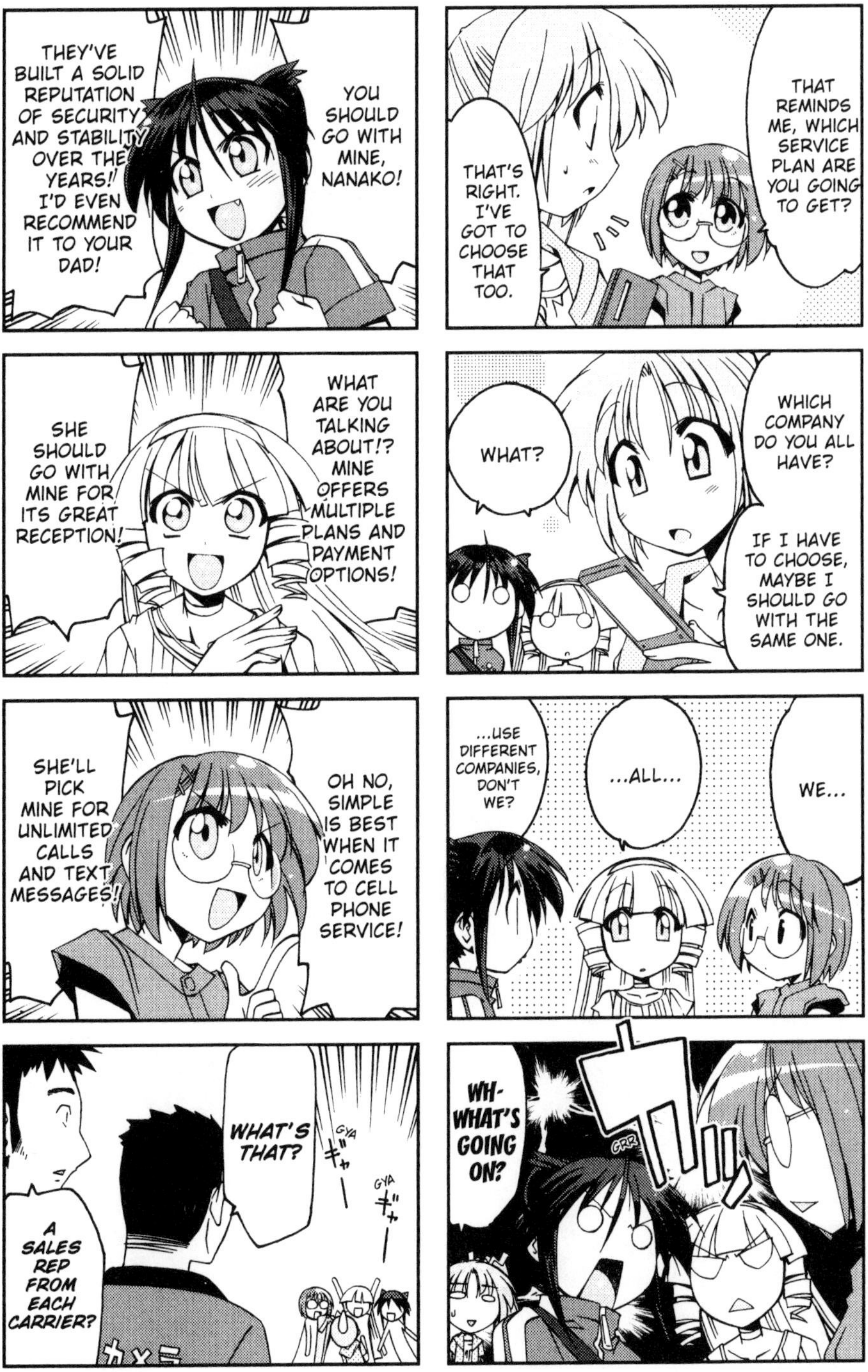
THAT REMINDS ME, WHICH SERVICE PLAN ARE YOU GOING TO GET?
THAT'S RIGHT. I'VE GOT TO CHOOSE THAT TOO.
WHICH COMPANY DO YOU ALL HAVE?
IF I HAVE TO CHOOSE, MAYBE I SHOULD GO WITH THE SAME ONE.
WHAT?
WE...
...ALL...
...USE DIFFERENT COMPANIES, DON'T WE?
GRR
WH- WHAT'S GOING ON?
YOU SHOULD GO WITH MINE, NANAKO!
THEY'VE BUILT A SOLID REPUTATION OF SECURITY AND STABILITY OVER THE YEARS! I'D EVEN RECOMMEND IT TO YOUR DAD!
WHAT ARE YOU TALKING ABOUT!? MINE OFFERS MULTIPLE PLANS AND PAYMENT OPTIONS!
SHE SHOULD GO WITH MINE FOR ITS GREAT RECEPTION!
OH NO, SIMPLE IS BEST WHEN IT COMES TO CELL PHONE SERVICE!
SHE'LL PICK MINE FOR UNLIMITED CALLS AND TEXT MESSAGES!
GYA
GYA
WHAT'S THAT?
A SALES REP FROM EACH CARRIER?

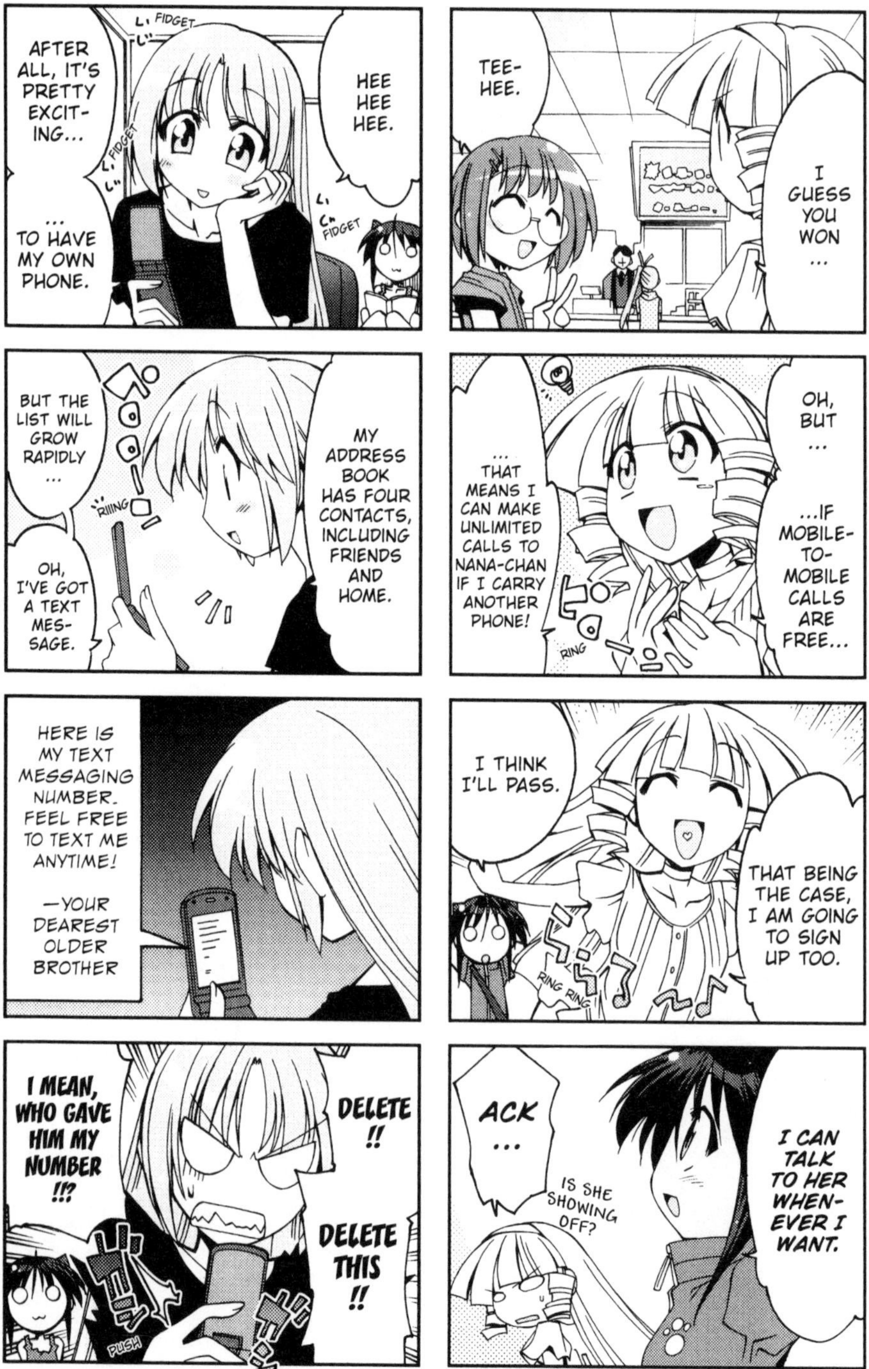
I GUESS YOU WON ...
TEE-HEE.
HEE HEE HEE.
FIDGET
AFTER ALL, IT'S PRETTY EXCIT-ING...
FIDGET
FIDGET
... TO HAVE MY OWN PHONE.
OH, BUT ...
...IF MOBILE-TO-MOBILE CALLS ARE FREE...
... THAT MEANS I CAN MAKE UNLIMITED CALLS TO NANA-CHAN IF I CARRY ANOTHER PHONE!
RING
MY ADDRESS BOOK HAS FOUR CONTACTS, INCLUDING FRIENDS AND HOME.
BUT THE LIST WILL GROW RAPIDLY ...
RIIING
OH, I'VE GOT A TEXT MES-SAGE.
THAT BEING THE CASE, I AM GOING TO SIGN UP TOO.
I THINK I'LL PASS.
RING RING
HERE IS MY TEXT MESSAGING NUMBER. FEEL FREE TO TEXT ME ANYTIME!
—YOUR DEAREST OLDER BROTHER
I CAN TALK TO HER WHEN-EVER I WANT.
ACK ...
IS SHE SHOWING OFF?
DELETE !!
DELETE THIS !!
I MEAN, WHO GAVE HIM MY NUMBER !!?
PUSH
PUSH

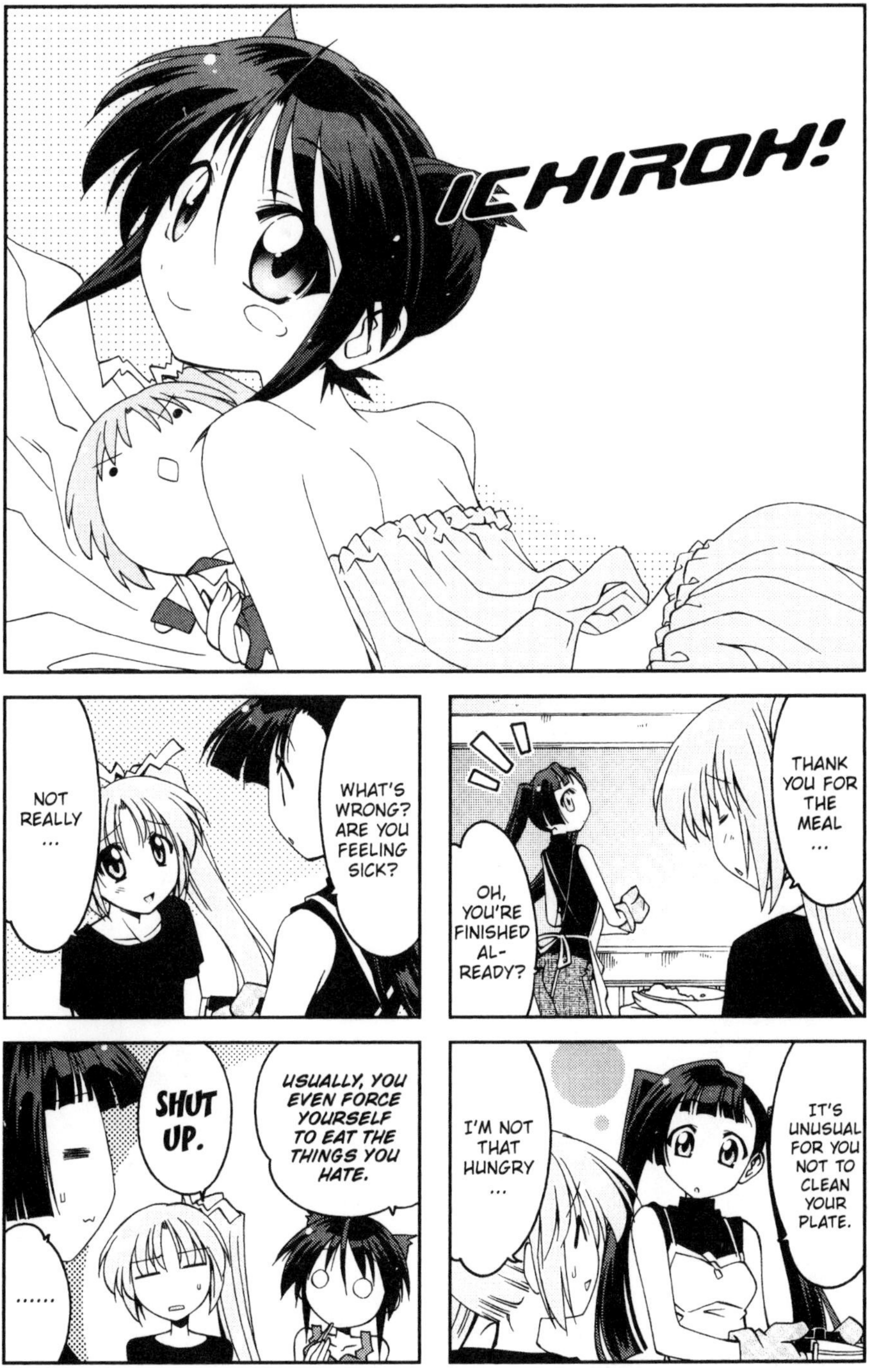
ICHIROH!
THANK YOU FOR THE MEAL ...
OH, YOU'RE FINISHED AL-READY?
WHAT'S WRONG? ARE YOU FEELING SICK?
NOT REALLY ...
IT'S UNUSUAL FOR YOU NOT TO CLEAN YOUR PLATE.
I'M NOT THAT HUNGRY ...
USUALLY, YOU EVEN FORCE YOURSELF TO EAT THE THINGS YOU HATE.
SHUT UP.
......

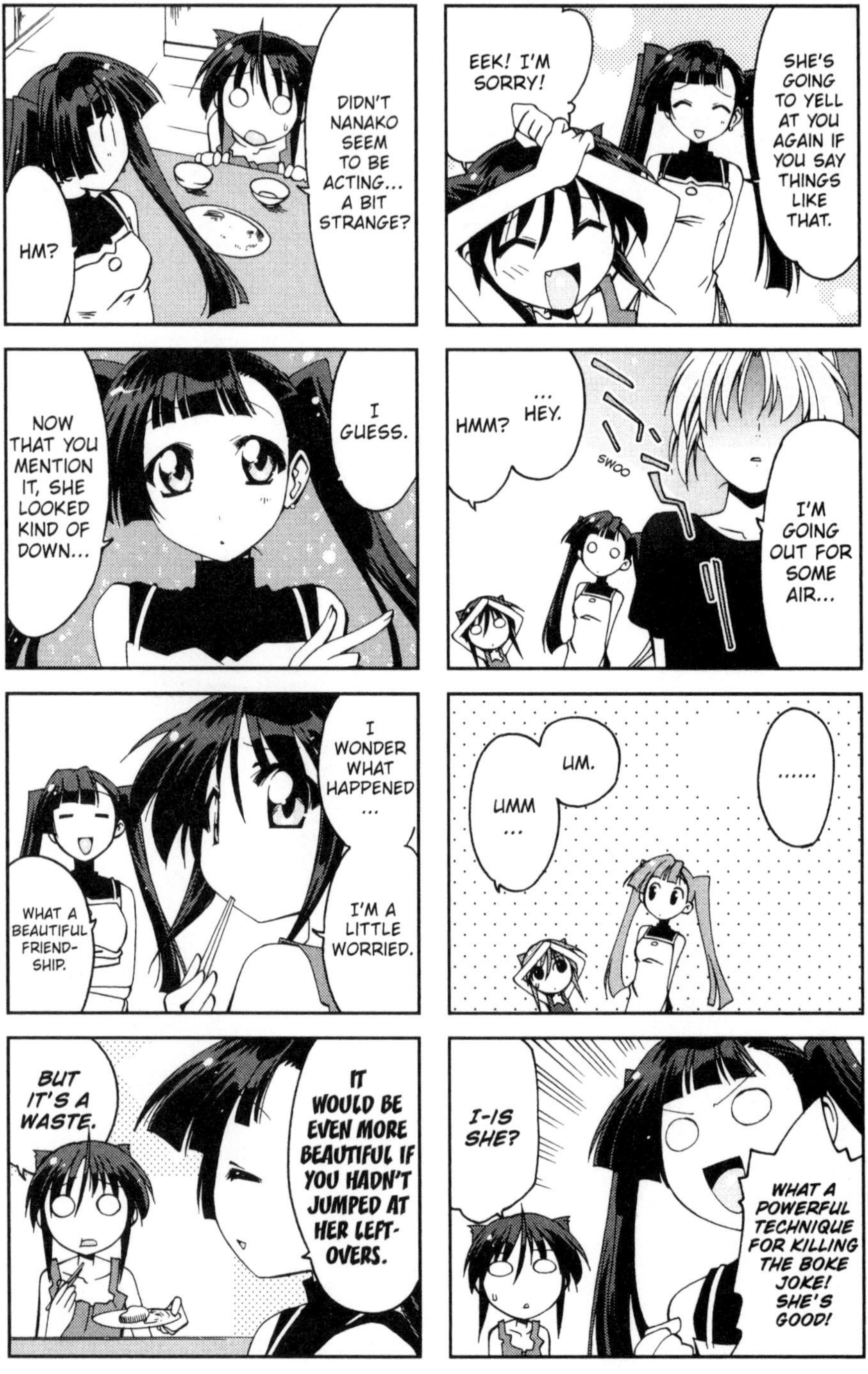
SHE'S GOING TO YELL AT YOU AGAIN IF YOU SAY THINGS LIKE THAT.
EEK! I'M SORRY!
... HEY.
HMM?
SWOO
I'M GOING OUT FOR SOME AIR...
......
UM.
UMM ...
WHAT A POWERFUL TECHNIQUE FOR KILLING THE BOKE JOKE! SHE'S GOOD!
I-IS SHE?
DIDN'T NANAKO SEEM TO BE ACTING... A BIT STRANGE?
HM?
I GUESS.
NOW THAT YOU MENTION IT, SHE LOOKED KIND OF DOWN...
I WONDER WHAT HAPPENED ...
I'M A LITTLE WORRIED.
WHAT A BEAUTIFUL FRIEND-SHIP.
IT WOULD BE EVEN MORE BEAUTIFUL IF YOU HADN'T JUMPED AT HER LEFT-OVERS.
BUT IT'S A WASTE.

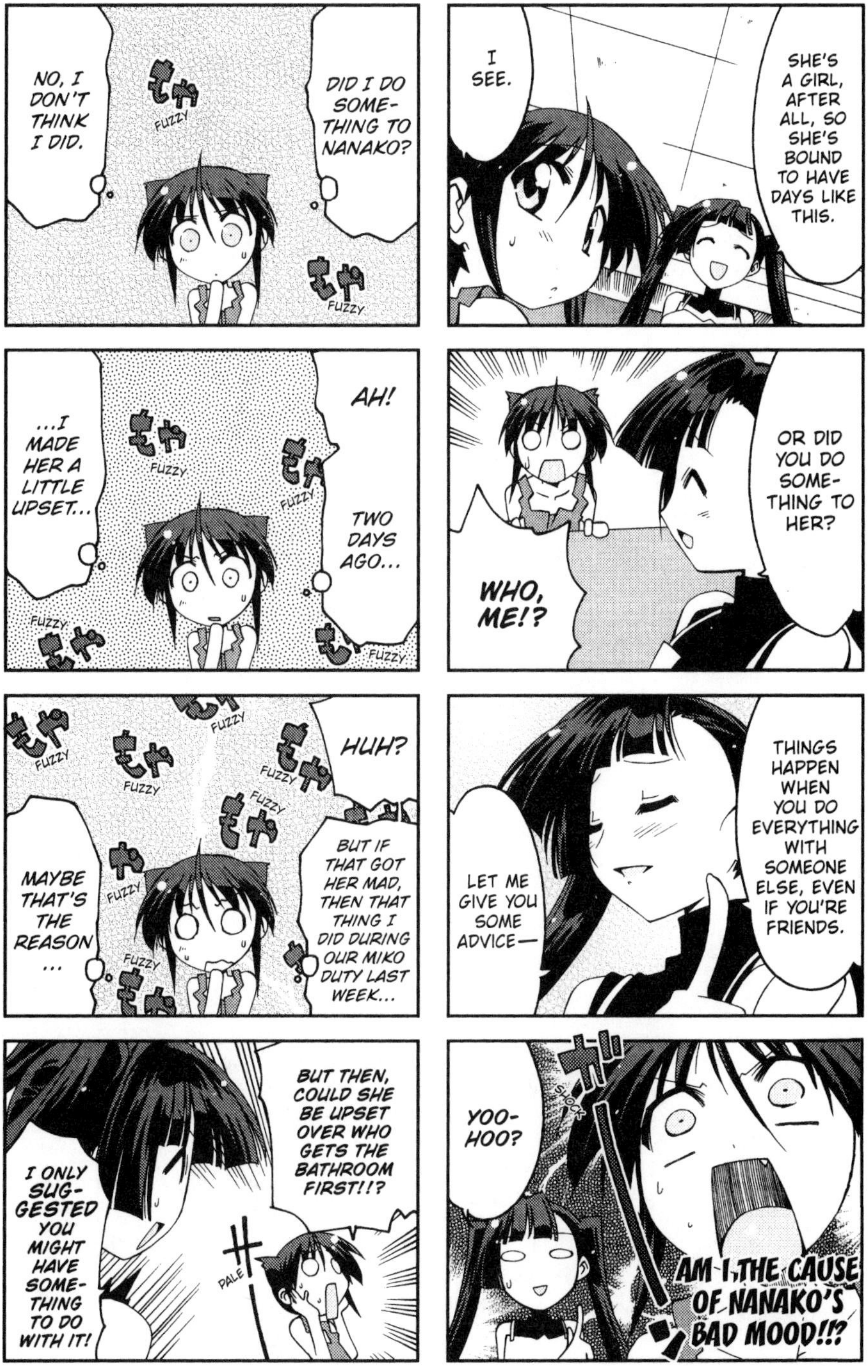
SHE'S A GIRL, AFTER ALL, SO SHE'S BOUND TO HAVE DAYS LIKE THIS.
I SEE.
DID I DO SOME-THING TO NANAKO?
FUZZY
FUZZY
NO, I DON'T THINK I DID.
OR DID YOU DO SOME-THING TO HER?
WHO, ME!?
AH!
TWO DAYS AGO...
FUZZY
FUZZY
FUZZY
FUZZY
...I MADE HER A LITTLE UPSET...
THINGS HAPPEN WHEN YOU DO EVERYTHING WITH SOMEONE ELSE, EVEN IF YOU'RE FRIENDS.
LET ME GIVE YOU SOME ADVICE—
HUH?
FUZZY
FUZZY
FUZZY
FUZZY
FUZZY
FUZZY
BUT IF THAT GOT HER MAD, THEN THAT THING I DID DURING OUR MIKO DUTY LAST WEEK...
MAYBE THAT'S THE REASON...
SHOCK
YOO-HOO?
AM I THE CAUSE OF NANAKO'S BAD MOOD!!?
BUT THEN, COULD SHE BE UPSET OVER WHO GETS THE BATHROOM FIRST!!?
PALE
I ONLY SUG-GESTED YOU MIGHT HAVE SOME-THING TO DO WITH IT!

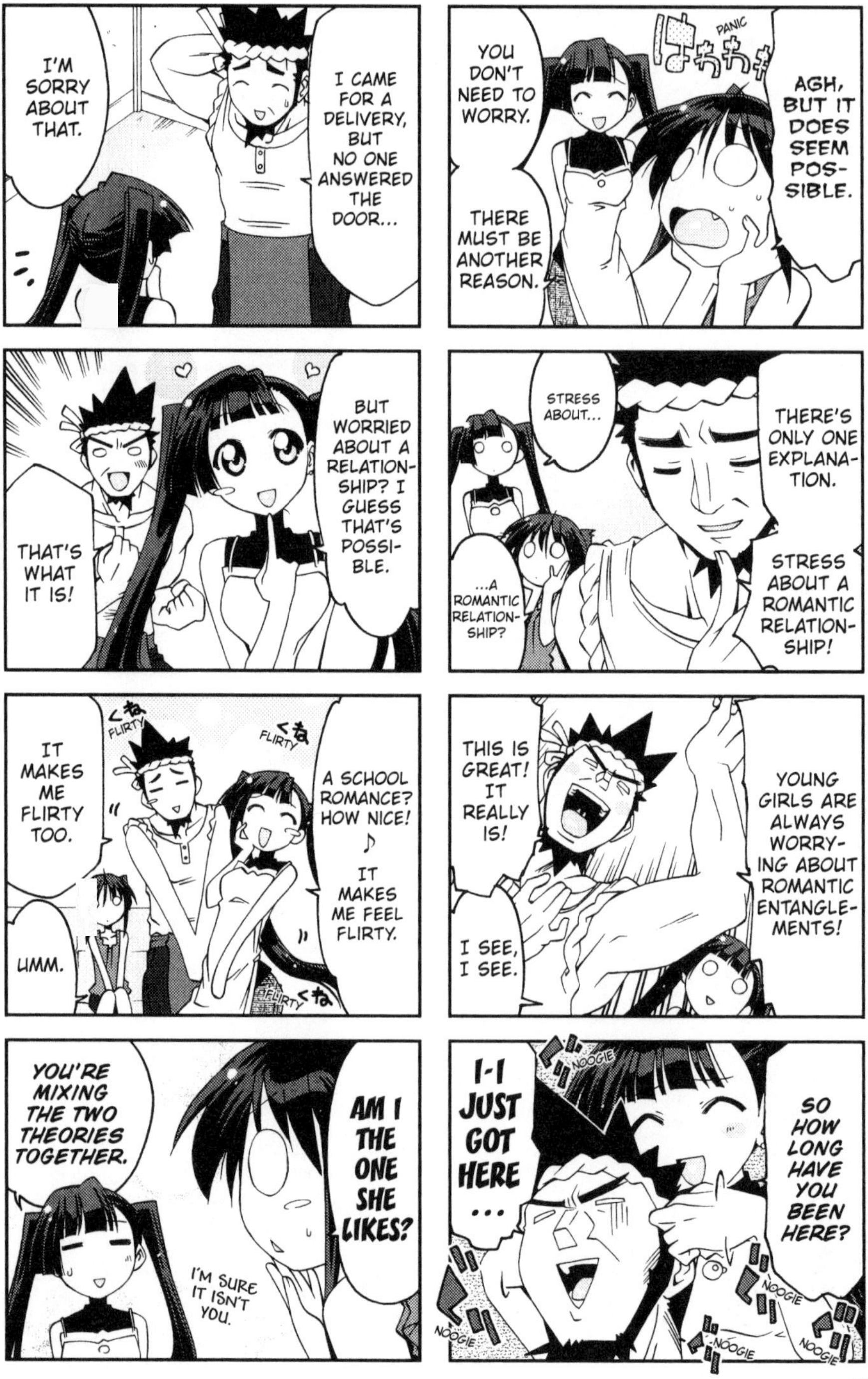
PANIC
AGH, BUT IT DOES SEEM POSSIBLE.
YOU DON'T NEED TO WORRY.
THERE MUST BE ANOTHER REASON.
THERE'S ONLY ONE EXPLANATION.
STRESS ABOUT A ROMANTIC RELATIONSHIP!
STRESS ABOUT...
...A ROMANTIC RELATIONSHIP?
YOUNG GIRLS ARE ALWAYS WORRYING ABOUT ROMANTIC ENTANGLEMENTS!
THIS IS GREAT! IT REALLY IS!
I SEE, I SEE.
NOOGIE
SO HOW LONG HAVE YOU BEEN HERE?
I-I JUST GOT HERE...
NOOGIE
NOOGIE
NOOGIE
NOOGIE
I CAME FOR A DELIVERY, BUT NO ONE ANSWERED THE DOOR...
I'M SORRY ABOUT THAT.
BUT WORRIED ABOUT A RELATIONSHIP? I GUESS THAT'S POSSIBLE.
THAT'S WHAT IT IS!
くね FLIRTY
A SCHOOL ROMANCE? HOW NICE! ♪
IT MAKES ME FEEL FLIRTY.
くね FLIRTY
IT MAKES ME FLIRTY TOO.
UMM.
FLIRTY くね
AM I THE ONE SHE LIKES?
I'M SURE IT ISN'T YOU.
YOU'RE MIXING THE TWO THEORIES TOGETHER.

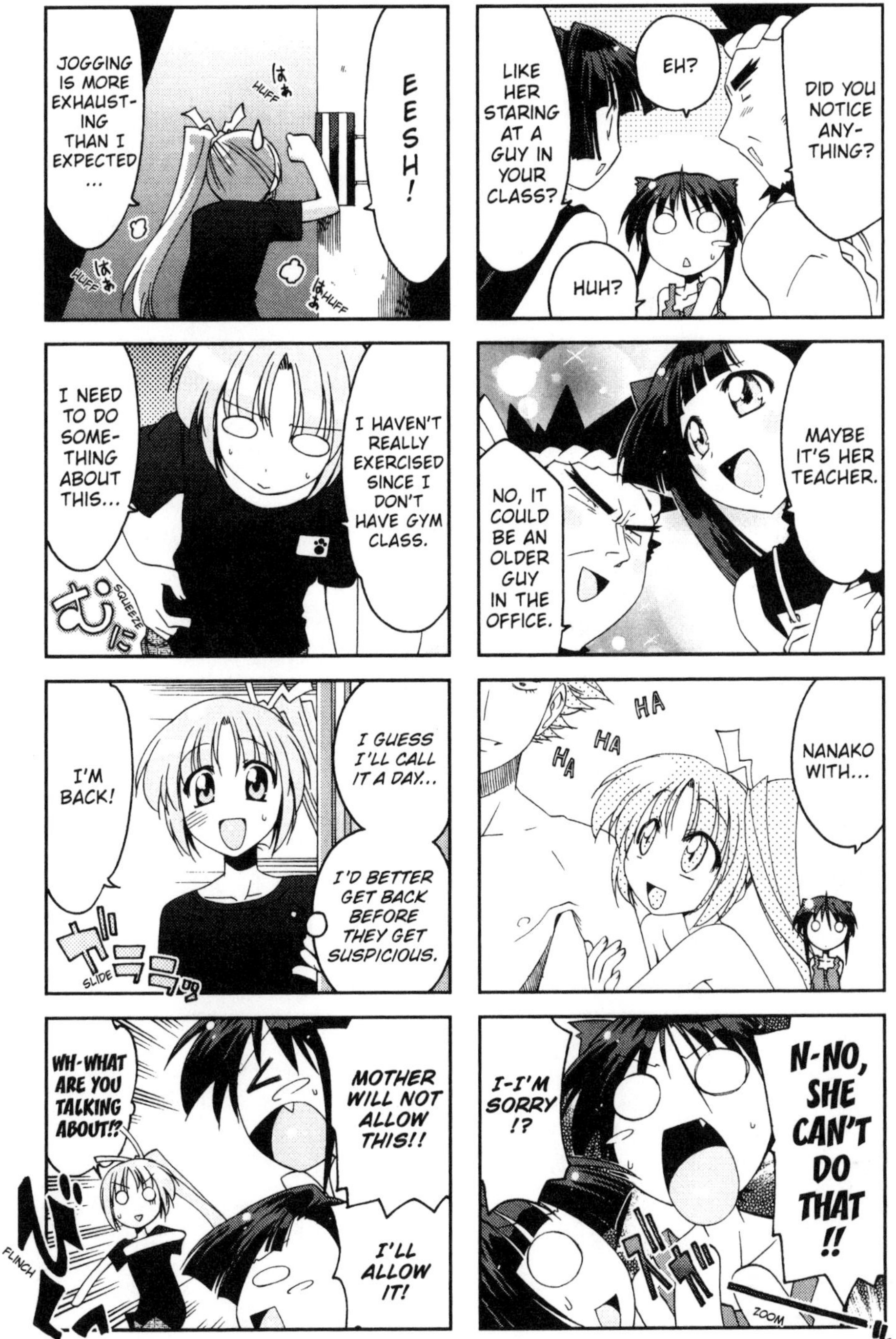
DID YOU NOTICE ANYTHING?
EH?
LIKE HER STARING AT A GUY IN YOUR CLASS?
HUH?
MAYBE IT'S HER TEACHER.
NO, IT COULD BE AN OLDER GUY IN THE OFFICE.
NANAKO WITH...
HA HA HA
N-NO, SHE CAN'T DO THAT!!
I-I'M SORRY!?
ZOOM
EESH!
はぁ HUFF
JOGGING IS MORE EXHAUSTING THAN I EXPECTED...
はぁ HUFF
はぁ HUFF
I HAVEN'T REALLY EXERCISED SINCE I DON'T HAVE GYM CLASS.
I NEED TO DO SOMETHING ABOUT THIS...
ぷに SQUEEZE
I GUESS I'LL CALL IT A DAY...
I'D BETTER GET BACK BEFORE THEY GET SUSPICIOUS.
I'M BACK!
SLIDE
MOTHER WILL NOT ALLOW THIS!!
I'LL ALLOW IT!
WH-WHAT ARE YOU TALKING ABOUT!?
FLINCH

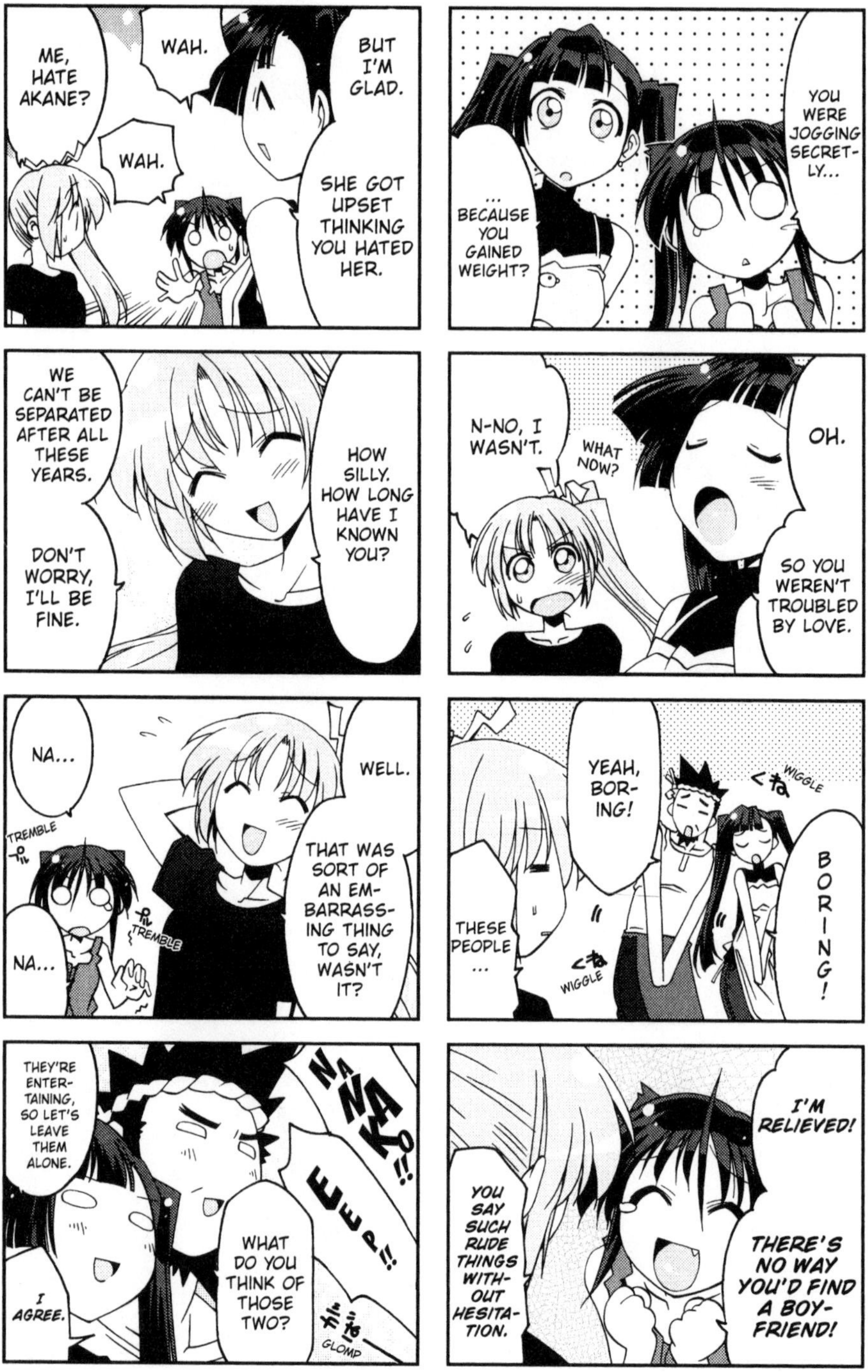
YOU WERE JOGGING SECRET-LY...
... BECAUSE YOU GAINED WEIGHT?
OH.
SO YOU WEREN'T TROUBLED BY LOVE.
WHAT NOW?
N-NO, I WASN'T.
BORING!
WIGGLE
YEAH, BOR-ING!
THESE PEOPLE ...
WIGGLE
I'M RELIEVED!
THERE'S NO WAY YOU'D FIND A BOY-FRIEND!
YOU SAY SUCH RUDE THINGS WITH-OUT HESITA-TION.
BUT I'M GLAD.
SHE GOT UPSET THINKING YOU HATED HER.
WAH.
WAH.
ME, HATE AKANE?
HOW SILLY. HOW LONG HAVE I KNOWN YOU?
WE CAN'T BE SEPARATED AFTER ALL THESE YEARS.
DON'T WORRY, I'LL BE FINE.
WELL.
THAT WAS SORT OF AN EM-BARRASS-ING THING TO SAY, WASN'T IT?
NA...
TREMBLE
TREMBLE
NA...
NANAKO!!
EEEP!!
WHAT DO YOU THINK OF THOSE TWO?
GLOMP
THEY'RE ENTER-TAINING, SO LET'S LEAVE THEM ALONE.
I AGREE.

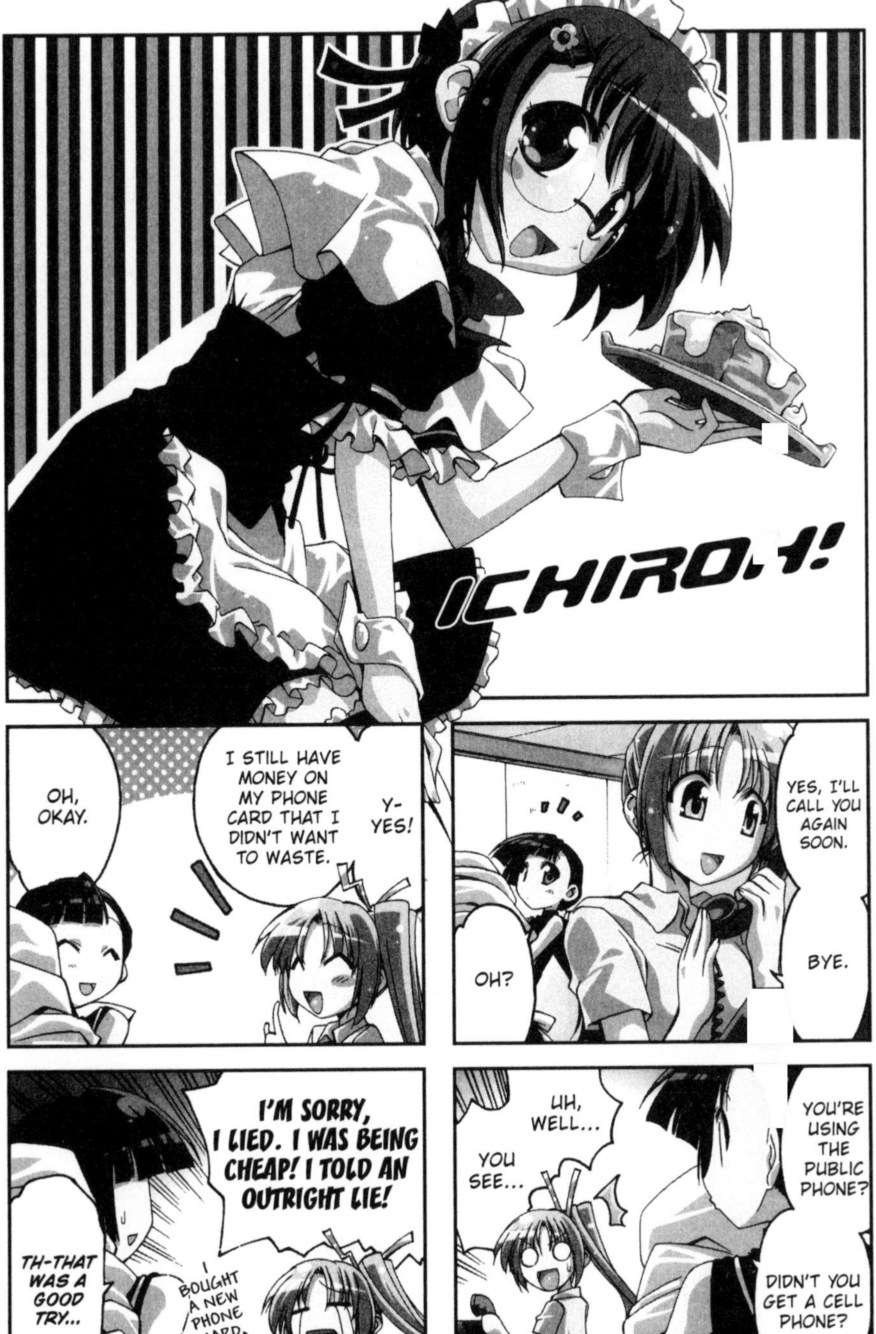
ICHIROH!
YES, I'LL CALL YOU AGAIN SOON.
BYE.
OH?
YOU'RE USING THE PUBLIC PHONE?
DIDN'T YOU GET A CELL PHONE?
UH, WELL...
YOU SEE...
Y-YES!
I STILL HAVE MONEY ON MY PHONE CARD THAT I DIDN'T WANT TO WASTE.
OH, OKAY.
I'M SORRY, I LIED. I WAS BEING CHEAP! I TOLD AN OUTRIGHT LIE!
I BOUGHT A NEW PHONE CARD TOO! WAHH!
TH-THAT WAS A GOOD TRY...

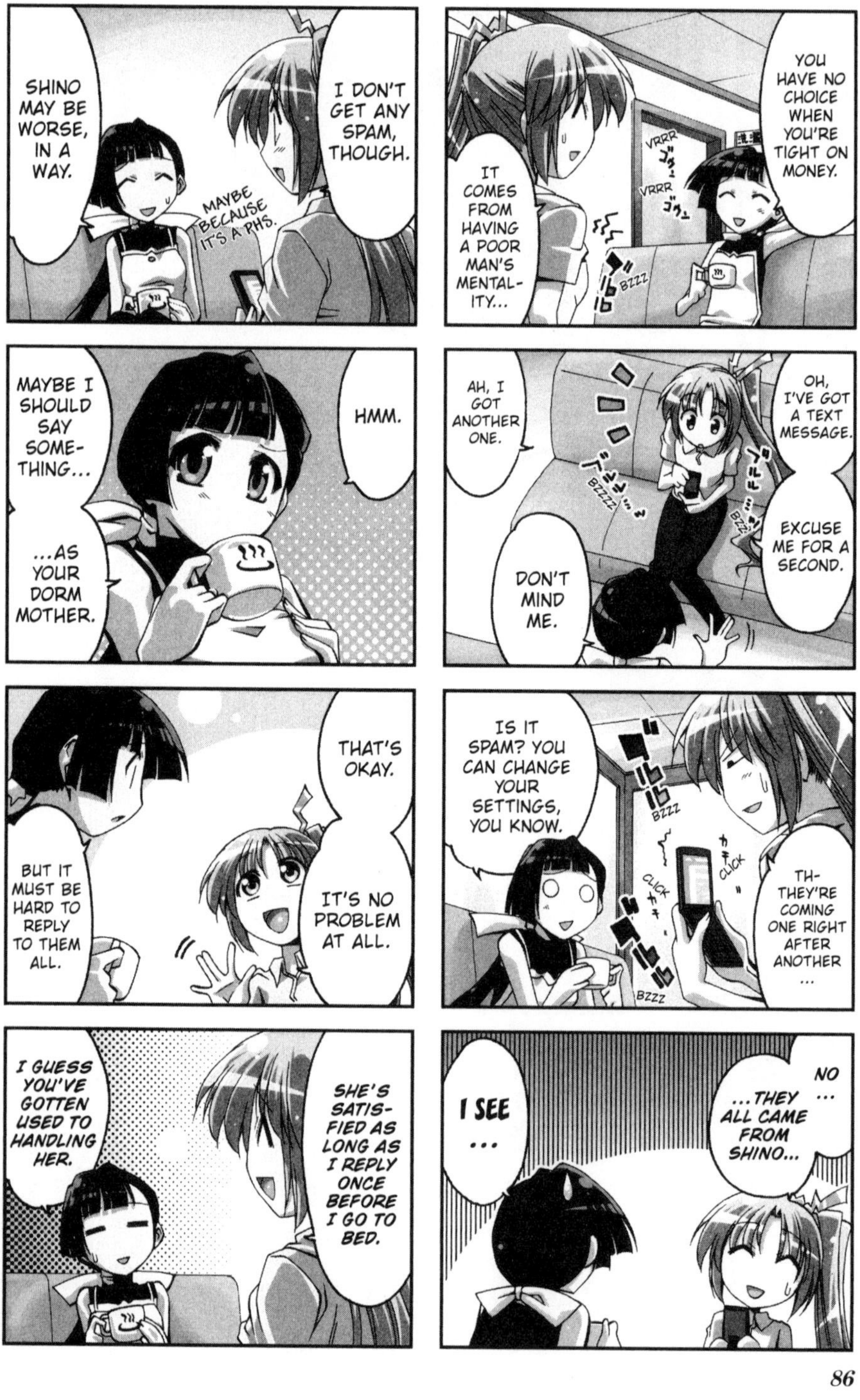
YOU HAVE NO CHOICE WHEN YOU'RE TIGHT ON MONEY.
VRRR
VRRR
IT COMES FROM HAVING A POOR MAN'S MENTAL-ITY...
BZZZ
OH, I'VE GOT A TEXT MESSAGE.
EXCUSE ME FOR A SECOND.
BZZZ
AH, I GOT ANOTHER ONE.
BZZZZZ
DON'T MIND ME.
TH-THEY'RE COMING ONE RIGHT AFTER ANOTHER ...
IS IT SPAM? YOU CAN CHANGE YOUR SETTINGS, YOU KNOW.
BZZZ
CLICK
CLICK
BZZZ
NO ... ...THEY ALL CAME FROM SHINO...
I SEE ...
I DON'T GET ANY SPAM, THOUGH.
MAYBE BECAUSE IT'S A PHS.
SHINO MAY BE WORSE, IN A WAY.
HMM.
MAYBE I SHOULD SAY SOME-THING...
...AS YOUR DORM MOTHER.
THAT'S OKAY.
IT'S NO PROBLEM AT ALL.
BUT IT MUST BE HARD TO REPLY TO THEM ALL.
SHE'S SATIS-FIED AS LONG AS I REPLY ONCE BEFORE I GO TO BED.
I GUESS YOU'VE GOTTEN USED TO HANDLING HER.

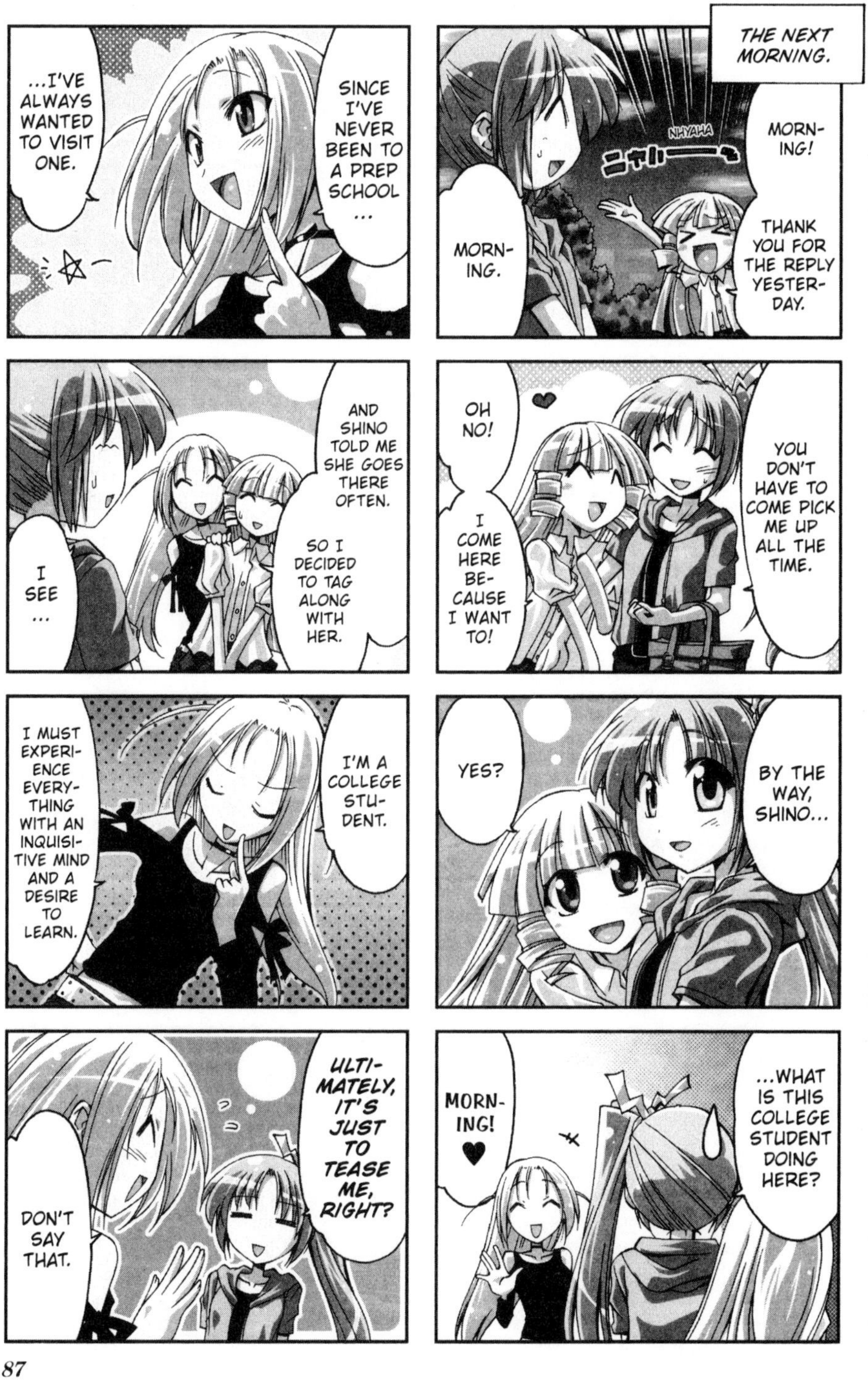
THE NEXT MORNING.
MORN-ING!
NHYAHA
ニャハー
THANK YOU FOR THE REPLY YESTER-DAY.
MORN-ING.
YOU DON'T HAVE TO COME PICK ME UP ALL THE TIME.
OH NO!
I COME HERE BE-CAUSE I WANT TO!
BY THE WAY, SHINO...
YES?
...WHAT IS THIS COLLEGE STUDENT DOING HERE?
MORN-ING! ♥
SINCE I'VE NEVER BEEN TO A PREP SCHOOL ...
...I'VE ALWAYS WANTED TO VISIT ONE.
AND SHINO TOLD ME SHE GOES THERE OFTEN.
SO I DECIDED TO TAG ALONG WITH HER.
I SEE ...
I'M A COLLEGE STU-DENT.
I MUST EXPERI-ENCE EVERY-THING WITH AN INQUISI-TIVE MIND AND A DESIRE TO LEARN.
ULTI-MATELY, IT'S JUST TO TEASE ME, RIGHT?
DON'T SAY THAT.

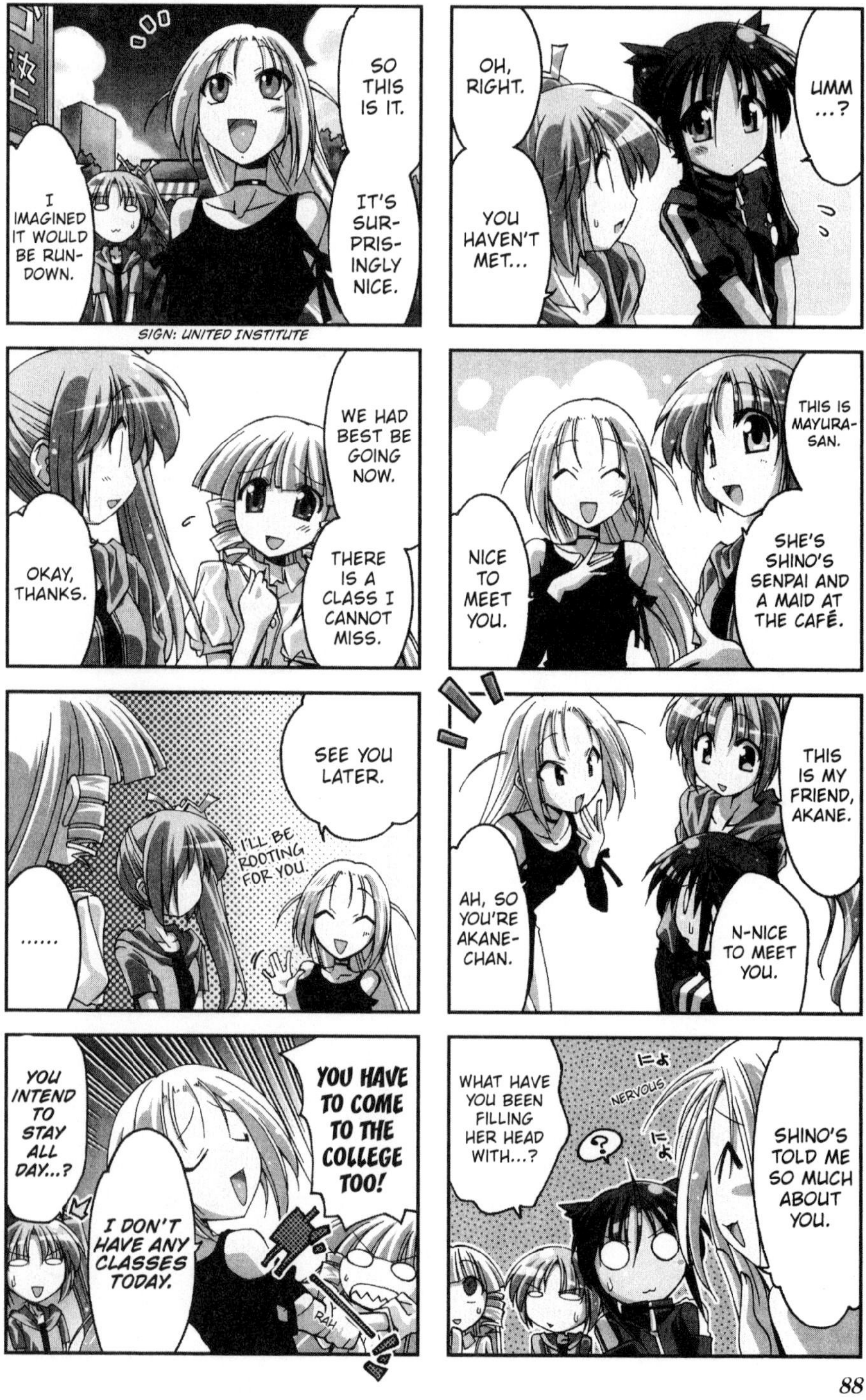
UMM ...?
OH, RIGHT.
YOU HAVEN'T MET...
THIS IS MAYURA-SAN.
SHE'S SHINO'S SENPAI AND A MAID AT THE CAFÉ.
NICE TO MEET YOU.
THIS IS MY FRIEND, AKANE.
AH, SO YOU'RE AKANE-CHAN.
N-NICE TO MEET YOU.
SHINO'S TOLD ME SO MUCH ABOUT YOU.
NERVOUS
WHAT HAVE YOU BEEN FILLING HER HEAD WITH...?
SO THIS IS IT.
IT'S SURPRISINGLY NICE.
I IMAGINED IT WOULD BE RUN-DOWN.
SIGN: UNITED INSTITUTE
WE HAD BEST BE GOING NOW.
THERE IS A CLASS I CANNOT MISS.
OKAY, THANKS.
SEE YOU LATER.
I'LL BE ROOTING FOR YOU.
......
YOU HAVE TO COME TO THE COLLEGE TOO!
I DON'T HAVE ANY CLASSES TODAY.
YOU INTEND TO STAY ALL DAY...?
RAH

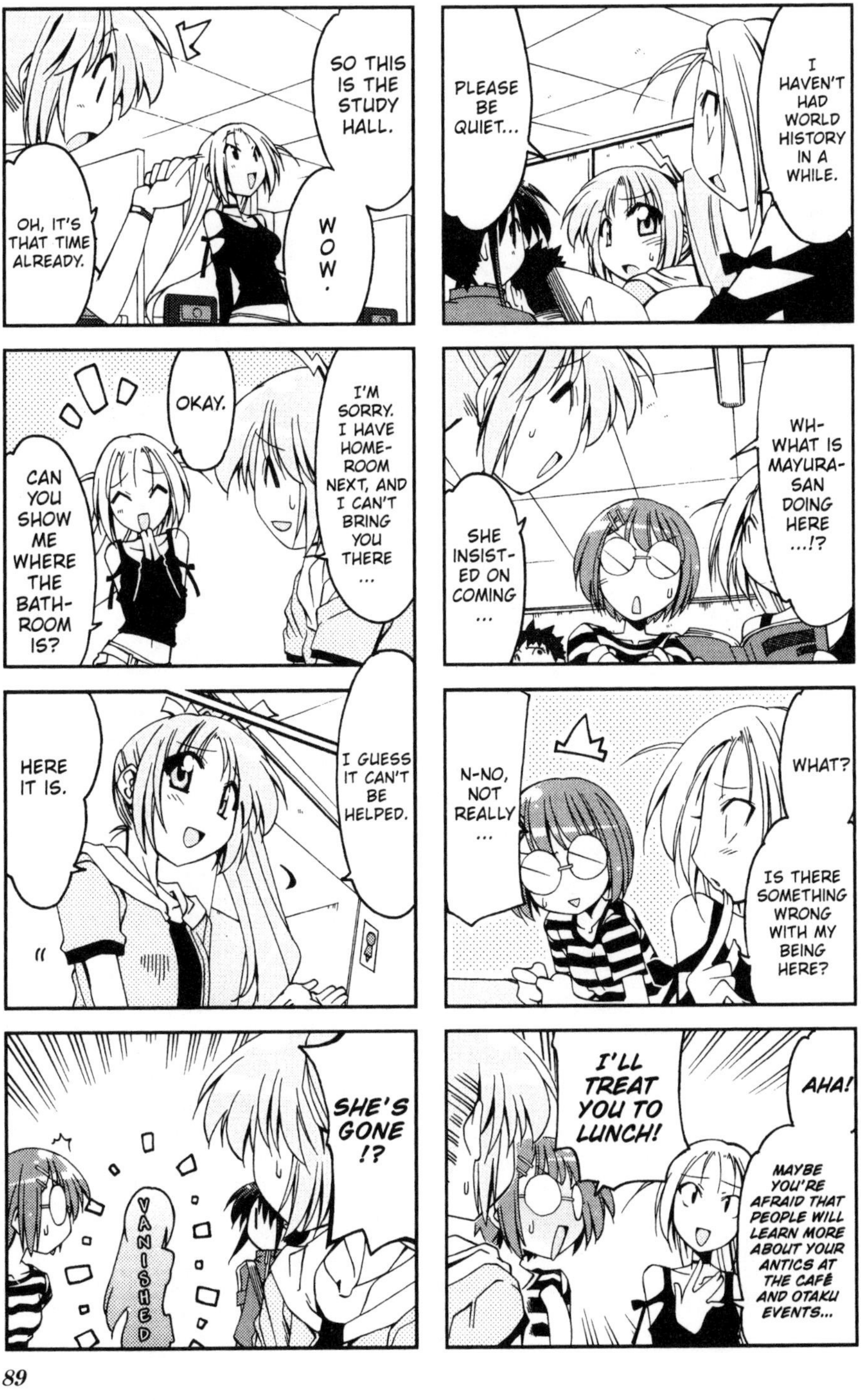
I HAVEN'T HAD WORLD HISTORY IN A WHILE.
PLEASE BE QUIET...
WH-WHAT IS MAYURA-SAN DOING HERE ...!?
SHE INSISTED ON COMING ...
WHAT?
IS THERE SOMETHING WRONG WITH MY BEING HERE?
N-NO, NOT REALLY ...
AHA!
MAYBE YOU'RE AFRAID THAT PEOPLE WILL LEARN MORE ABOUT YOUR ANTICS AT THE CAFÉ AND OTAKU EVENTS...
I'LL TREAT YOU TO LUNCH!
SO THIS IS THE STUDY HALL.
WOW.
OH, IT'S THAT TIME ALREADY.
I'M SORRY. I HAVE HOME-ROOM NEXT, AND I CAN'T BRING YOU THERE ...
OKAY.
CAN YOU SHOW ME WHERE THE BATH-ROOM IS?
I GUESS IT CAN'T BE HELPED.
HERE IT IS.
SHE'S GONE !?
VANISHED

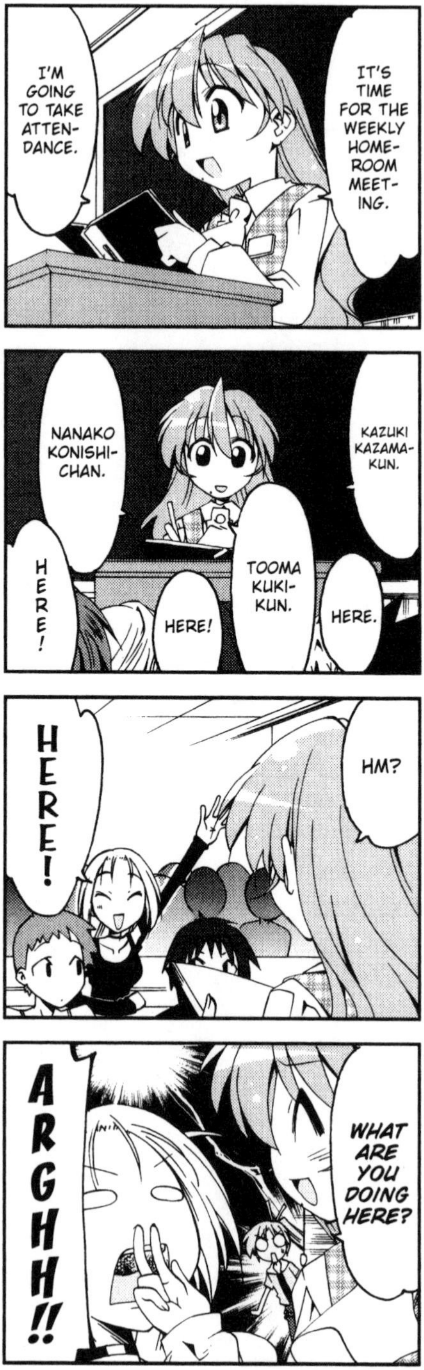
IT'S TIME FOR THE WEEKLY HOMEROOM MEETING.
I'M GOING TO TAKE ATTENDANCE.
KAZUKI KAZAMA-KUN.
HERE.
TOOMA KUKI-KUN.
HERE!
NANAKO KONISHI-CHAN.
HERE!
HM?
HERE!
WHAT ARE YOU DOING HERE?
ARGHH!!

AFTER HOMEROOM.

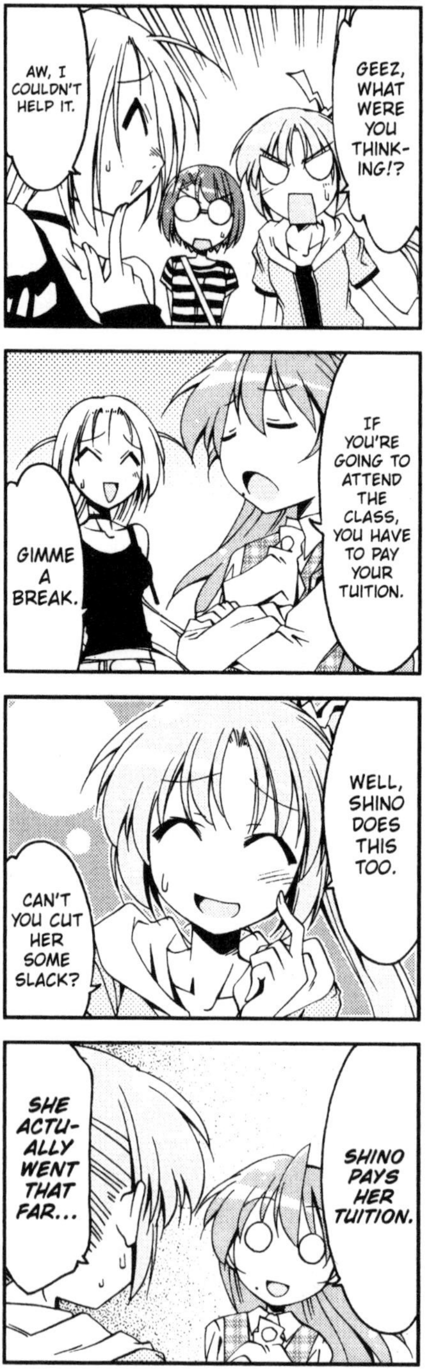
GEEZ, WHAT WERE YOU THINKING!?
AW, I COULDN'T HELP IT.
IF YOU'RE GOING TO ATTEND THE CLASS, YOU HAVE TO PAY YOUR TUITION.
GIMME A BREAK.
WELL, SHINO DOES THIS TOO.
CAN'T YOU CUT HER SOME SLACK?
SHINO PAYS HER TUITION.
SHE ACTUALLY WENT THAT FAR...

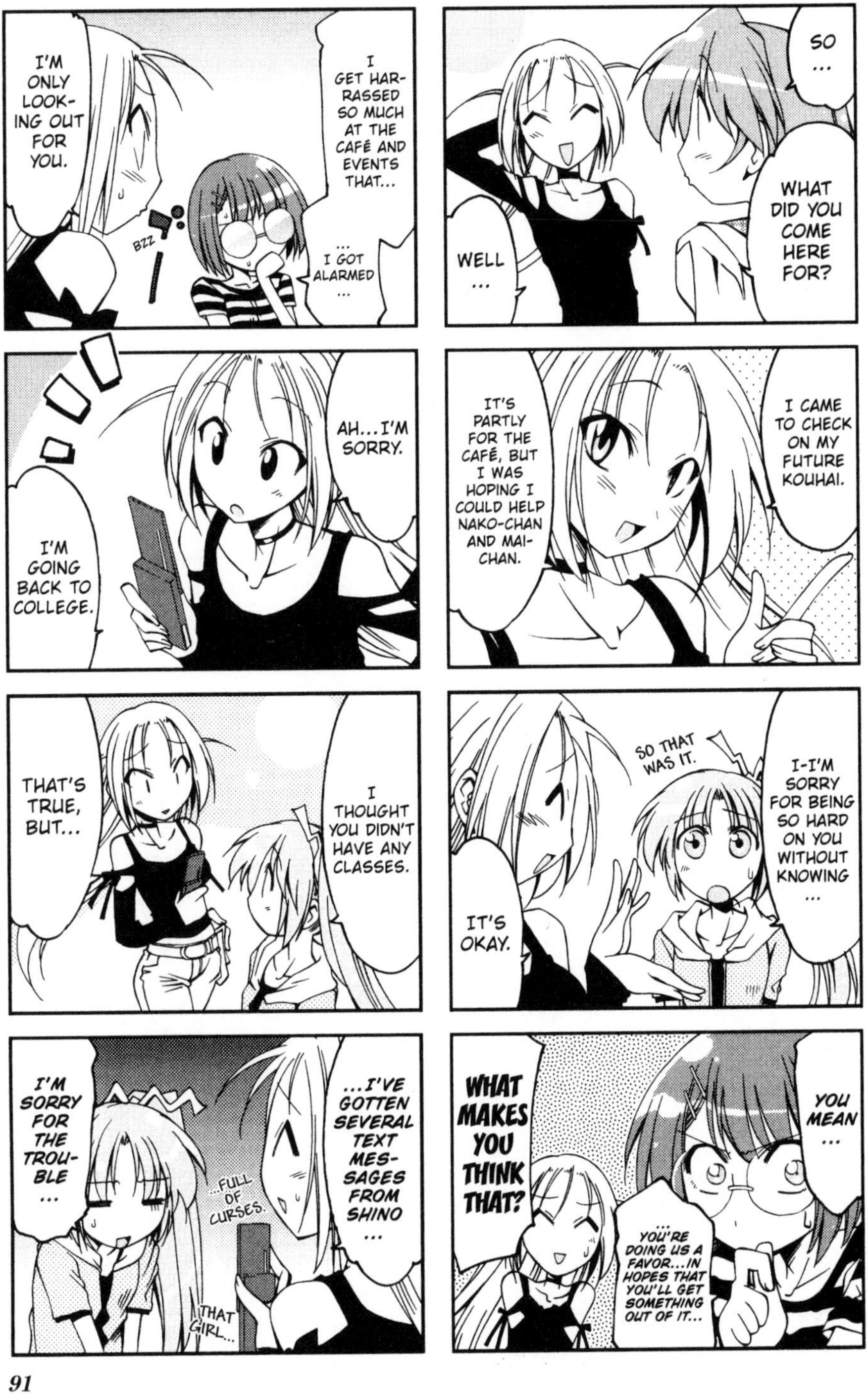

SO ...
WHAT DID YOU COME HERE FOR?
WELL ...
I GET HARRASSED SO MUCH AT THE CAFÉ AND EVENTS THAT...
... I GOT ALARMED ...
I'M ONLY LOOKING OUT FOR YOU.
BZZ
I CAME TO CHECK ON MY FUTURE KOUHAI.
IT'S PARTLY FOR THE CAFÉ, BUT I WAS HOPING I COULD HELP NAKO-CHAN AND MAI-CHAN.
AH...I'M SORRY.
I'M GOING BACK TO COLLEGE.
I-I'M SORRY FOR BEING SO HARD ON YOU WITHOUT KNOWING ...
SO THAT WAS IT.
IT'S OKAY.
I THOUGHT YOU DIDN'T HAVE ANY CLASSES.
THAT'S TRUE, BUT...
YOU MEAN ...
... YOU'RE DOING US A FAVOR...IN HOPES THAT YOU'LL GET SOMETHING OUT OF IT...
WHAT MAKES YOU THINK THAT?
...I'VE GOTTEN SEVERAL TEXT MESSAGES FROM SHINO ...
...FULL OF CURSES.
THAT GIRL...
I'M SORRY FOR THE TROUBLE ...

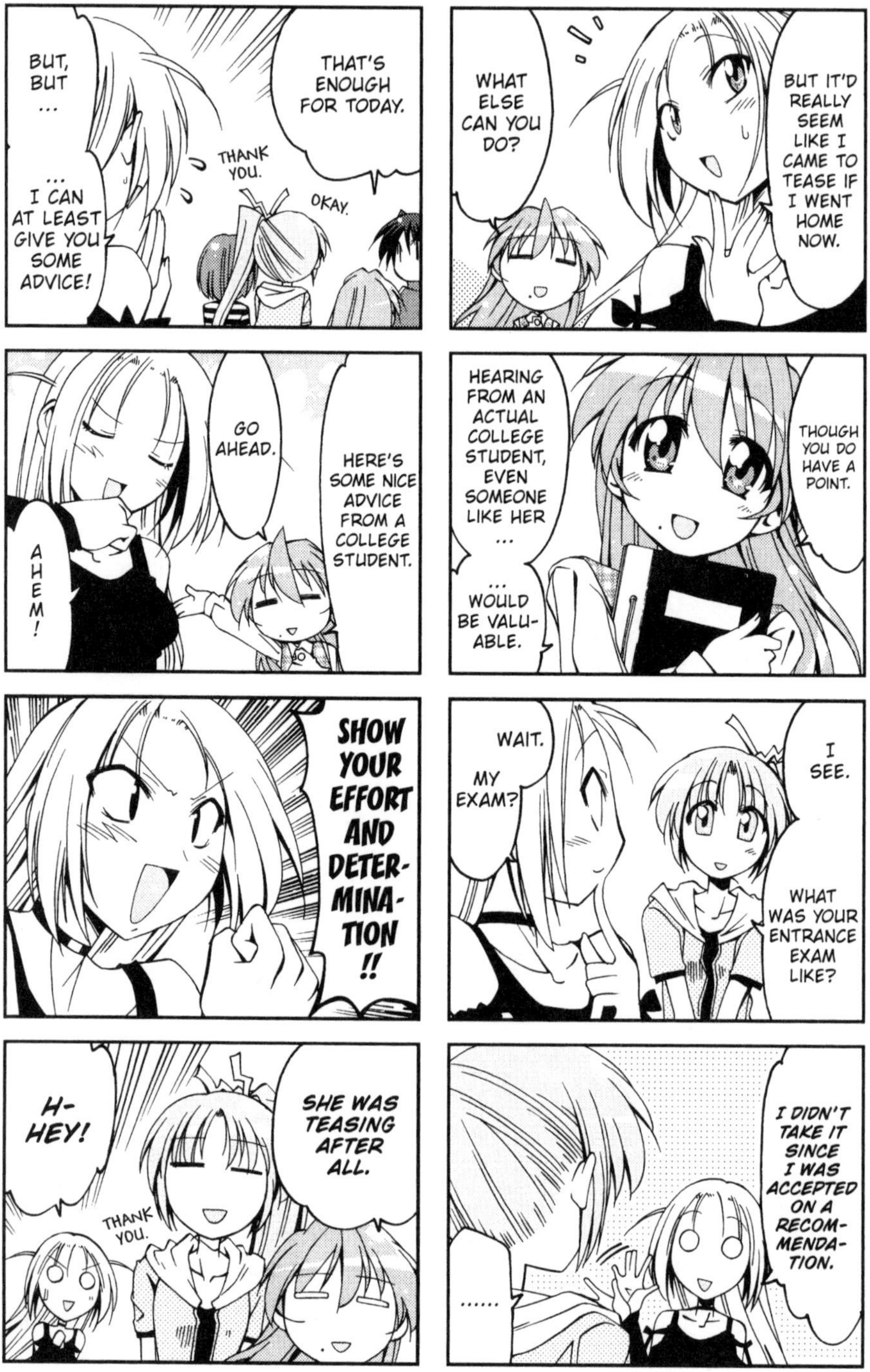
BUT IT'D REALLY SEEM LIKE I CAME TO TEASE IF I WENT HOME NOW.
WHAT ELSE CAN YOU DO?
THAT'S ENOUGH FOR TODAY.
OKAY.
THANK YOU.
BUT, BUT ...
... I CAN AT LEAST GIVE YOU SOME ADVICE!
THOUGH YOU DO HAVE A POINT.
HEARING FROM AN ACTUAL COLLEGE STUDENT, EVEN SOMEONE LIKE HER ...
... WOULD BE VALU-ABLE.
HERE'S SOME NICE ADVICE FROM A COLLEGE STUDENT.
GO AHEAD.
AHEM!
I SEE.
WHAT WAS YOUR ENTRANCE EXAM LIKE?
WAIT.
MY EXAM?
SHOW YOUR EFFORT AND DETER-MINA-TION!!
I DIDN'T TAKE IT SINCE I WAS ACCEPTED ON A RECOM-MENDA-TION.
......
SHE WAS TEASING AFTER ALL.
H-HEY!
THANK YOU.

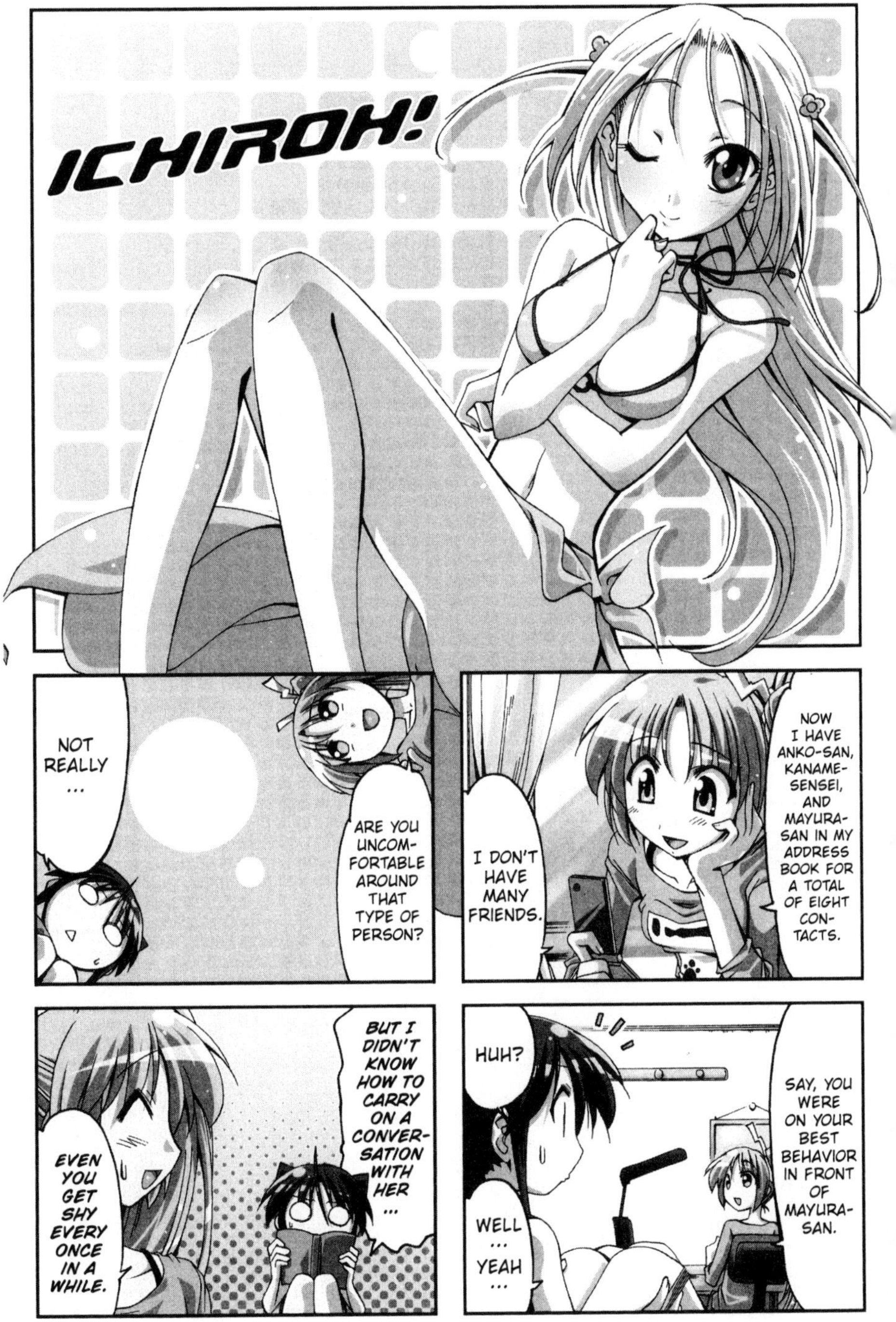
ICHIROH!
NOW I HAVE ANKO-SAN, KANAME-SENSEI, AND MAYURA-SAN IN MY ADDRESS BOOK FOR A TOTAL OF EIGHT CONTACTS.
I DON'T HAVE MANY FRIENDS.
ARE YOU UNCOMFORTABLE AROUND THAT TYPE OF PERSON?
NOT REALLY ...
SAY, YOU WERE ON YOUR BEST BEHAVIOR IN FRONT OF MAYURA-SAN.
HUH?
WELL ... YEAH ...
BUT I DIDN'T KNOW HOW TO CARRY ON A CONVERSATION WITH HER ...
EVEN YOU GET SHY EVERY ONCE IN A WHILE.

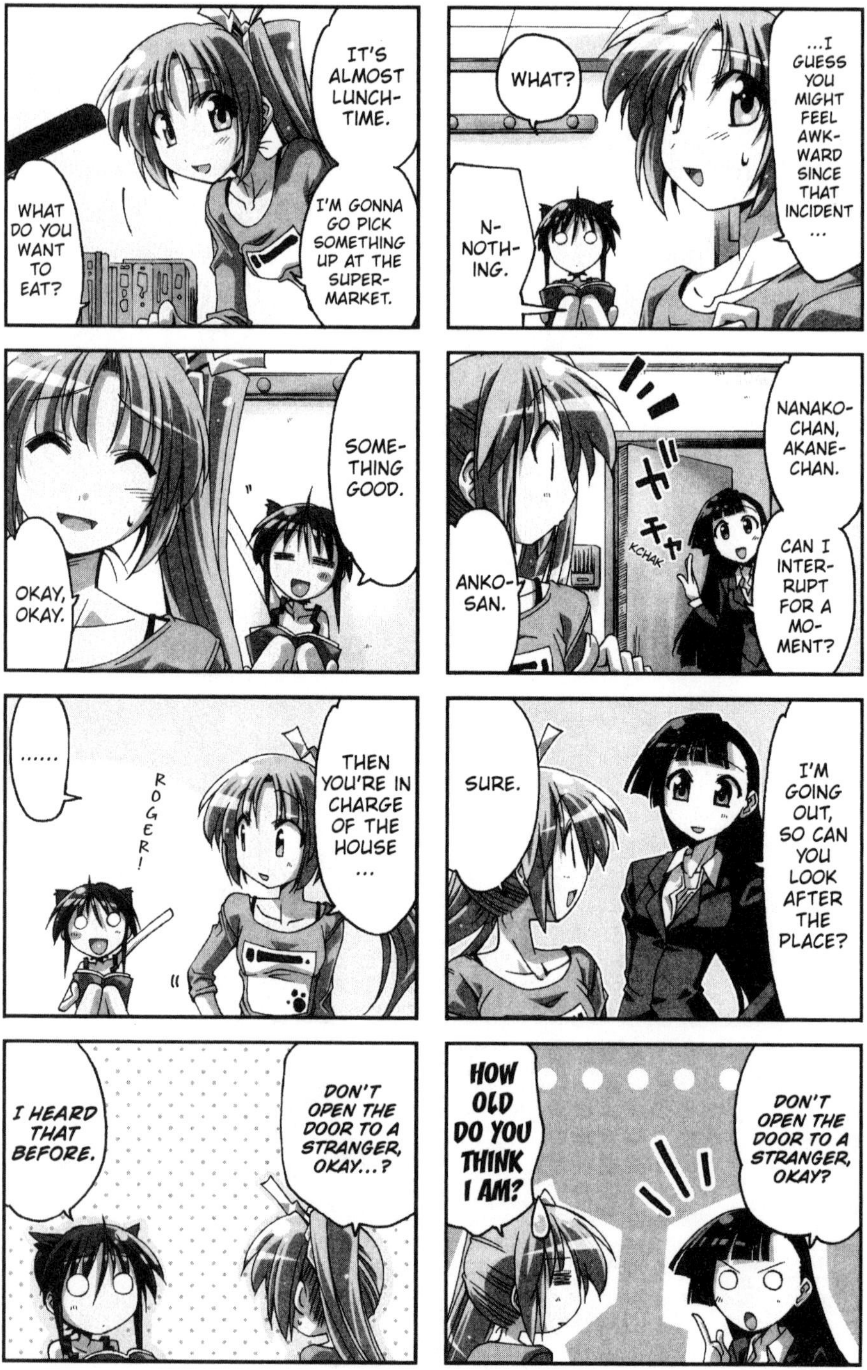
...I GUESS YOU MIGHT FEEL AWKWARD SINCE THAT INCIDENT...
WHAT?
N-NOTHING.
IT'S ALMOST LUNCHTIME.
I'M GONNA GO PICK SOMETHING UP AT THE SUPERMARKET.
WHAT DO YOU WANT TO EAT?
NANAKO-CHAN, AKANE-CHAN.
CAN I INTERRUPT FOR A MOMENT?
KCHAK
ANKO-SAN.
SOMETHING GOOD.
OKAY, OKAY.
I'M GOING OUT, SO CAN YOU LOOK AFTER THE PLACE?
SURE.
THEN YOU'RE IN CHARGE OF THE HOUSE...
ROGER!
......
DON'T OPEN THE DOOR TO A STRANGER, OKAY?
HOW OLD DO YOU THINK I AM?
DON'T OPEN THE DOOR TO A STRANGER, OKAY...?
I HEARD THAT BEFORE.

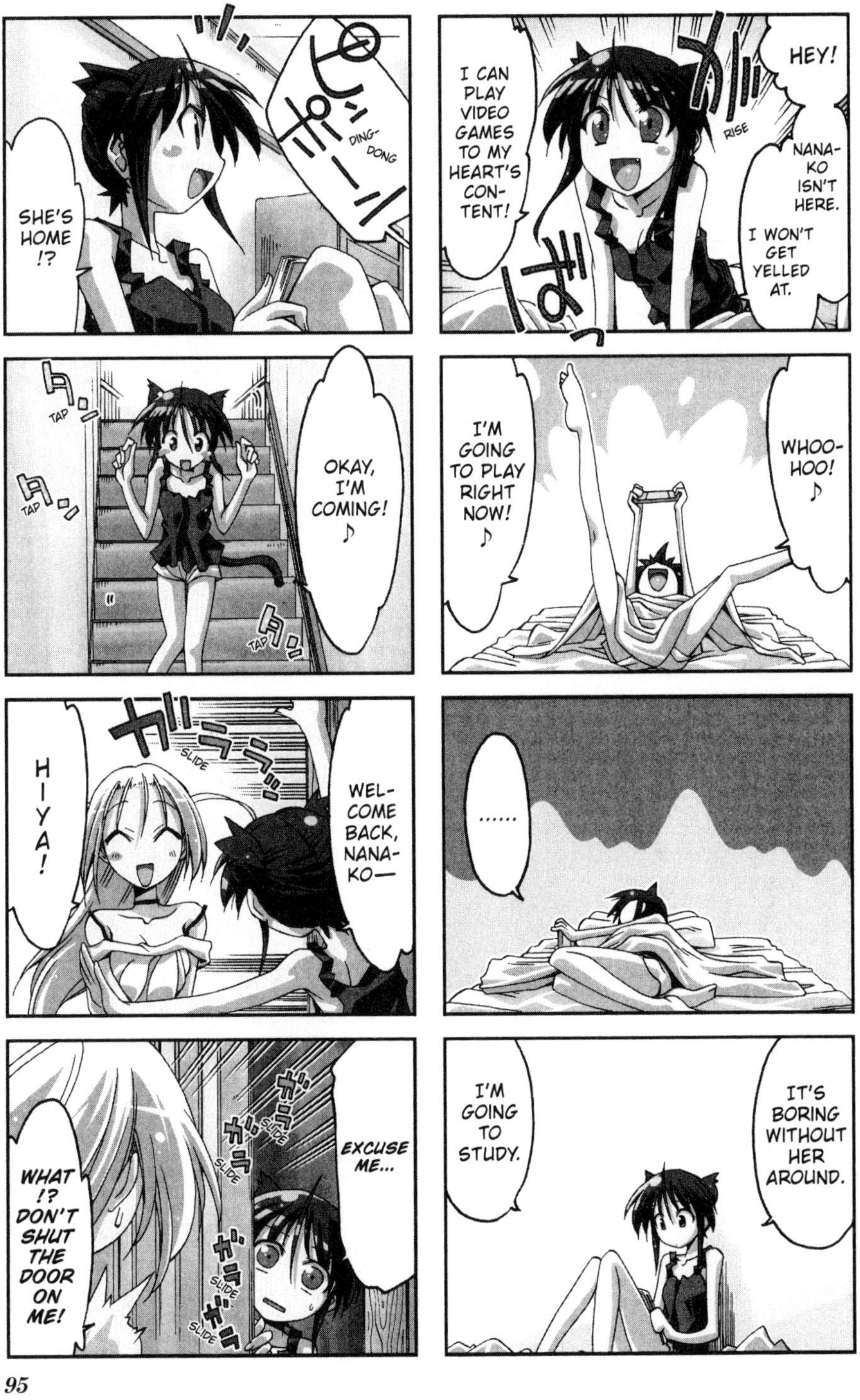
HEY!
RISE
NANA-KO ISN'T HERE.
I WON'T GET YELLED AT.
I CAN PLAY VIDEO GAMES TO MY HEART'S CON-TENT!
DING-DONG
SHE'S HOME !?
WHOO-HOO! ♪
I'M GOING TO PLAY RIGHT NOW! ♪
OKAY, I'M COMING! ♪
TAP
TAP
TAP
......
WEL-COME BACK, NANA-KO—
SLIDE
HIYA!
IT'S BORING WITHOUT HER AROUND.
I'M GOING TO STUDY.
EXCUSE ME...
SLIDE
SLIDE
SLIDE
SLIDE
WHAT !? DON'T SHUT THE DOOR ON ME!

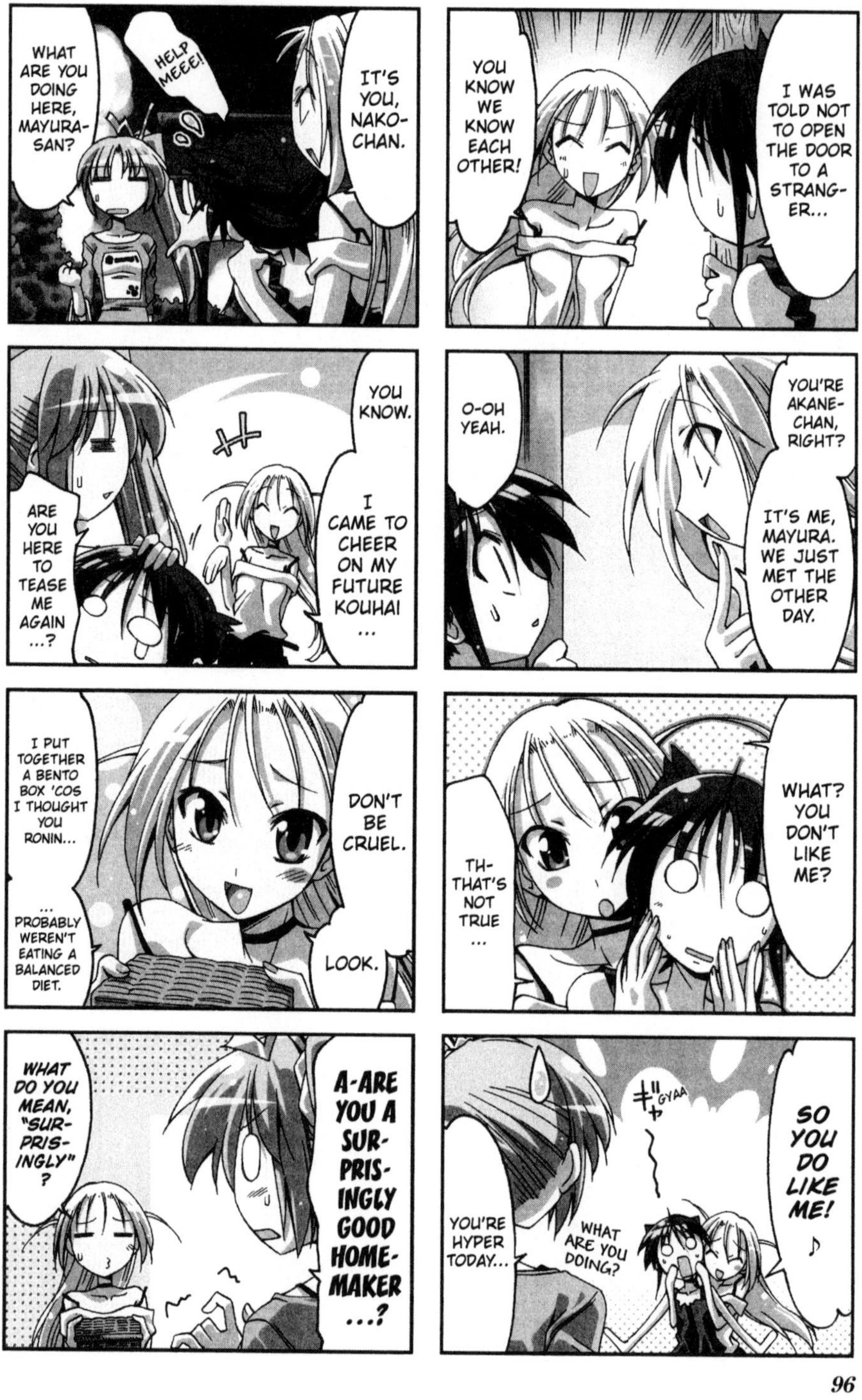
I WAS TOLD NOT TO OPEN THE DOOR TO A STRANGER...
YOU KNOW WE KNOW EACH OTHER!
IT'S YOU, NAKO-CHAN.
HELP MEEE!
WHAT ARE YOU DOING HERE, MAYURA-SAN?
YOU'RE AKANE-CHAN, RIGHT?
IT'S ME, MAYURA. WE JUST MET THE OTHER DAY.
O-OH YEAH.
YOU KNOW.
I CAME TO CHEER ON MY FUTURE KOUHAI...
ARE YOU HERE TO TEASE ME AGAIN...?
WHAT? YOU DON'T LIKE ME?
TH-THAT'S NOT TRUE...
DON'T BE CRUEL.
LOOK.
I PUT TOGETHER A BENTO BOX 'COS I THOUGHT YOU RONIN...
...PROBABLY WEREN'T EATING A BALANCED DIET.
SO YOU DO LIKE ME! ♪
GYAA
WHAT ARE YOU DOING?
YOU'RE HYPER TODAY...
A-ARE YOU A SURPRISINGLY GOOD HOMEMAKER...?
WHAT DO YOU MEAN, "SURPRISINGLY"?

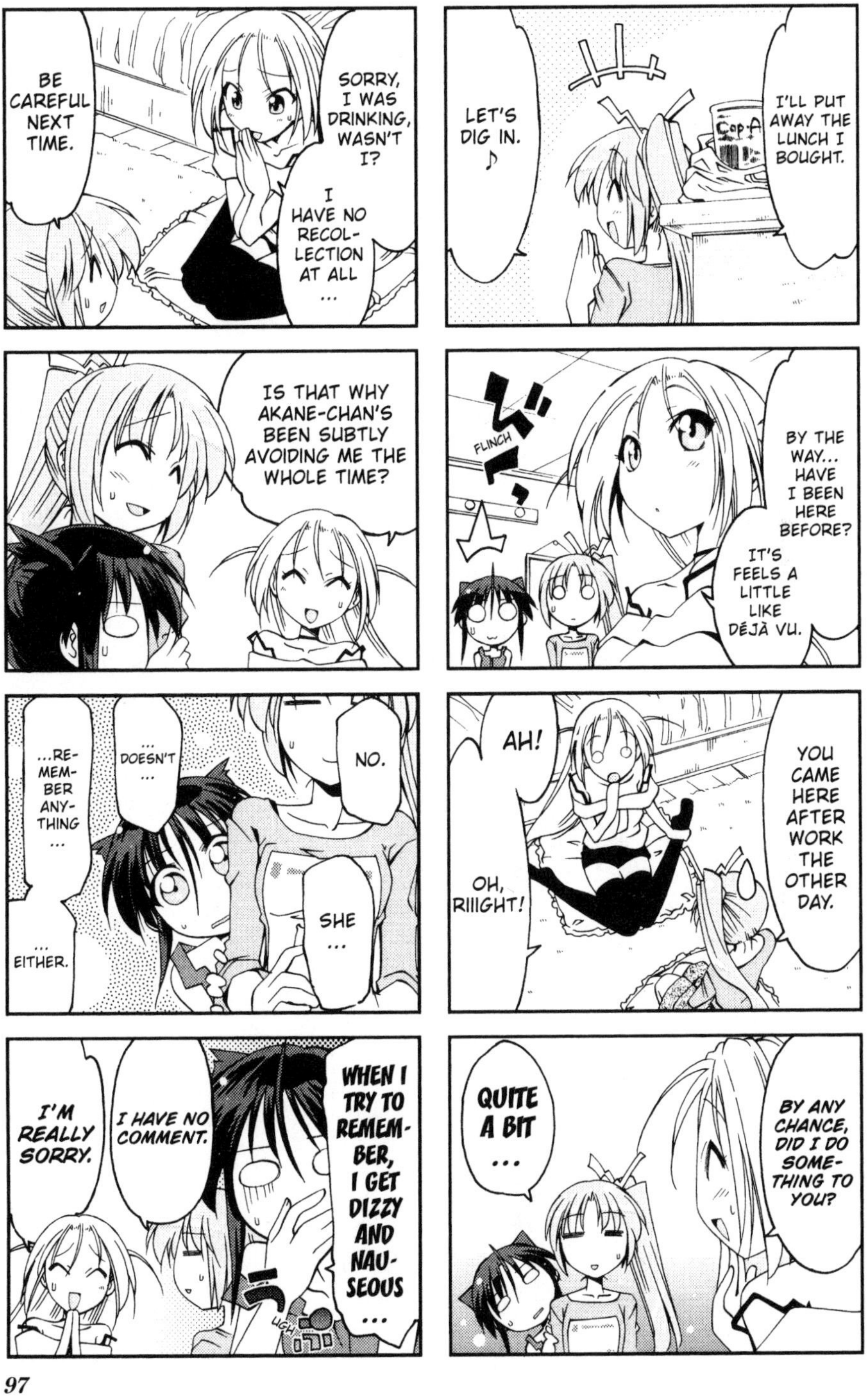

I'LL PUT AWAY THE LUNCH I BOUGHT.
LET'S DIG IN. ♪
SORRY, I WAS DRINKING, WASN'T I?
I HAVE NO RECOL-LECTION AT ALL ...
BE CAREFUL NEXT TIME.
BY THE WAY... HAVE I BEEN HERE BEFORE?
IT'S FEELS A LITTLE LIKE DÉJÀ VU.
FLINCH
IS THAT WHY AKANE-CHAN'S BEEN SUBTLY AVOIDING ME THE WHOLE TIME?
YOU CAME HERE AFTER WORK THE OTHER DAY.
AH!
OH, RIIIGHT!
NO.
SHE ...
... DOESN'T ...
...RE-MEM-BER ANY-THING ...
... EITHER.
BY ANY CHANCE, DID I DO SOME-THING TO YOU?
QUITE A BIT ...
WHEN I TRY TO REMEM-BER, I GET DIZZY AND NAU-SEOUS ...
UGH
I HAVE NO COMMENT.
I'M REALLY SORRY.

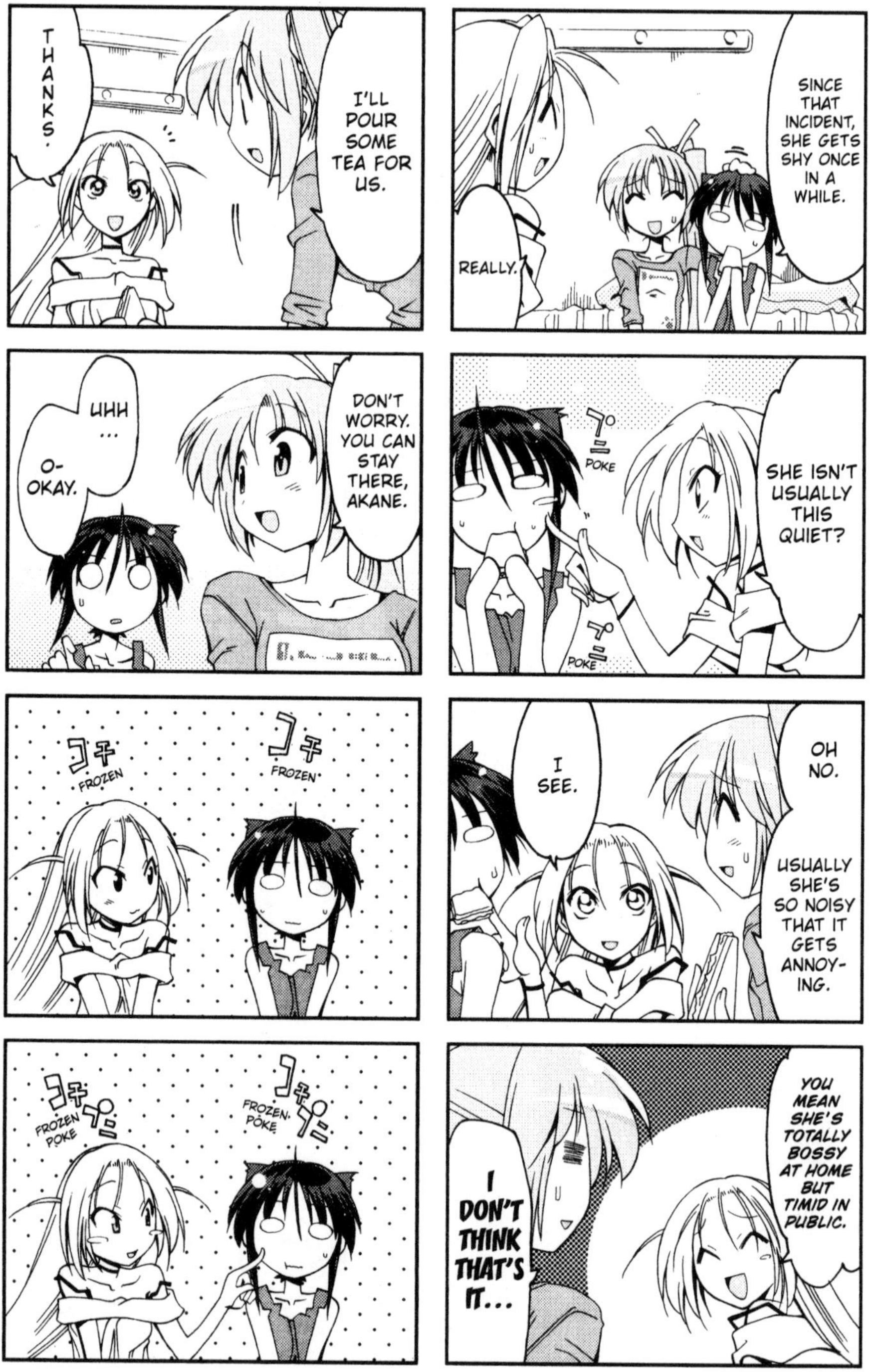
SINCE THAT INCIDENT, SHE GETS SHY ONCE IN A WHILE.
REALLY.
プニ POKE
SHE ISN'T USUALLY THIS QUIET?
プニ POKE
OH NO.
USUALLY SHE'S SO NOISY THAT IT GETS ANNOY-ING.
I SEE.
YOU MEAN SHE'S TOTALLY BOSSY AT HOME BUT TIMID IN PUBLIC.
I DON'T THINK THAT'S IT...
I'LL POUR SOME TEA FOR US.
THANKS.
DON'T WORRY. YOU CAN STAY THERE, AKANE.
UHH ... O-OKAY.
コチ FROZEN
コチ FROZEN
コチ プニ FROZEN POKE
コチ プニ FROZEN. POKE

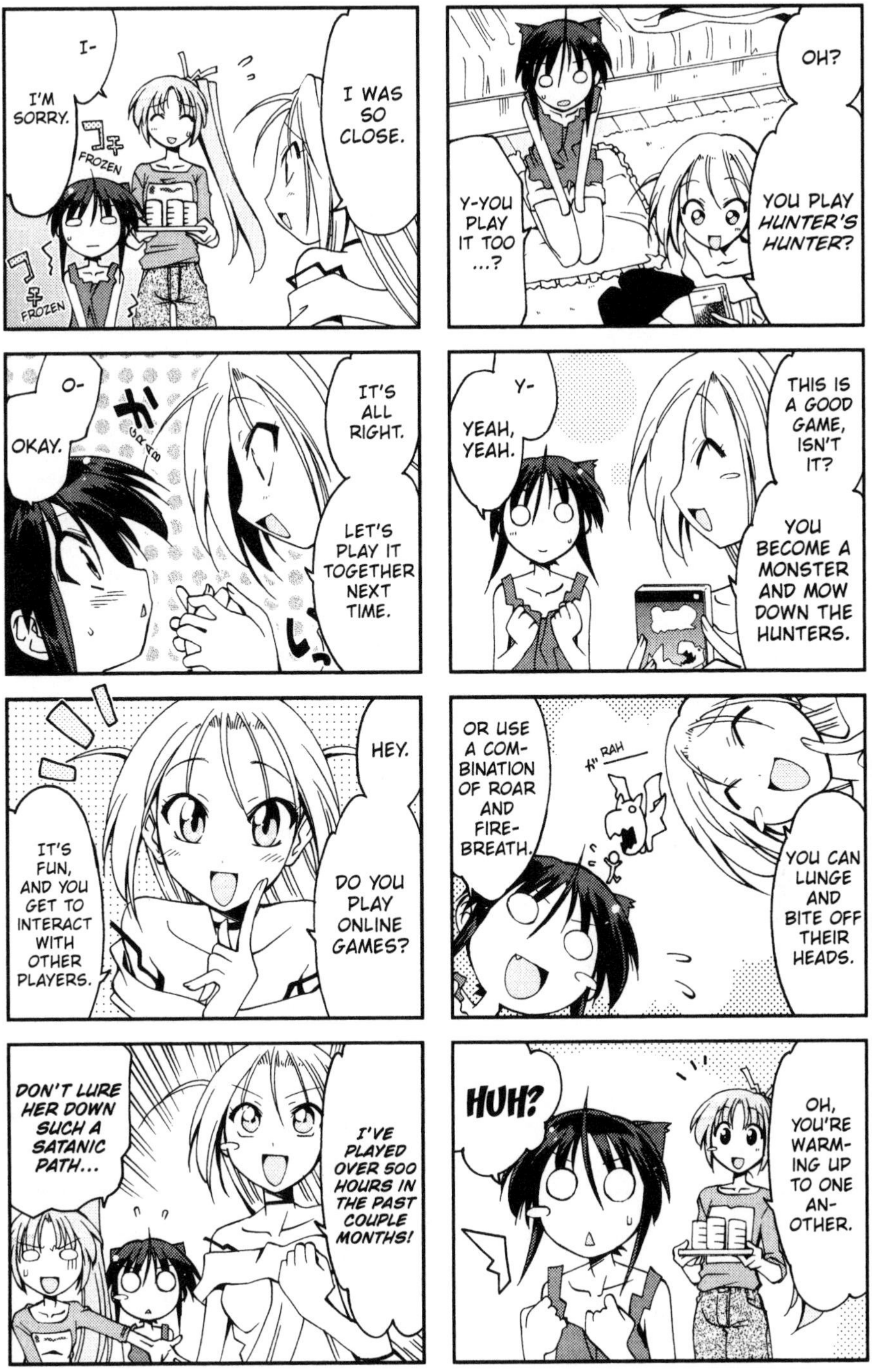
OH?
YOU PLAY *HUNTER'S HUNTER?*
Y-YOU PLAY IT TOO ...?
THIS IS A GOOD GAME, ISN'T IT?
YOU BECOME A MONSTER AND MOW DOWN THE HUNTERS.
Y-
YEAH, YEAH.
YOU CAN LUNGE AND BITE OFF THEIR HEADS.
RAH
OR USE A COMBINATION OF ROAR AND FIRE-BREATH.
OH, YOU'RE WARMING UP TO ONE ANOTHER.
HUH?
I WAS SO CLOSE.
I-
I'M SORRY.
FROZEN
FROZEN
IT'S ALL RIGHT.
LET'S PLAY IT TOGETHER NEXT TIME.
GRAB
O-
OKAY.
HEY.
DO YOU PLAY ONLINE GAMES?
IT'S FUN, AND YOU GET TO INTERACT WITH OTHER PLAYERS.
*I'VE PLAYED OVER 500 HOURS IN THE PAST COUPLE MONTHS!*
*DON'T LURE HER DOWN SUCH A SATANIC PATH...*

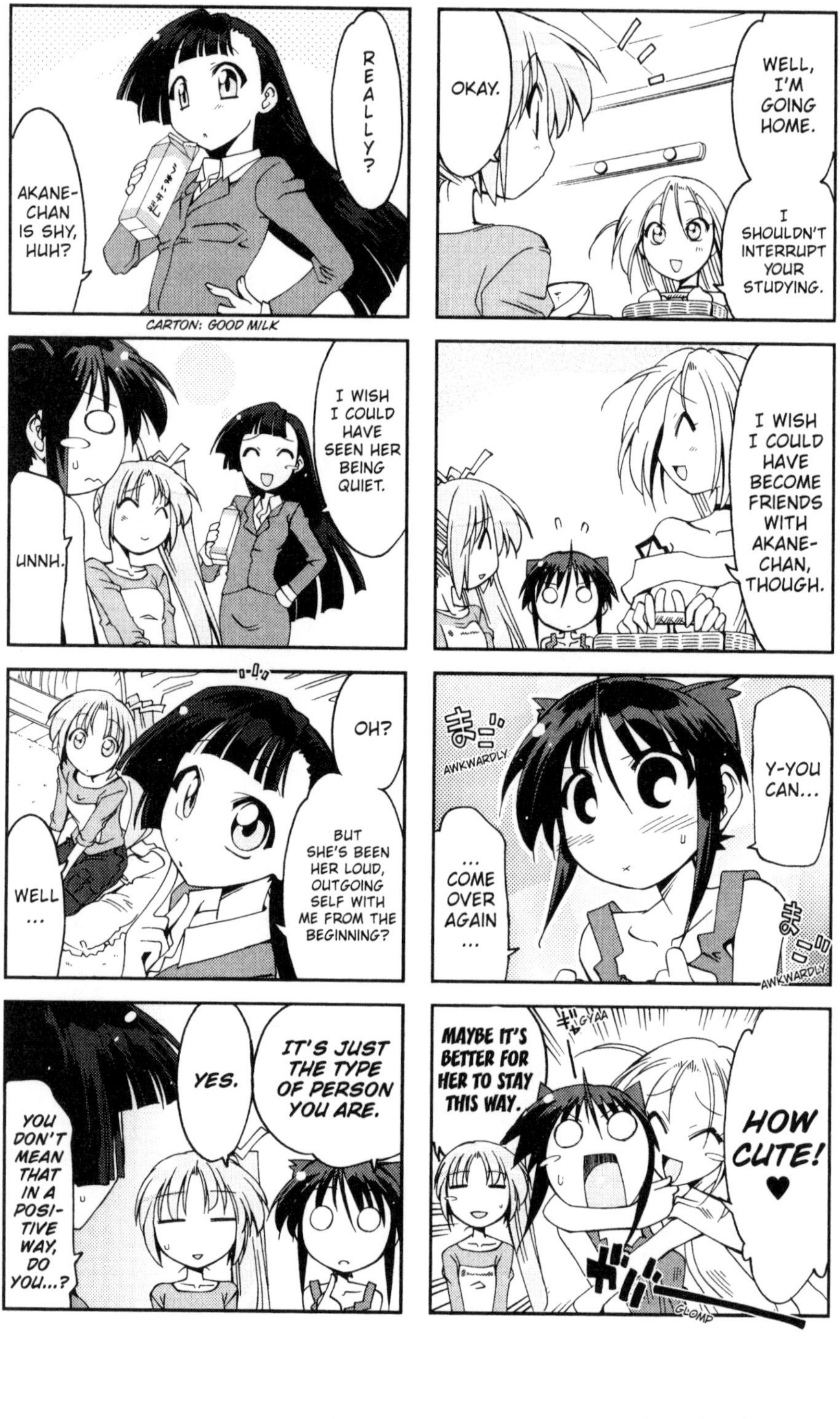
WELL, I'M GOING HOME.
I SHOULDN'T INTERRUPT YOUR STUDYING.
OKAY.
I WISH I COULD HAVE BECOME FRIENDS WITH AKANE-CHAN, THOUGH.
まご
AWKWARDLY
Y-YOU CAN...
...COME OVER AGAIN...
まご
AWKWARDLY
HOW CUTE! ♥
ギャ
GYAA
MAYBE IT'S BETTER FOR HER TO STAY THIS WAY.
GLOMP
REALLY?
AKANE-CHAN IS SHY, HUH?
CARTON: GOOD MILK
I WISH I COULD HAVE SEEN HER BEING QUIET.
UNNH.
OH?
BUT SHE'S BEEN HER LOUD, OUTGOING SELF WITH ME FROM THE BEGINNING?
WELL...
IT'S JUST THE TYPE OF PERSON YOU ARE.
YES.
YOU DON'T MEAN THAT IN A POSITIVE WAY, DO YOU...?

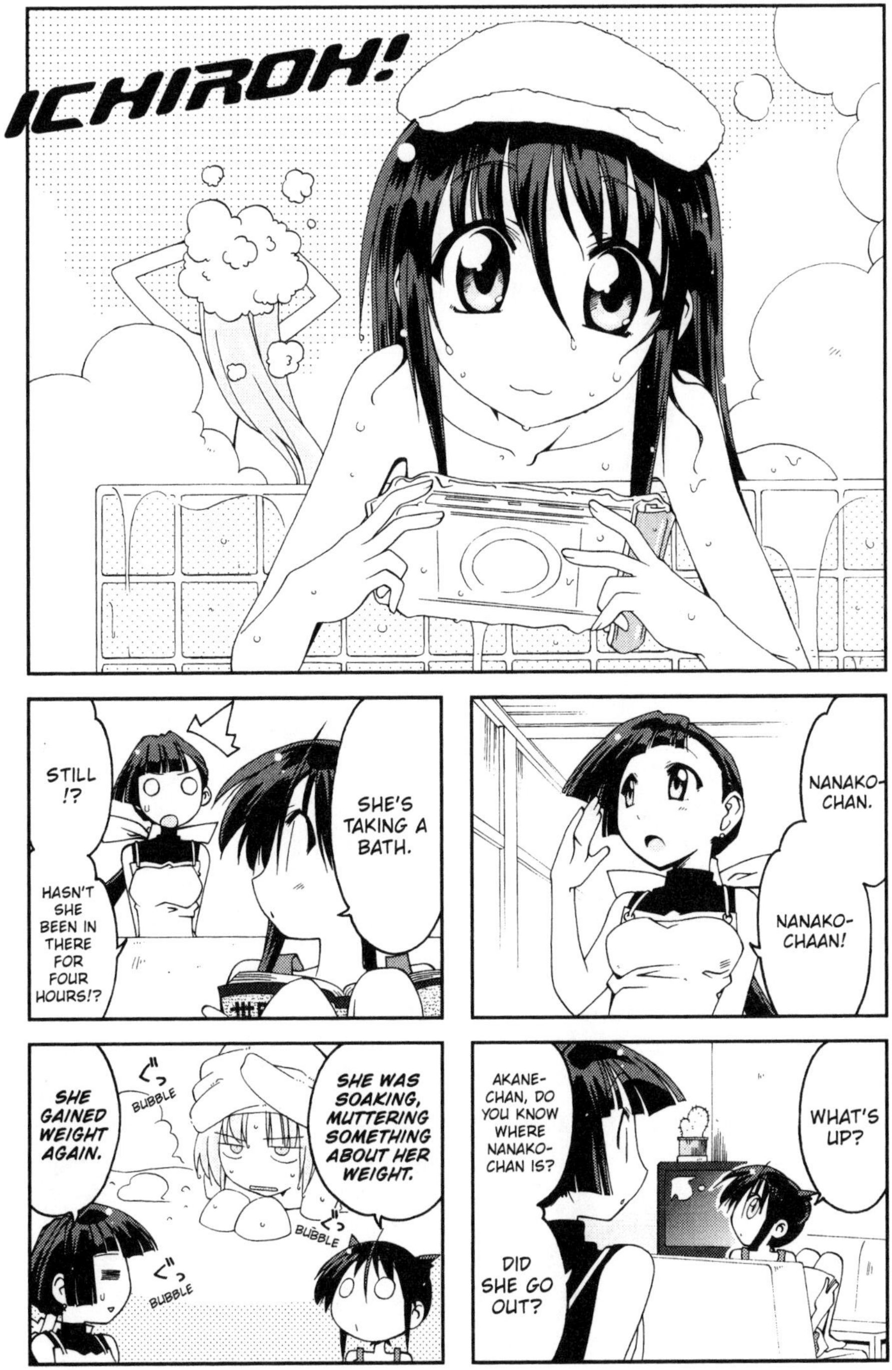
ICHIROH!
NANAKO-CHAN.
NANAKO-CHAAN!
SHE'S TAKING A BATH.
STILL!?
HASN'T SHE BEEN IN THERE FOR FOUR HOURS!?
WHAT'S UP?
AKANE-CHAN, DO YOU KNOW WHERE NANAKO-CHAN IS?
DID SHE GO OUT?
SHE WAS SOAKING, MUTTERING SOMETHING ABOUT HER WEIGHT.
BUBBLE
SHE GAINED WEIGHT AGAIN.
BUBBLE
BUBBLE

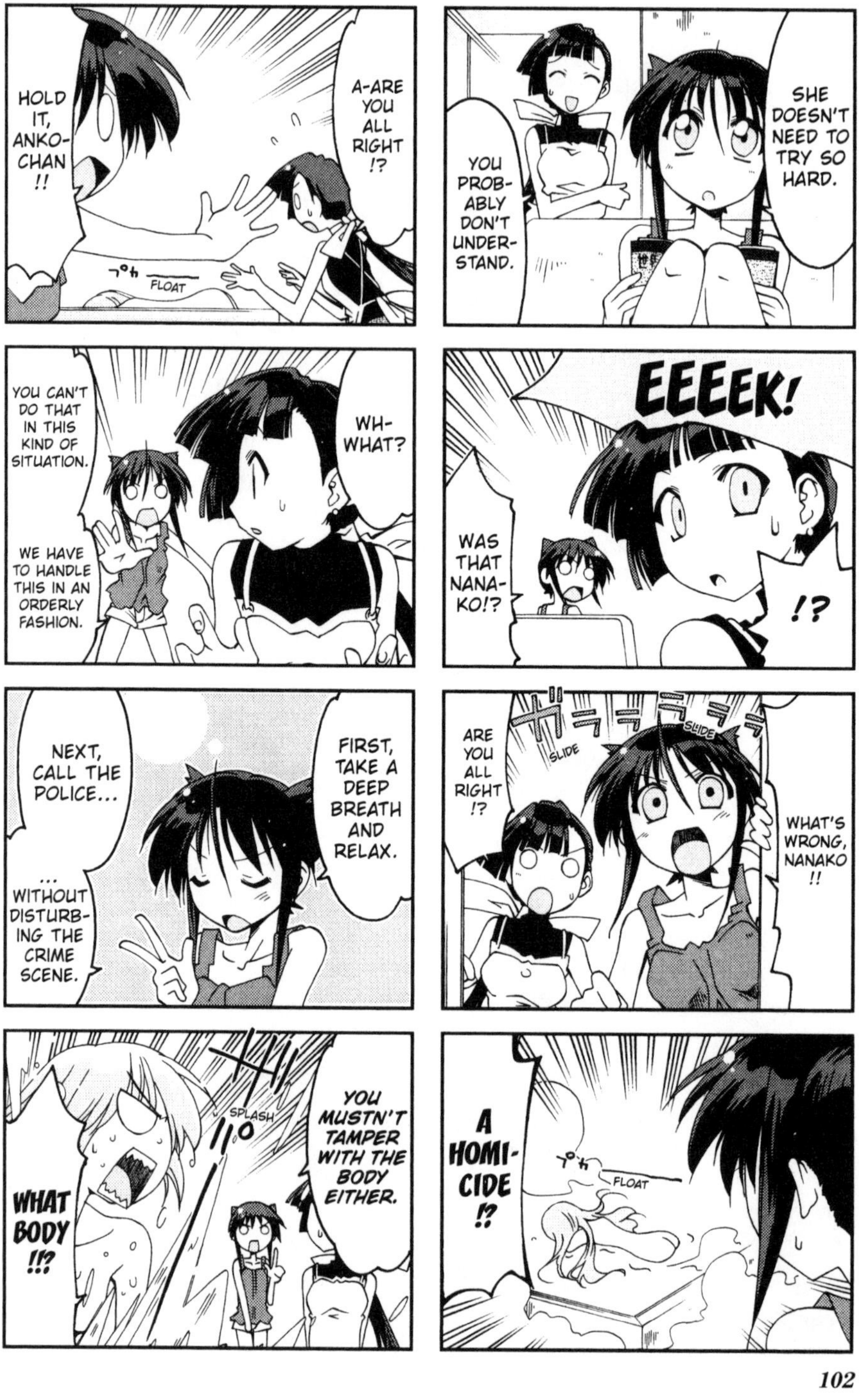

SHE DOESN'T NEED TO TRY SO HARD.
YOU PROBABLY DON'T UNDERSTAND.
EEEEK!
WAS THAT NANAKO!?
!?
WHAT'S WRONG, NANAKO !!
SLIDE
SLIDE
ARE YOU ALL RIGHT !?
A HOMICIDE !?
FLOAT
A-ARE YOU ALL RIGHT !?
HOLD IT, ANKO-CHAN !!
FLOAT
WH-WHAT?
YOU CAN'T DO THAT IN THIS KIND OF SITUATION.
WE HAVE TO HANDLE THIS IN AN ORDERLY FASHION.
FIRST, TAKE A DEEP BREATH AND RELAX.
NEXT, CALL THE POLICE...
...WITHOUT DISTURBING THE CRIME SCENE.
YOU MUSTN'T TAMPER WITH THE BODY EITHER.
SPLASH
WHAT BODY !!?

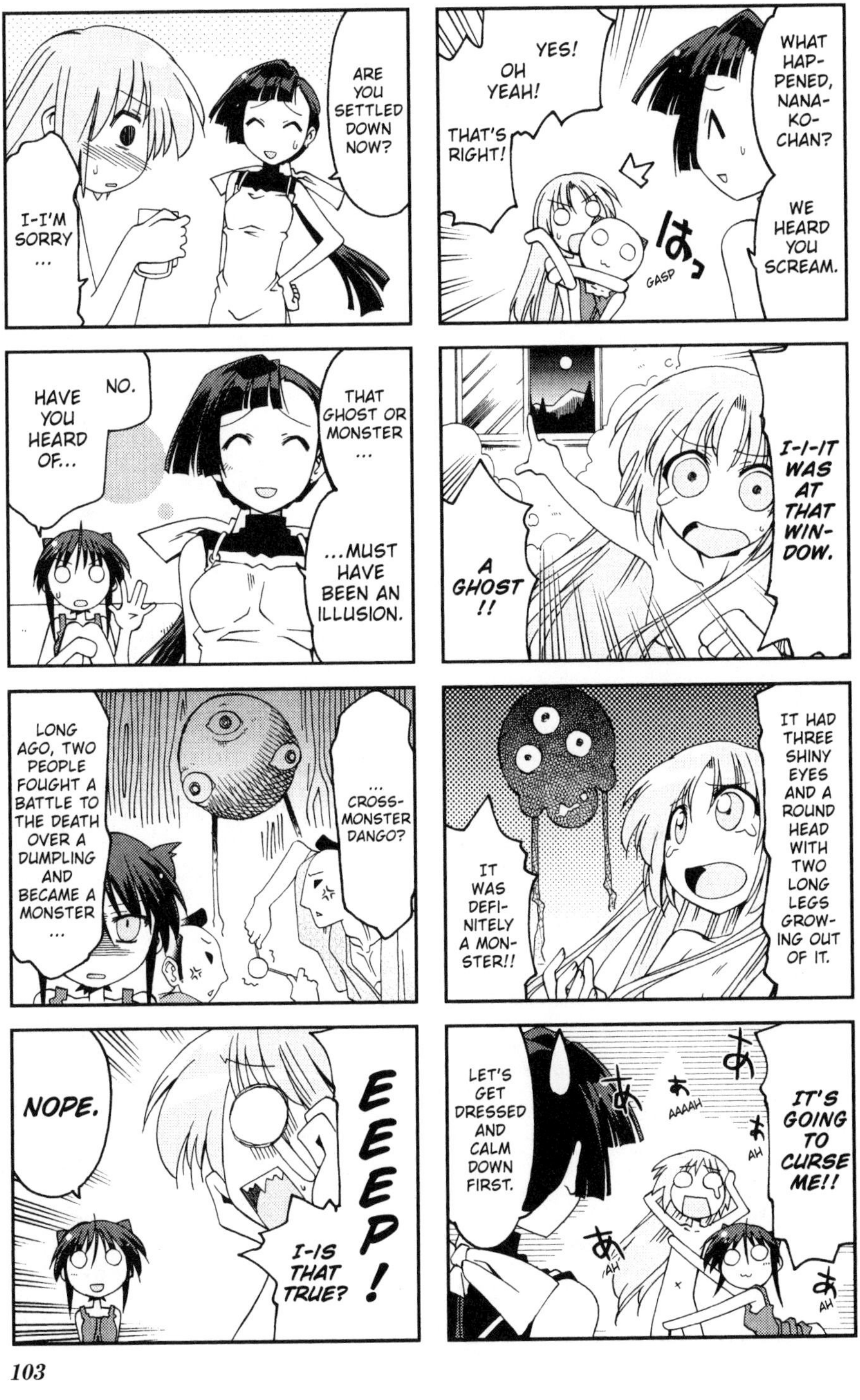
WHAT HAPPENED, NANAKO-CHAN?
WE HEARD YOU SCREAM.
はっ
GASP
YES!
OH YEAH!
THAT'S RIGHT!
ARE YOU SETTLED DOWN NOW?
I-I'M SORRY ...
I-I-IT WAS AT THAT WINDOW.
A GHOST!!
THAT GHOST OR MONSTER ...
...MUST HAVE BEEN AN ILLUSION.
NO.
HAVE YOU HEARD OF...
IT HAD THREE SHINY EYES AND A ROUND HEAD WITH TWO LONG LEGS GROWING OUT OF IT.
IT WAS DEFINITELY A MONSTER!!
... CROSS-MONSTER DANGO?
LONG AGO, TWO PEOPLE FOUGHT A BATTLE TO THE DEATH OVER A DUMPLING AND BECAME A MONSTER ...
あ
IT'S GOING TO CURSE ME!!
あ
AH
あ
AAAAH
あ
LET'S GET DRESSED AND CALM DOWN FIRST.
あ
AH
あ
AH
EEEEP!
I-IS THAT TRUE?
NOPE.

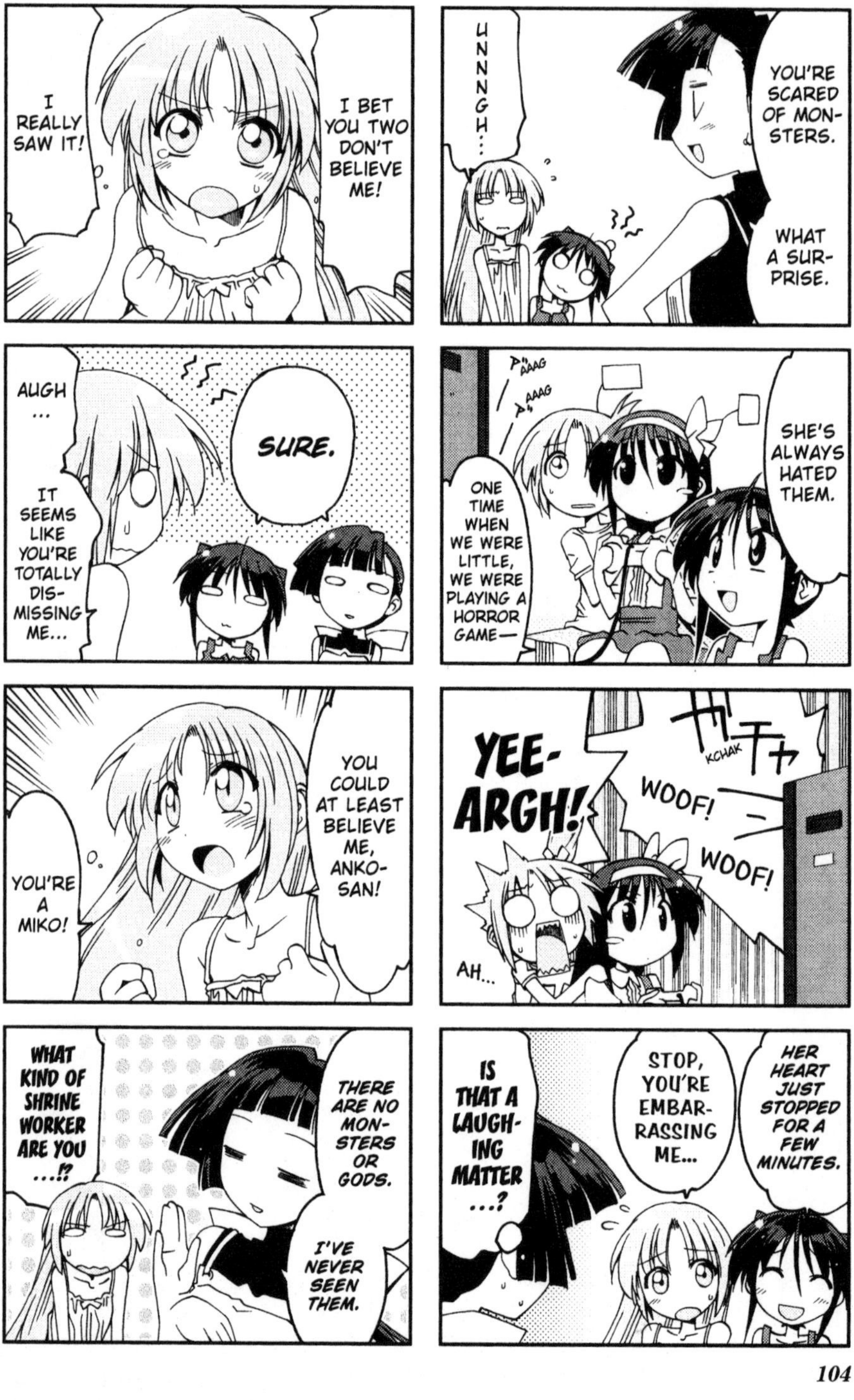
YOU'RE SCARED OF MON-STERS.
WHAT A SUR-PRISE.
UNNNGH...
SHE'S ALWAYS HATED THEM.
ONE TIME WHEN WE WERE LITTLE, WE WERE PLAYING A HORROR GAME—
AAAG
AAAG
KCHAK
WOOF!
WOOF!
YEE-ARGH!
AH...
HER HEART JUST STOPPED FOR A FEW MINUTES.
STOP, YOU'RE EMBAR-RASSING ME...
IS THAT A LAUGH-ING MATTER ...?
I BET YOU TWO DON'T BELIEVE ME!
I REALLY SAW IT!
SURE.
AUGH ...
IT SEEMS LIKE YOU'RE TOTALLY DIS-MISSING ME...
YOU COULD AT LEAST BELIEVE ME, ANKO-SAN!
YOU'RE A MIKO!
THERE ARE NO MON-STERS OR GODS.
I'VE NEVER SEEN THEM.
WHAT KIND OF SHRINE WORKER ARE YOU ...!?

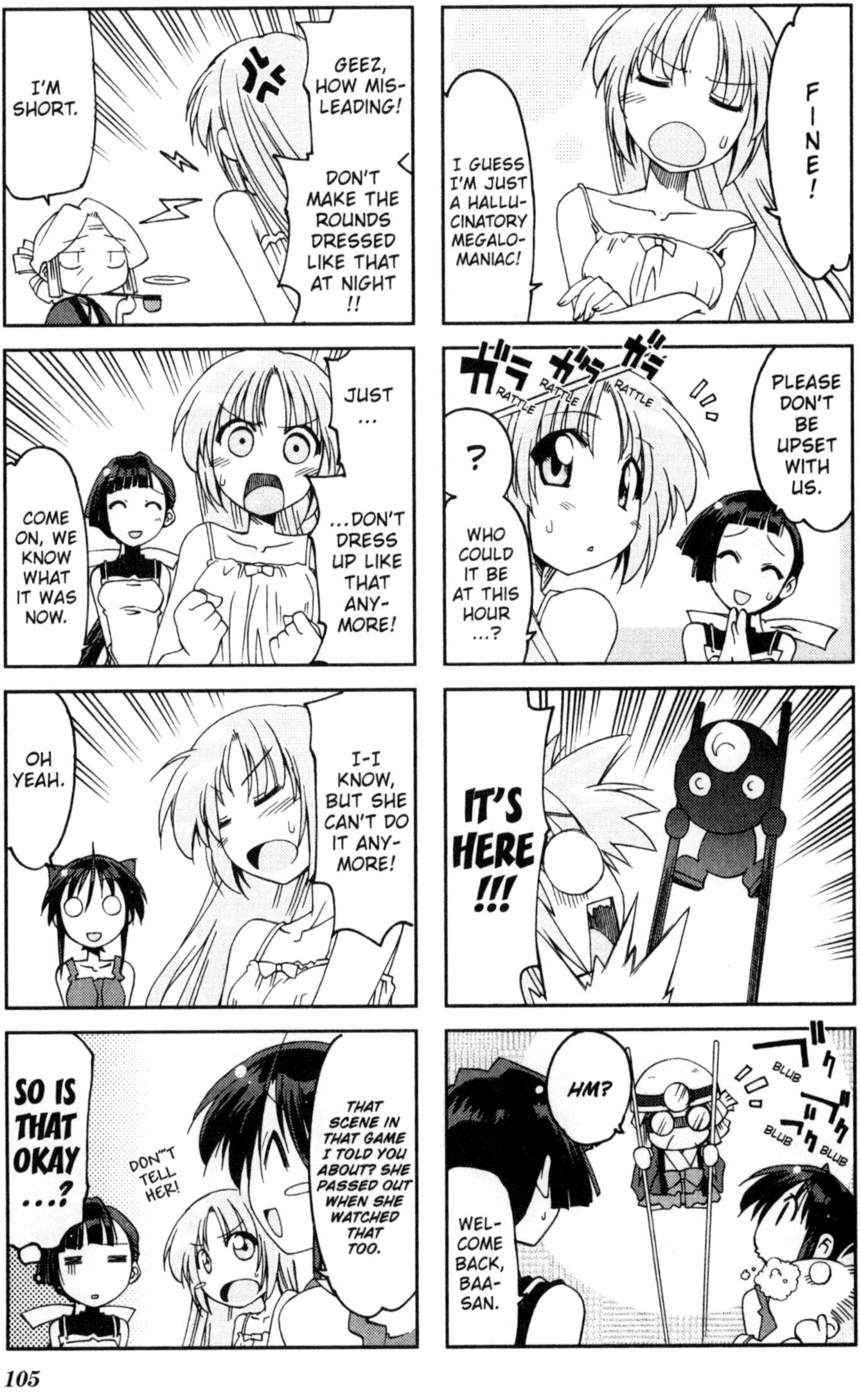
FINE!
I GUESS I'M JUST A HALLUCINATORY MEGALOMANIAC!
ガラ ガラ ガラ
RATTLE RATTLE RATTLE
PLEASE DON'T BE UPSET WITH US.
?
WHO COULD IT BE AT THIS HOUR ...?
IT'S HERE!!!
ブク ブク ブク
BLUB BLUB BLUB
HM?
WELCOME BACK, BAA-SAN.
GEEZ, HOW MIS-LEADING!
DON'T MAKE THE ROUNDS DRESSED LIKE THAT AT NIGHT!!
I'M SHORT.
JUST ...
...DON'T DRESS UP LIKE THAT ANY-MORE!
COME ON, WE KNOW WHAT IT WAS NOW.
I-I KNOW, BUT SHE CAN'T DO IT ANY-MORE!
OH YEAH.
THAT SCENE IN THAT GAME I TOLD YOU ABOUT? SHE PASSED OUT WHEN SHE WATCHED THAT TOO.
DON'T TELL HER!
SO IS THAT OKAY ...?

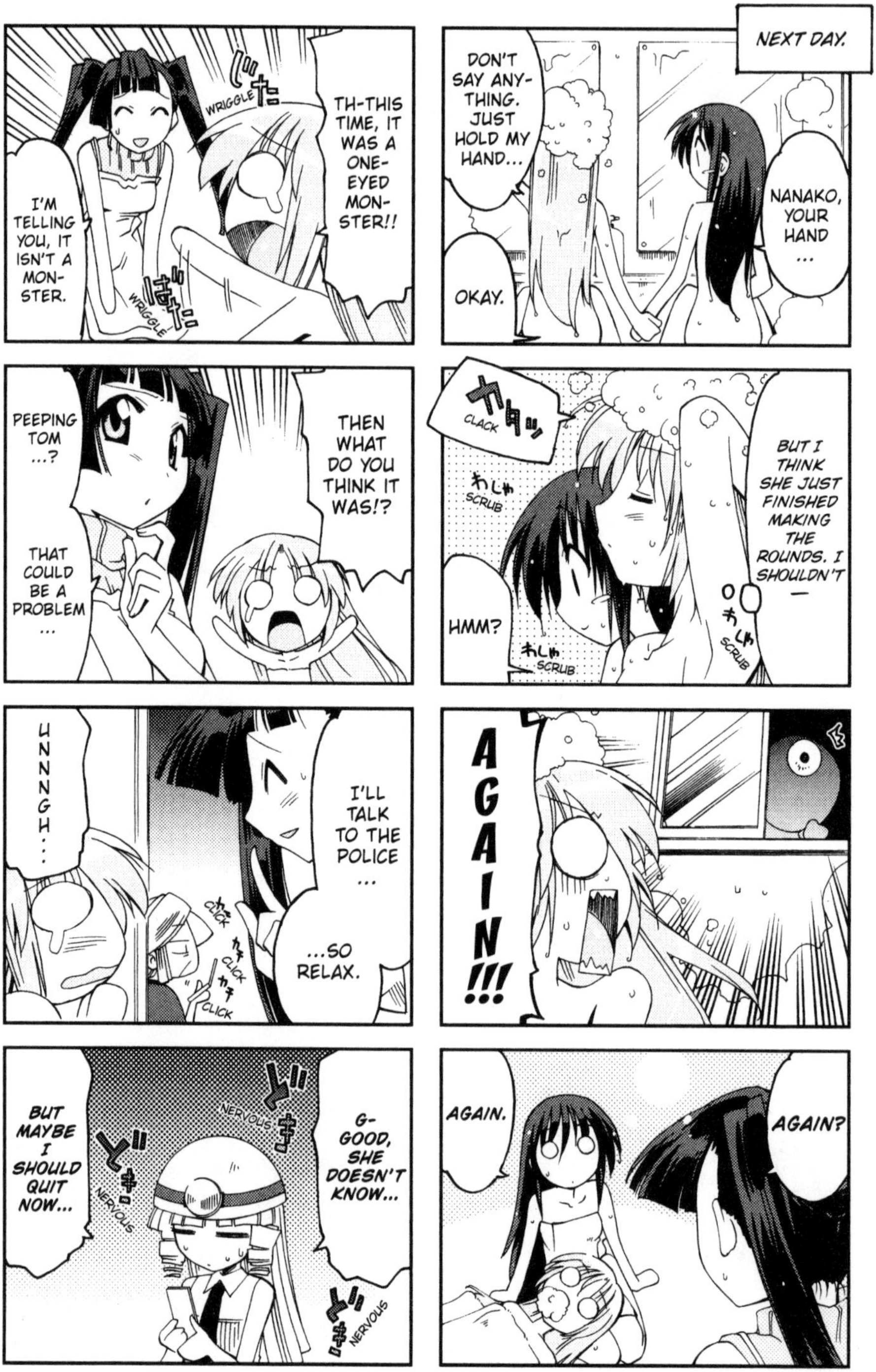
NEXT DAY.
NANAKO, YOUR HAND...
DON'T SAY ANY-THING. JUST HOLD MY HAND...
OKAY.
CLACK
BUT I THINK SHE JUST FINISHED MAKING THE ROUNDS. I SHOULDN'T—
SCRUB
SCRUB
HMM?
AGAIN!!!
AGAIN?
AGAIN.
TH-THIS TIME, IT WAS A ONE-EYED MON-STER!!
WRIGGLE
WRIGGLE
I'M TELLING YOU, IT ISN'T A MON-STER.
THEN WHAT DO YOU THINK IT WAS!?
PEEPING TOM...?
THAT COULD BE A PROBLEM...
I'LL TALK TO THE POLICE...
...SO RELAX.
UNNNGH...
CLICK
CLICK
CLICK
G-GOOD, SHE DOESN'T KNOW...
NERVOUS
NERVOUS
NERVOUS
BUT MAYBE I SHOULD QUIT NOW...

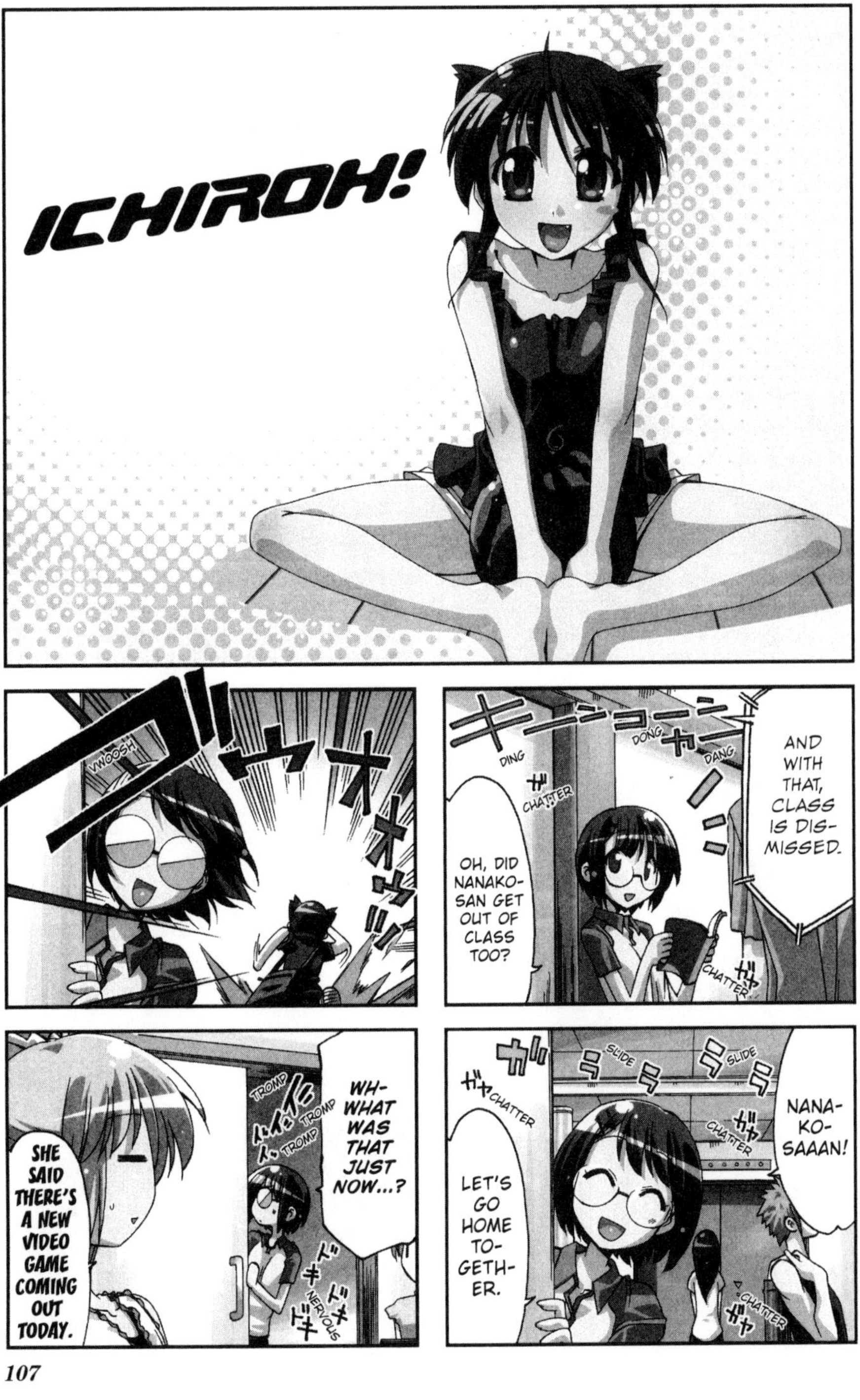
ICHIROH!
DING
DONG
DANG
CHATTER
AND WITH THAT, CLASS IS DISMISSED.
OH, DID NANAKO-SAN GET OUT OF CLASS TOO?
CHATTER
VWOOSH
NANA-KO-SAAAN!
SLIDE
SLIDE
CHATTER
CHATTER
LET'S GO HOME TO-GETH-ER.
CHATTER
WH-WHAT WAS THAT JUST NOW...?
TROMP
TROMP
TROMP
NERVOUS
SHE SAID THERE'S A NEW VIDEO GAME COMING OUT TODAY.

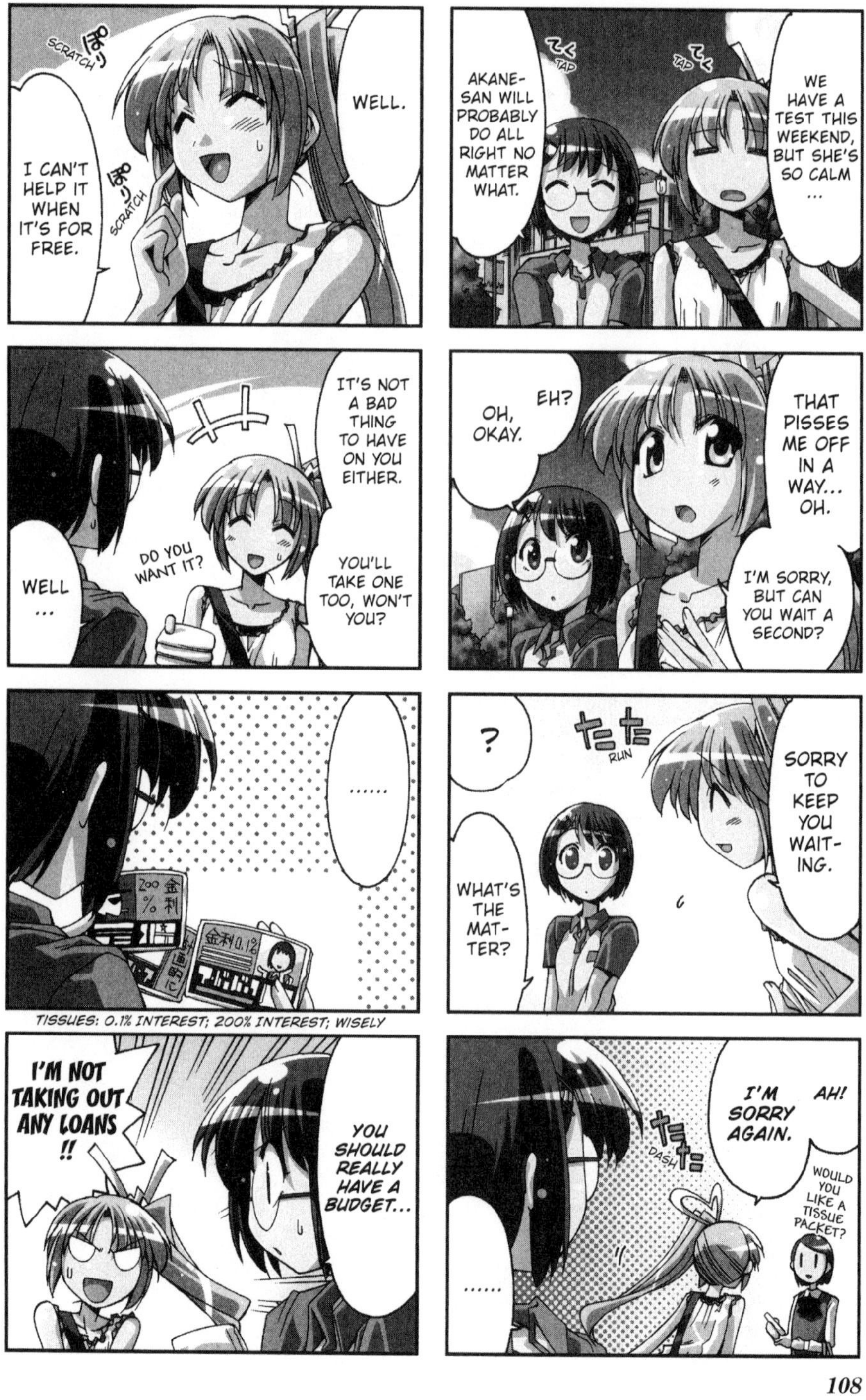
てく
TAP
てく
TAP
WE HAVE A TEST THIS WEEKEND, BUT SHE'S SO CALM ...
AKANE-SAN WILL PROBABLY DO ALL RIGHT NO MATTER WHAT.
THAT PISSES ME OFF IN A WAY... OH.
EH?
I'M SORRY, BUT CAN YOU WAIT A SECOND?
OH, OKAY.
たたた
RUN
SORRY TO KEEP YOU WAIT-ING.
?
WHAT'S THE MAT-TER?
AH!
I'M SORRY AGAIN.
たたた
DASH
WOULD YOU LIKE A TISSUE PACKET?
......
WELL.
ぽり
SCRATCH
ぽり
SCRATCH
I CAN'T HELP IT WHEN IT'S FOR FREE.
IT'S NOT A BAD THING TO HAVE ON YOU EITHER.
YOU'LL TAKE ONE TOO, WON'T YOU?
DO YOU WANT IT?
WELL ...
......
TISSUES: 0.1% INTEREST; 200% INTEREST; WISELY
YOU SHOULD REALLY HAVE A BUDGET...
I'M NOT TAKING OUT ANY LOANS !!

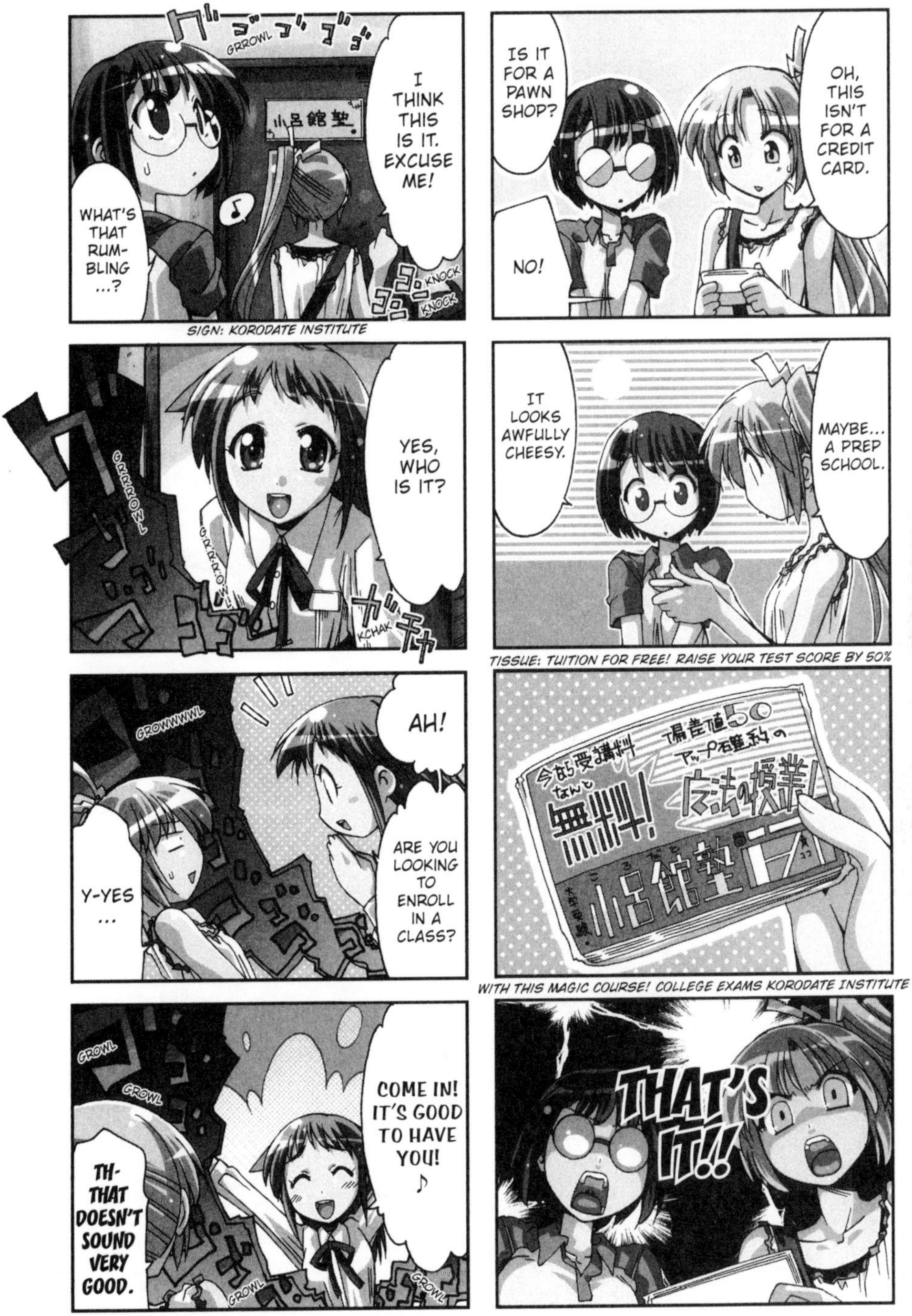
OH, THIS ISN'T FOR A CREDIT CARD.
IS IT FOR A PAWN SHOP?
NO!
MAYBE... A PREP SCHOOL.
IT LOOKS AWFULLY CHEESY.
TISSUE: TUITION FOR FREE! RAISE YOUR TEST SCORE BY 50%
WITH THIS MAGIC COURSE! COLLEGE EXAMS KORODATE INSTITUTE
THAT'S IT!!
GRROWL
I THINK THIS IS IT. EXCUSE ME!
WHAT'S THAT RUM-BLING ...?
KNOCK KNOCK
SIGN: KORODATE INSTITUTE
YES, WHO IS IT?
GRRROWL
GRRROWL
KCHAK
AH!
GROWWWWL
ARE YOU LOOKING TO ENROLL IN A CLASS?
Y-YES ...
COME IN! IT'S GOOD TO HAVE YOU! ♪
GROWL
GROWL
TH-THAT DOESN'T SOUND VERY GOOD.
GROWL
GROWL

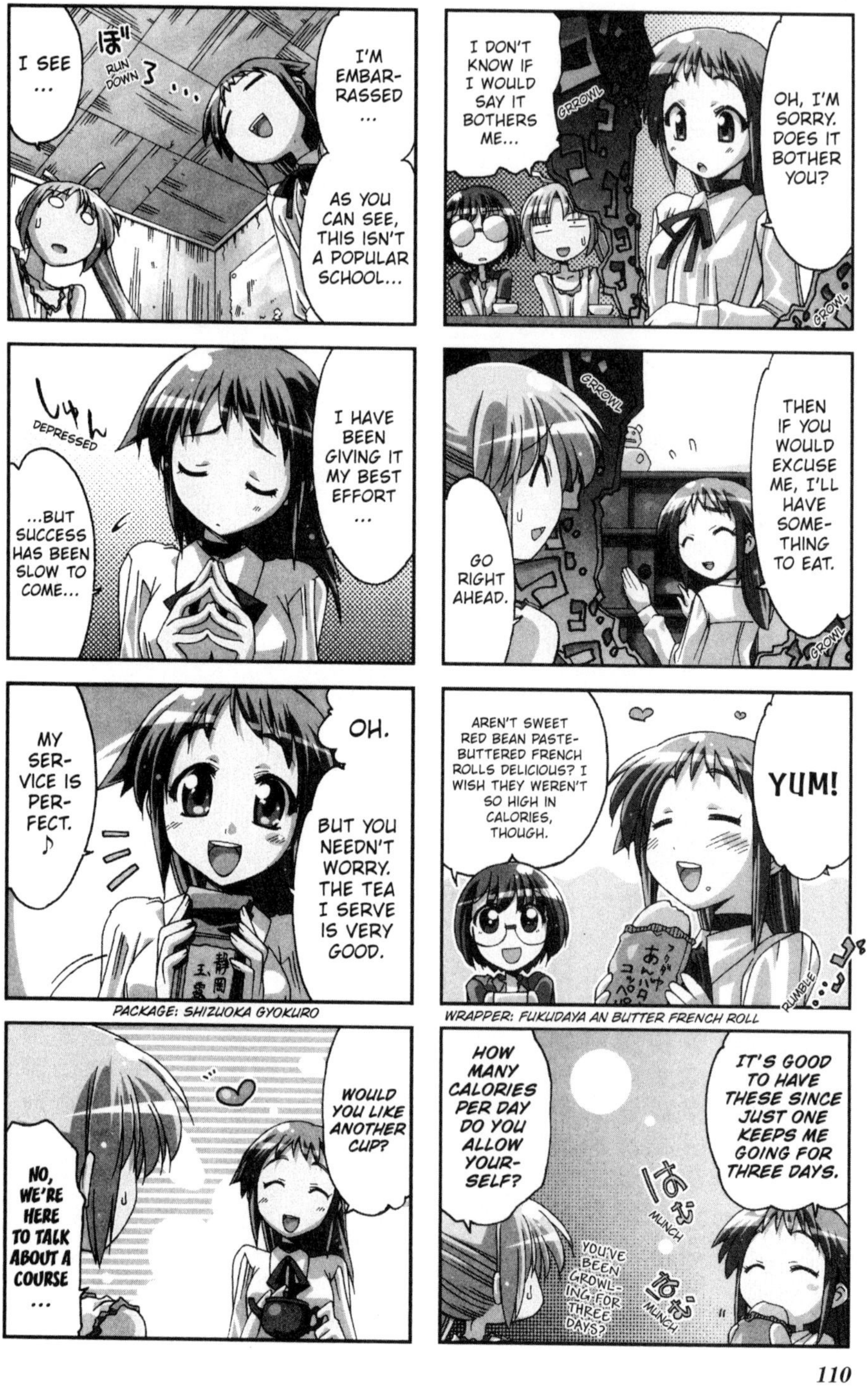

OH, I'M SORRY. DOES IT BOTHER YOU?
I DON'T KNOW IF I WOULD SAY IT BOTHERS ME...
GRROWL
GROWL
THEN IF YOU WOULD EXCUSE ME, I'LL HAVE SOME-THING TO EAT.
GO RIGHT AHEAD.
GRROWL
GROWL
YUM!
AREN'T SWEET RED BEAN PASTE-BUTTERED FRENCH ROLLS DELICIOUS? I WISH THEY WEREN'T SO HIGH IN CALORIES, THOUGH.
RUMBLE
WRAPPER: FUKUDAYA AN BUTTER FRENCH ROLL
IT'S GOOD TO HAVE THESE SINCE JUST ONE KEEPS ME GOING FOR THREE DAYS.
HOW MANY CALORIES PER DAY DO YOU ALLOW YOUR-SELF?
はむ MUNCH
はむ MUNCH
YOU'VE BEEN GROWL-ING FOR THREE DAYS?
I'M EMBAR-RASSED...
AS YOU CAN SEE, THIS ISN'T A POPULAR SCHOOL...
ぼろ RUN DOWN
I SEE...
しゅん DEPRESSED
I HAVE BEEN GIVING IT MY BEST EFFORT...
...BUT SUCCESS HAS BEEN SLOW TO COME...
OH.
BUT YOU NEEDN'T WORRY. THE TEA I SERVE IS VERY GOOD.
MY SER-VICE IS PER-FECT. ♪
PACKAGE: SHIZUOKA GYOKURO
WOULD YOU LIKE ANOTHER CUP?
NO, WE'RE HERE TO TALK ABOUT A COURSE...

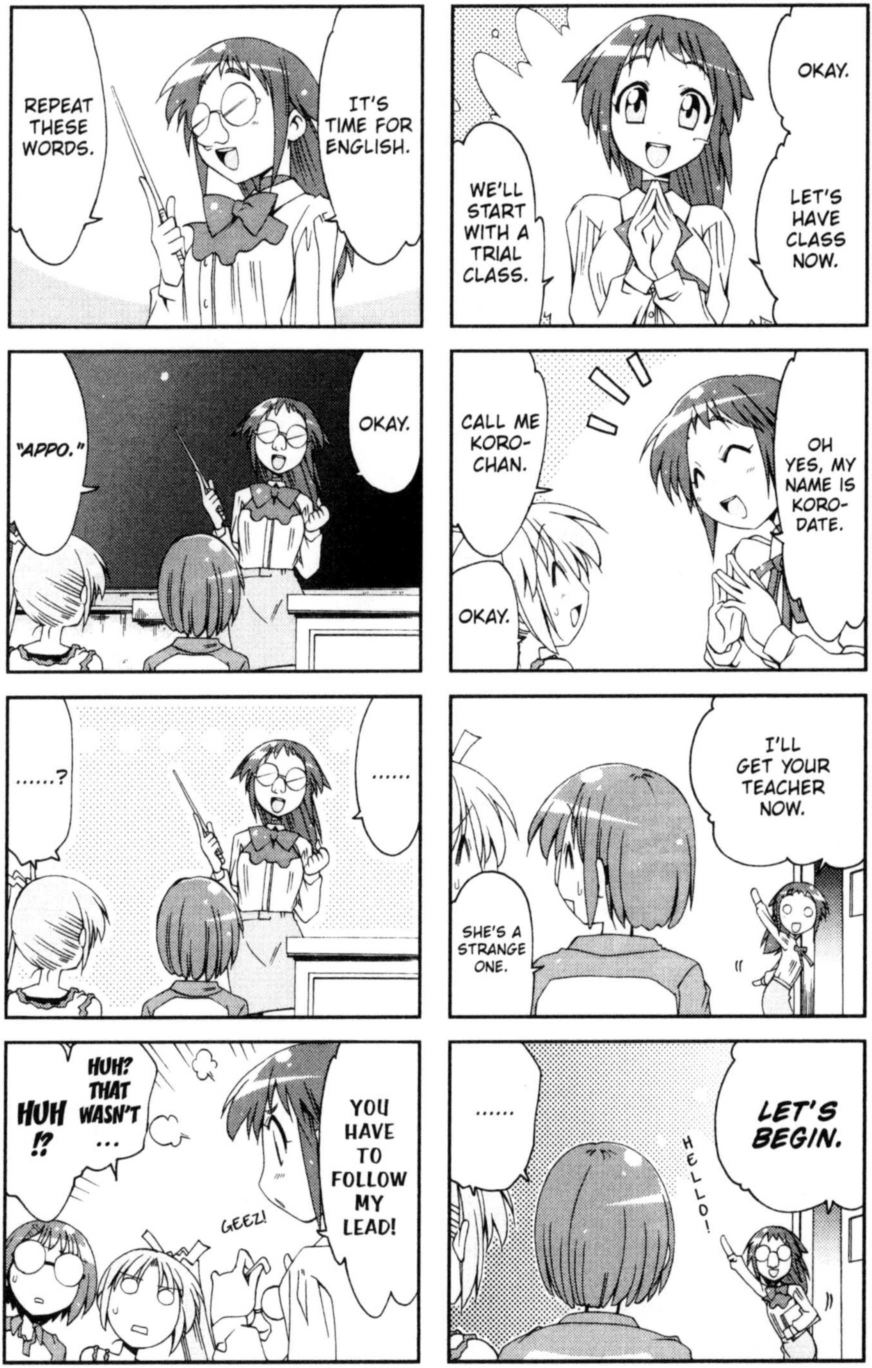
OKAY.
LET'S HAVE CLASS NOW.
WE'LL START WITH A TRIAL CLASS.
IT'S TIME FOR ENGLISH.
REPEAT THESE WORDS.
OH YES, MY NAME IS KORO-DATE.
CALL ME KORO-CHAN.
OKAY.
OKAY.
"APPO."
I'LL GET YOUR TEACHER NOW.
SHE'S A STRANGE ONE.
......
......?
LET'S BEGIN.
HELLO!
......
YOU HAVE TO FOLLOW MY LEAD!
GEEZ!
HUH? THAT WASN'T ...
HUH !?

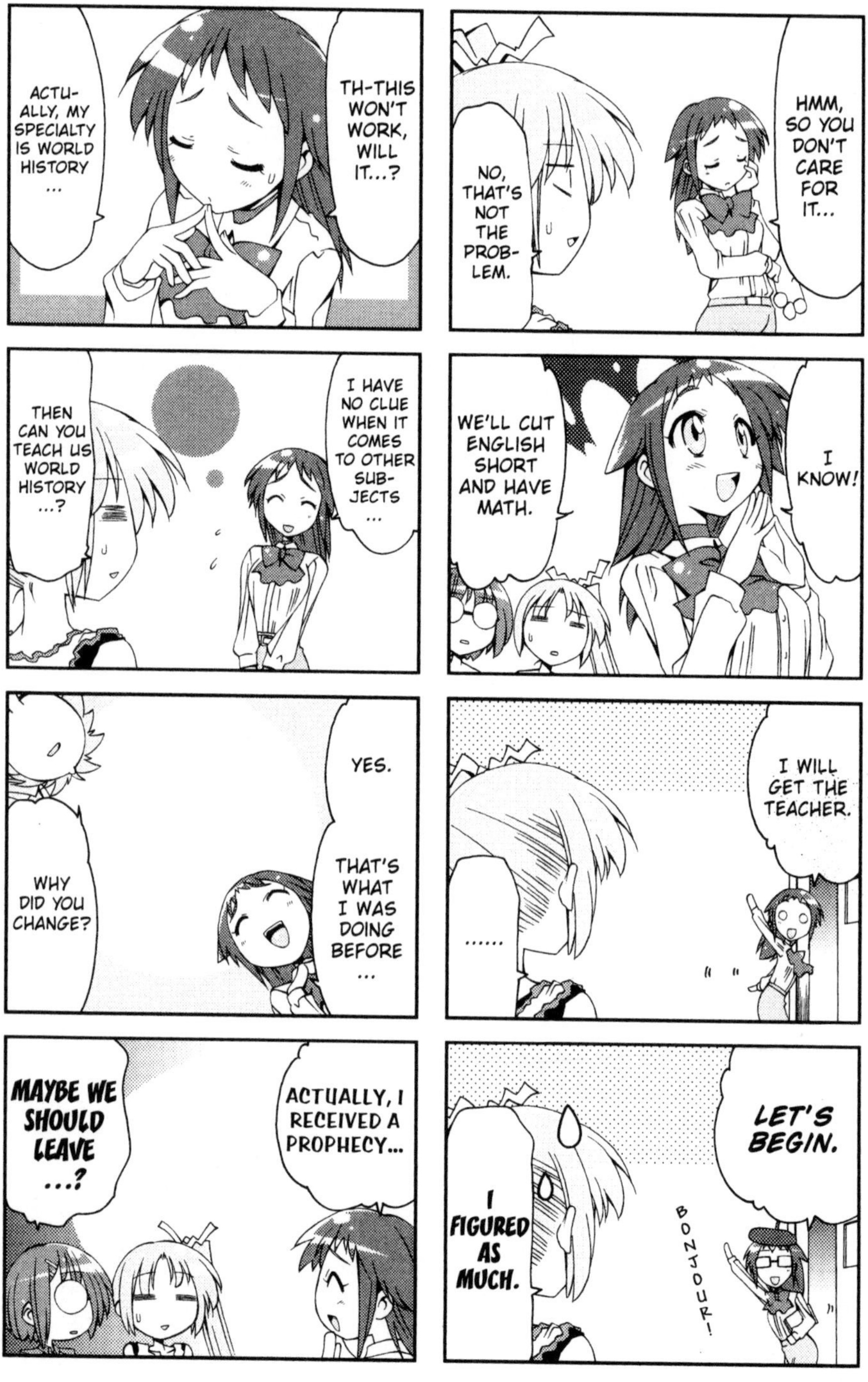
HMM, SO YOU DON'T CARE FOR IT...
NO, THAT'S NOT THE PROBLEM.
TH-THIS WON'T WORK, WILL IT...?
ACTUALLY, MY SPECIALTY IS WORLD HISTORY...
I KNOW!
WE'LL CUT ENGLISH SHORT AND HAVE MATH.
I HAVE NO CLUE WHEN IT COMES TO OTHER SUBJECTS...
THEN CAN YOU TEACH US WORLD HISTORY...?
I WILL GET THE TEACHER.
......
YES.
THAT'S WHAT I WAS DOING BEFORE...
WHY DID YOU CHANGE?
LET'S BEGIN.
BONJOUR!
I FIGURED AS MUCH.
ACTUALLY, I RECEIVED A PROPHECY...
MAYBE WE SHOULD LEAVE...?

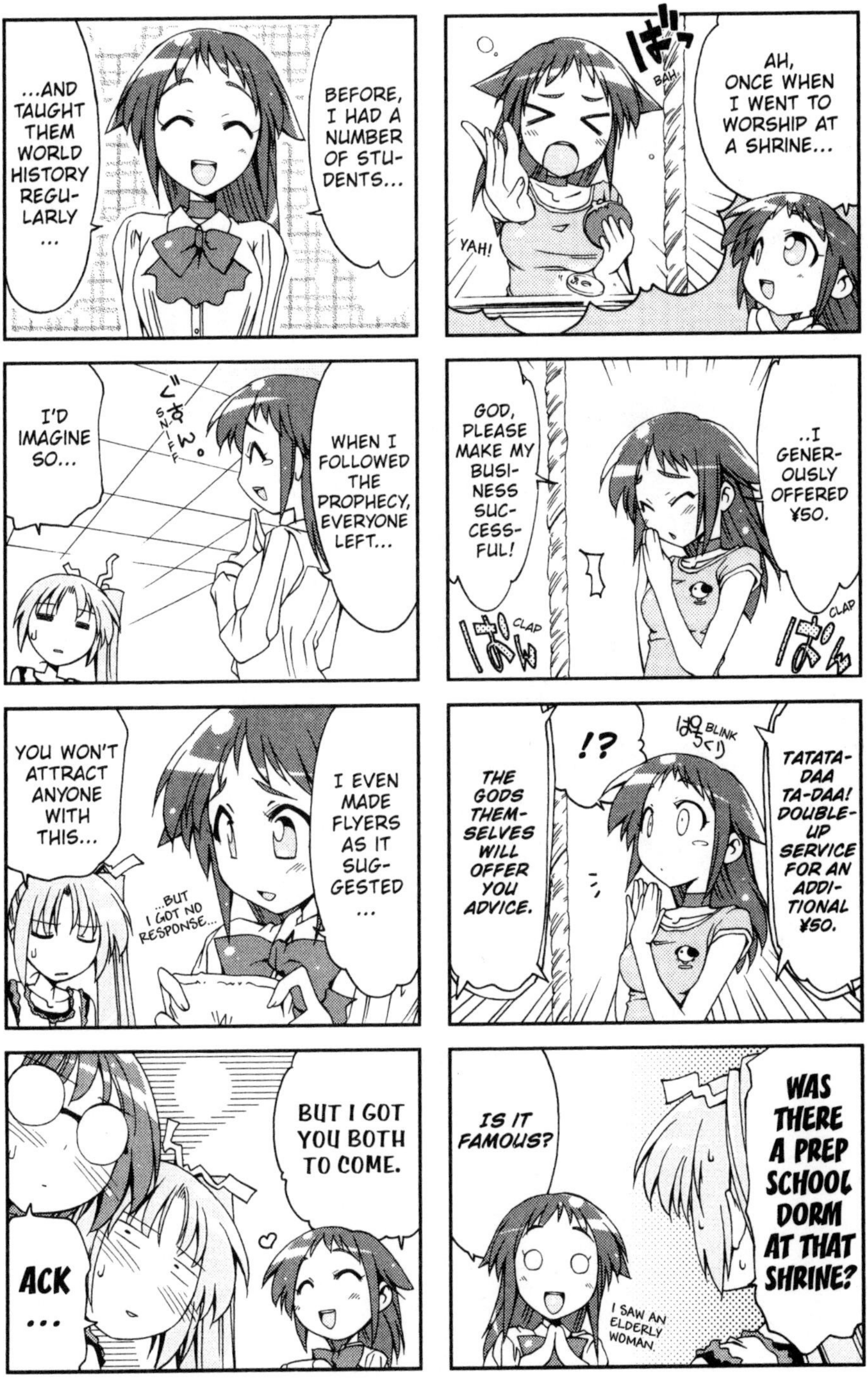
AH, ONCE WHEN I WENT TO WORSHIP AT A SHRINE...
ばっ BAH
YAH!
..I GENEROUSLY OFFERED ¥50.
GOD, PLEASE MAKE MY BUSINESS SUCCESSFUL!
ぱん CLAP
ぱん CLAP
TATATA-DAA TA-DAA! DOUBLE-UP SERVICE FOR AN ADDITIONAL ¥50.
ぱちくり BLINK
!?
THE GODS THEMSELVES WILL OFFER YOU ADVICE.
WAS THERE A PREP SCHOOL DORM AT THAT SHRINE?
IS IT FAMOUS?
I SAW AN ELDERLY WOMAN.
BEFORE, I HAD A NUMBER OF STUDENTS...
...AND TAUGHT THEM WORLD HISTORY REGULARLY...
WHEN I FOLLOWED THE PROPHECY, EVERYONE LEFT...
ぐすん SNIFF
I'D IMAGINE SO...
I EVEN MADE FLYERS AS IT SUGGESTED...
...BUT I GOT NO RESPONSE...
YOU WON'T ATTRACT ANYONE WITH THIS...
BUT I GOT YOU BOTH TO COME.
ACK...

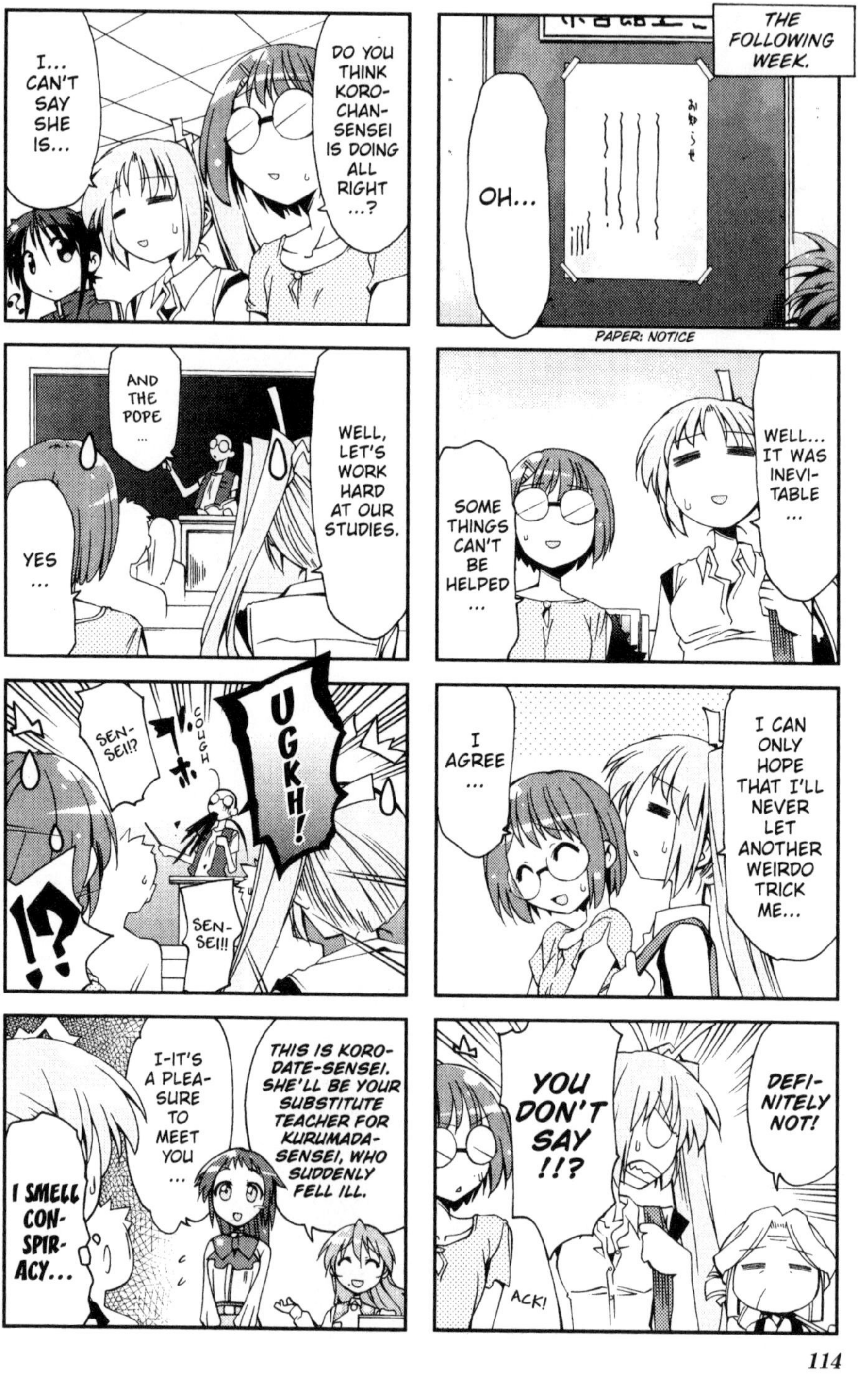
THE FOLLOWING WEEK.
OH...
おしらせ
PAPER: NOTICE
WELL... IT WAS INEVITABLE...
SOME THINGS CAN'T BE HELPED...
I CAN ONLY HOPE THAT I'LL NEVER LET ANOTHER WEIRDO TRICK ME...
I AGREE...
DEFINITELY NOT!
YOU DON'T SAY!!?
ACK!
DO YOU THINK KORO-CHAN-SENSEI IS DOING ALL RIGHT...?
I... CAN'T SAY SHE IS...
WELL, LET'S WORK HARD AT OUR STUDIES.
AND THE POPE...
YES...
UGKH!
COUGH
SEN-SEI!?
SEN-SEI!!
!?
THIS IS KORODATE-SENSEI. SHE'LL BE YOUR SUBSTITUTE TEACHER FOR KURUMADA-SENSEI, WHO SUDDENLY FELL ILL.
I-IT'S A PLEASURE TO MEET YOU...
I SMELL CONSPIRACY...

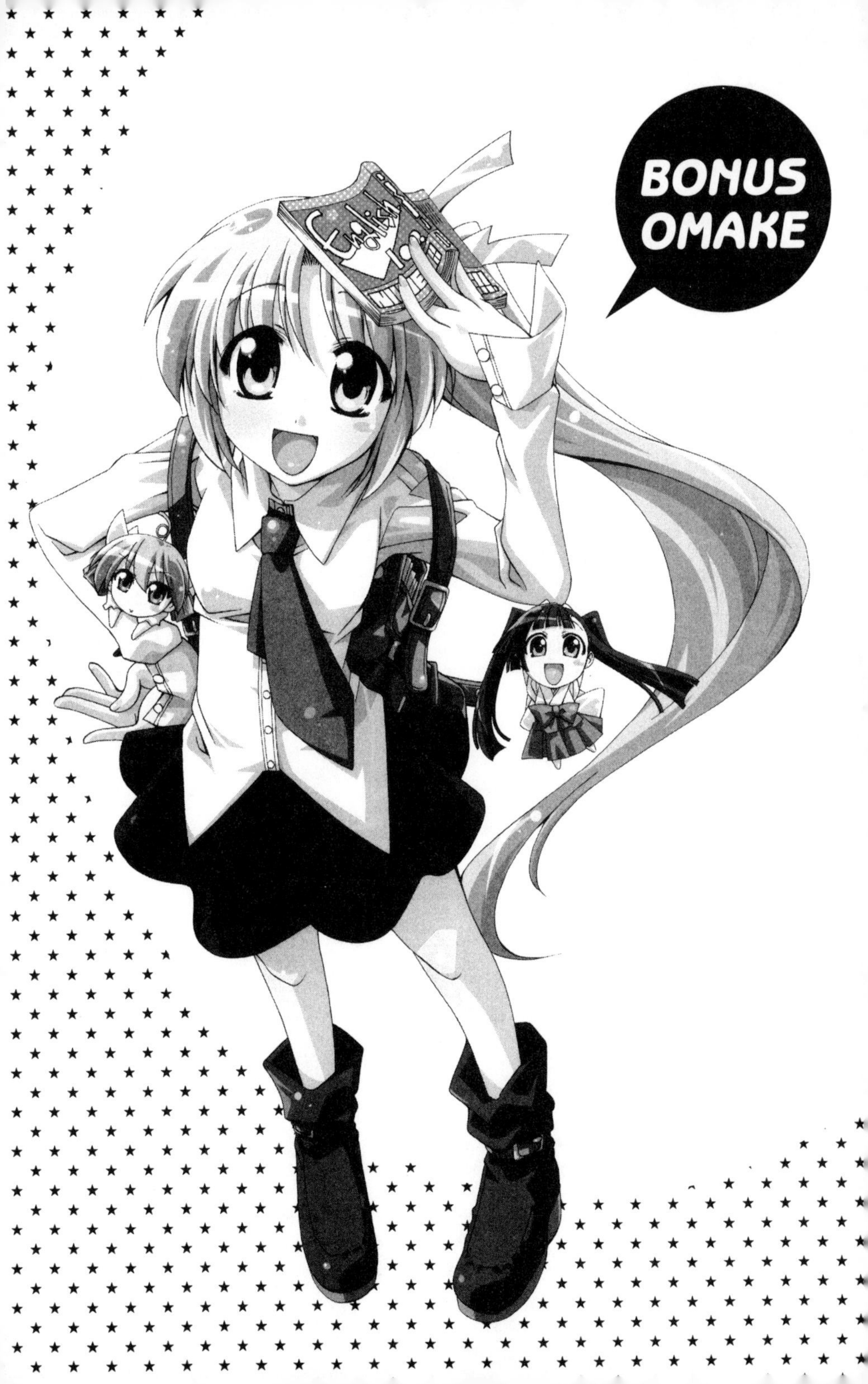
BONUS OMAKE
English 1

## MAYURA & SHINO'S SPLASH PAGE ILLUSTRATION COMMENT FEATURE ♪

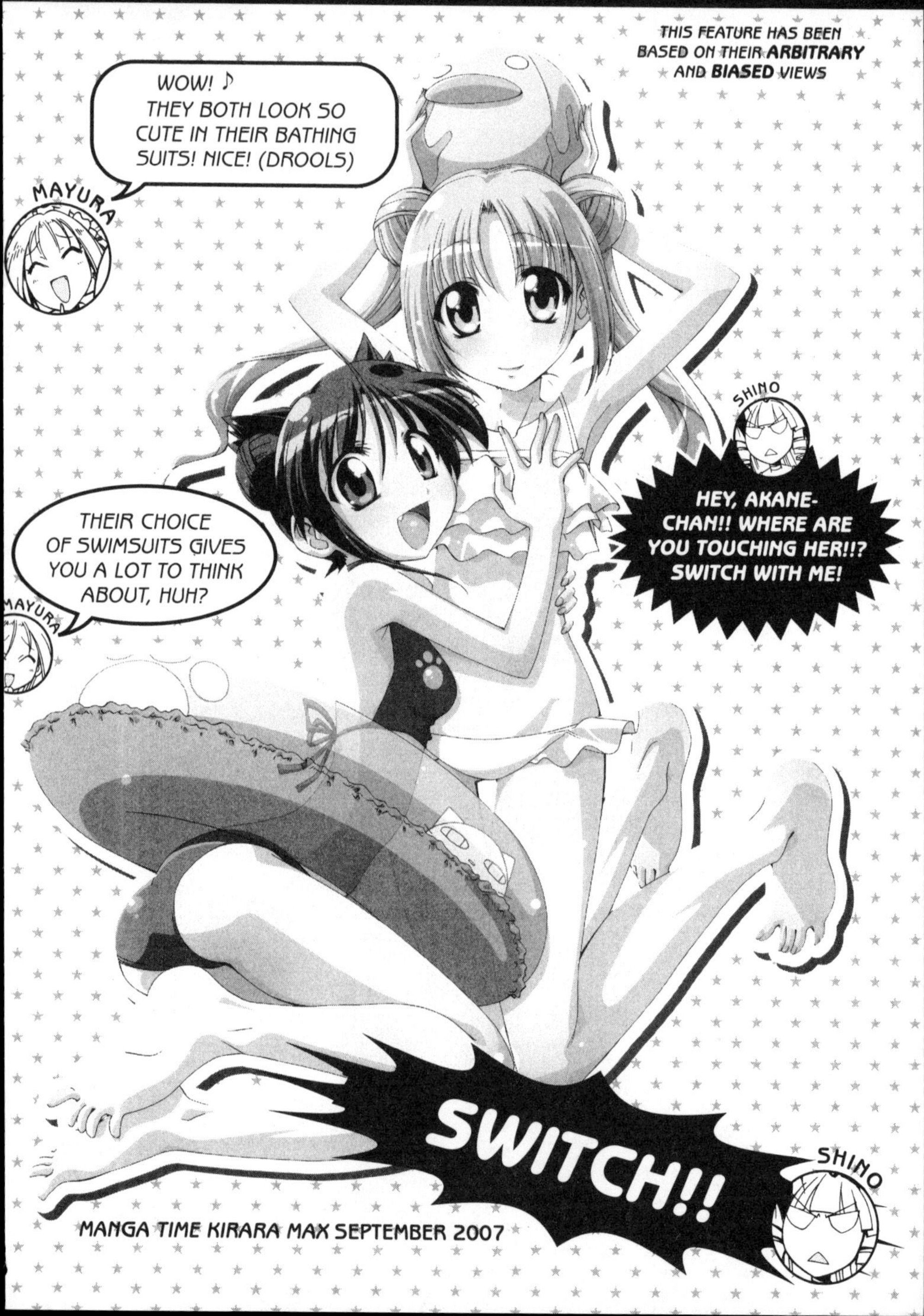
THIS FEATURE HAS BEEN BASED ON THEIR ARBITRARY AND BIASED VIEWS
WOW! ♪ THEY BOTH LOOK SO CUTE IN THEIR BATHING SUITS! NICE! (DROOLS)
MAYURA
SHINO
HEY, AKANE-CHAN!! WHERE ARE YOU TOUCHING HER!!? SWITCH WITH ME!
THEIR CHOICE OF SWIMSUITS GIVES YOU A LOT TO THINK ABOUT, HUH?
MAYURA
SWITCH!!
SHINO

MANGA TIME KIRARA MAX SEPTEMBER 2007

MANGA TIME KIRARA MAX SEPTEMBER 2007

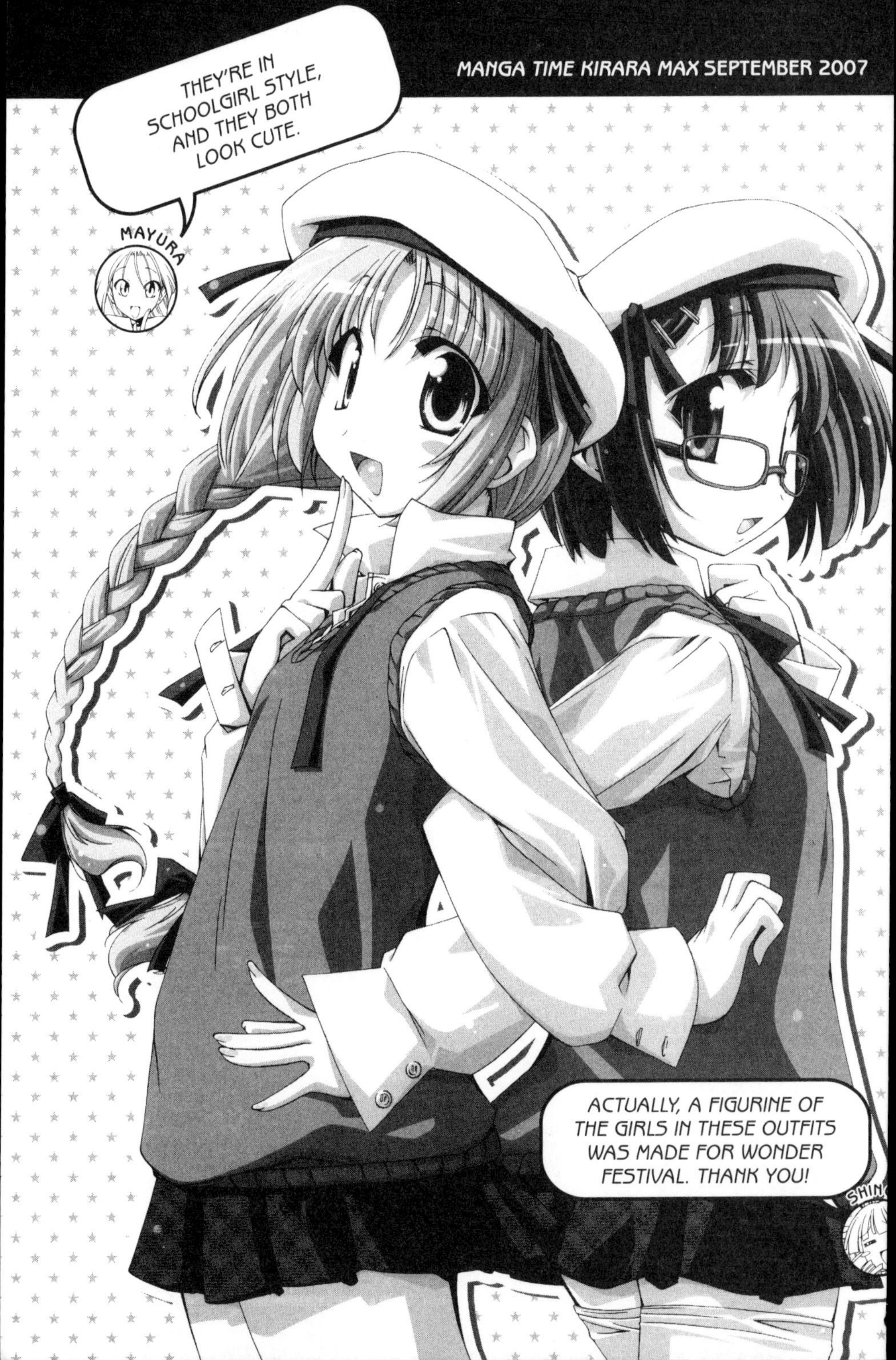
THEY'RE IN SCHOOLGIRL STYLE, AND THEY BOTH LOOK CUTE.
MAYURA
ACTUALLY, A FIGURINE OF THE GIRLS IN THESE OUTFITS WAS MADE FOR WONDER FESTIVAL. THANK YOU!
SHIN

HI, THIS IS MIKAGE. WE'RE ALREADY AT VOLUME 2; CAN YOU BELIEVE IT? THIS IS LIKE DOUBLING THE SALES!

NANAKO AND THE OTHERS SEEM TO PLAY MORE THAN THEY STUDY, BUT THAT'S THE WAY PREP SCHOOL STUDENTS ARE. AS FOR ME, MY ONLY MEMORIES OF PREP SCHOOL ARE OF GOING TO THE ARCADE AFTERWARD. BUT PREP SCHOOL STUDENTS SHOULD STUDY.

IT'LL BE SUMMER SOON, AND THEY'LL TAKE THEIR STUDIES A LITTLE MORE SERIOUSLY, I THINK... AT LEAST I HOPE THEY WILL.

I HOPE YOU'LL CONTIN-UE TO SUPPORT MY WORK!

SPECIAL THANKS!

SATOPON-SAMA,
I ALWAYS APPRECIATE YOUR HELPING ME.

AND MY EDITOR, I-SAMA,
I'M SORRY FOR ALWAYS CAUSING TROUBLE. orz ONCE AGAIN, I'M REALLY, REALLY SORRY... I LOOK FORWARD TO EATING OUT WITH YOU AGAIN.

I HOPE TO SEE YOU AGAIN IN THE NEXT VOLUME!

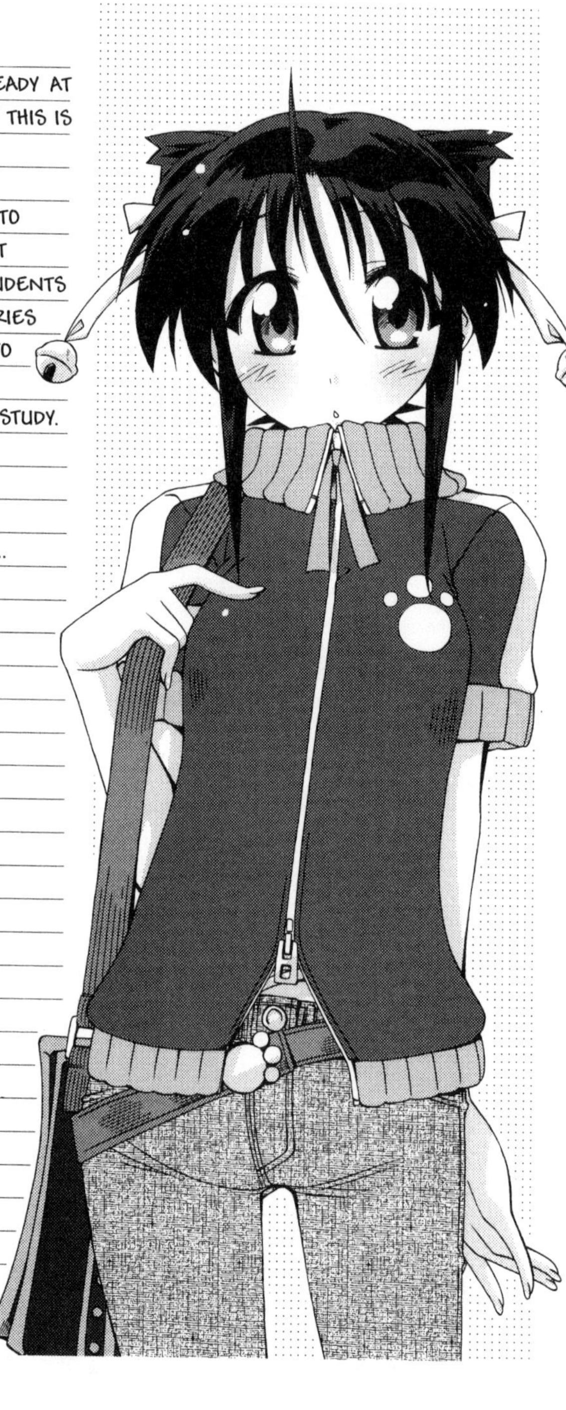

07. 11. 未影
MIKAGE

# TRANSLATION NOTES

## ICHIROH

The word *ichiroh* is derived from the word *ronin* — "a student who is preparing to take the annual entrance exam after failing it." Japanese count the number of years a student spends as a *ronin* as *ichiroh* ("first year"), *niroh* or *jiroh* ("second year"), and *sanroh* or *saburoh* ("third year").

### Page 6
Kindergarten classes are often named after flowers such as *sakura* or "cherry blossom."

### Page 7
*Nii-san* is a common honorific for "big brother."

### Page 13
An *onigiri* is a rice ball, typically triangular, usually stuffed with pickled plums, seasoned seaweed, or grilled salmon and wrapped with dry seaweed.

### Page 16
An *era prayer* is a Buddhist chant-like meditation used to usher in a new year, a new season, etc.

### Page 17
*Sensei* is an honorific title used to address teachers, doctors, and the like.

### Page 25
A general rule for Japanese monetary conversion is ¥100 to one USD.

### Page 34
*Miko*, or "shrine maidens," are female attendants serving at Shinto shrines who are well known for their red and white uniforms.

Underclassmen refer to their seniors as *senpai*, and upperclassmen refer to younger students as *kouhai*.

### Page 40
*Saisen* are monetary donations made when worshipping at a shrine or temple.

¥1,000 and ¥10,000 bills feature Hideyo Noguchi and Yukichi Fukuzawa respectively.

### Page 41
*Yaoya* means "vegetable store."

### Page 51
*Katakana* is a syllabic Japanese writing system. As readers advance, they tend to use more Chinese characters, called *kanji*, as a form of shorthand.

### Page 68
*Baa-san* and *obaa-san* are variant forms of "granny."

### Page 69
*Goukon* is like a group blind date.

*Hakama* are traditional pleated pants worn by *miko*.

### Page 80
A *boke* is the half of a typical Japanese comedy team that feigns misunderstanding to deliver puns, after which he is typically whacked by his partner.

### Page 86
PHS stands for personal handyphone system, a low-cost mobile network developed in Asia. PHS phones are designed to work inside and outside, with calls being transferred from one short-range signal station to another, allowing people to make calls in indoor or underground areas where many cell users cannot get a signal.

### Page 89
*Otaku* literally means "house" or "family" but has come to refer to people who are obsessed with anime, manga, and/or video games.

### Page 103
*Dango* is a Japanese dumpling made of glutinous rice flour.

### Page 110
*An* is a sweet red bean paste.

*Gyokuro* is the finest Japanese green tea.

### Page 111
*Appo* is a Japanese abbreviation of "appointment."

### Page 116
*MAX* is the name of the magazine that serializes *Ichiroh!*

### Page 117
Wonder Festival is a semiannual event for "garage kits," or model kits produced by fans, held in Tokyo.

# ICHIROH! ②

## MIKAGE

**Translation: Elina Ishikawa**

**Lettering: Hope Donovan**

ICHIROH! vol. 2 © 2007 Mikage. All rights reserved. First published in Japan in 2007 by HOUBUNSHA CO., LTD., Tokyo. English translation rights in United States, Canada, and United Kingdom arranged with HOUBUNSHA CO., LTD through Tuttle-Mori Agency, Inc., Tokyo.

Translation © 2009 by Hachette Book Group, Inc.

Yen Press
Hachette Book Group
237 Park Avenue, New York, NY 10017

Visit our websites at www.HachetteBookGroup.com and www.YenPress.com.

Yen Press is an imprint of Hachette Book Group, Inc. The Yen Press name and logo are trademarks of Hachette Book Group, Inc.

First Yen Press Edition: November 2009

ISBN: 978-0-7595-3071-3

10 9 8 7 6 5 4 3 2 1

BVG

Printed in the United States of America